THE FLOWERS OF EVIL

LES FLEURS DU MAL

(French and English Edition)

By CHARLES BAUDELAIRE

Translated by WILLIAM AGGELER

Introduction by FRANK PEARCE STURM

The Flowers of Evil / Les Fleurs du Mal (French and English Edition)
By Charles Baudelaire
Translated by William Aggeler
Introduction by Frank Pearce Sturm

Print ISBN 13: 978-1-4209-5120-2
eBook ISBN 13: 978-1-4209-5121-9

Cover Image: A detail of the illustration "Spleen et Idéal" by Carlos Schwabe which originally appeared in *Les Fleurs du Mal*, Paris, Charles Meunier, 1900.

Please visit *www.digireads.com*

CONTENTS

LA MORT — DEATH

PIÈCES CONDAMNÉES — CONDEMNED POEMS

Introduction

Charles Baudelaire was one of those who take the downward path which leads to salvation. There are men born to be the martyrs of the world and of their own time; men whose imagination carries them beyond all that we know or have learned to think of as law and order; who are so intoxicated with a vision of a beauty beyond the world that the world's beauty seems to them but a little paint above the face of the dead; who love God with a so consuming fire that they must praise evil for God's glory, and blaspheme His name that all sects and creeds may be melted away; who see beneath all there is of mortal loveliness, the invisible worm, feeding upon hopes and desires no less than upon the fair and perishable flesh; who are good and evil at the same time; and because the good and evil in their souls finds a so perfect instrument in the refined and tortured body of modern times, desire keener pleasure and more intolerable anguish than the world contains, and become materialists because the tortured heart cries out in denial of the soul that tortures it. Charles Baudelaire was one of these men; his art is the expression of his decadence; a study of his art is the understanding of that complex movement, that "inquietude of the Veil in the temple," as Mallarmé called it, that has changed the literature of the world; and, especially, made of poetry the subtle and delicate instrument of emotional expression it has become in our own day.

We used to hear a deal about Decadence in the arts, and now we hear as much about Symbolism, which is a flower sprung from the old corruption—but Baudelaire *is* decadence; his art is not a mere literary affectation, a mask of sorrow to be thrown aside when the curtain falls, but the voice of an imagination plunged into the contemplation of all the perverse and fallen loveliness of the world; that finds beauty most beautiful at the moment of its passing away, and regrets its perishing with a so poignant grief that it must follow it even into the narrow grave where those "dark comrades the worms, without ears, without eyes," whisper their secrets of terror and tell of yet another pang—

"Pour ce vieux corps sans âme et mort parmi les morts."

All his life Baudelaire was a victim to an unutterable weariness, that terrible malady of the soul born out of old times to prey upon civilizations that have reached their zenith—weariness, not of life, but of living, of continuing to labor and suffer in a world that has exhausted all its emotions and has no new thing to offer. Being an artist, therefore, he took his revenge upon life by a glorification of all the sorrowful things that it is life's continual desire to forget. His poems speak sweetly of decay and death, and whisper their graveyard secrets into the ears of beauty. His men are men whom the moon has touched with her own fantasy: who love the immense ungovernable sea, the unformed and multitudinous waters; the place where they are not; the woman they will never know; and all his women are enigmatic courtesans whose beauty is a transfiguration of sin; who hide the ugliness of the soul beneath the perfection of the body. He loves them and does not love; they are cruel and indolent and full of strange perversions; they are perfumed with exotic perfumes; they sleep to the sound of viols, or fan themselves languidly in the shadow, and only he sees that it is the shadow of death.

An art like this, rooted in a so tortured perception of the beauty and ugliness of a world where the spirit is mingled indistinguishably with the flesh, almost inevitably concerns itself with material things, with all the subtle raptures the soul feels, not by abstract contemplation, for that would mean content, but through the gateway of the senses; the lust of the flesh, the delight of the eye. Sound, color, odor, form: to him these are not the symbols that lead the soul towards the infinite: they are the soul; they are the infinite. He writes, always with a weary and laborious grace, about the abstruser and more enigmatic things of the flesh, colors and odors particularly; but, unlike those later writers who have been called realists, he apprehends, to borrow a phrase from Pater, "all those finer conditions wherein material things rise to that subtlety of operation which constitutes them spiritual, where only the finer nerve and the keener touch can follow."

In one of his sonnets he says:

"Je hais la passion et l'esprit me fait mal!"

and, indeed, he is a poet in whom the spirit, as modern thought understands the word, had little or no part. We feel, reading his terrible poems, that the body is indeed acutely conscious of the soul, distressfully and even angrily conscious, but its motions are not yet subdued by the soul's prophetic voice. It was to forget this voice, with its eternal *Esto memor*, that Baudelaire wrote imperishably of perishable things and their fading glory.

II

Charles Baudelaire was born at Paris, April 9th, 1821, in an old turreted house in the Rue Hautefeuille. His father, a distinguished gentleman of the eighteenth-century school, seems to have passed his old-world manners on to his son, for we learn from Baudelaire's friend and biographer, Théophile Gautier, that the poet "always preserved the forms of an extreme urbanity."

At school, during his childhood, he gained many distinctions, and passed for a kind of infant prodigy; but later on, when he sat for his examination as *bachlier ès lettres*, his extreme nervousness made him appear almost an idiot. Failing miserably, he made no second attempt. Then his father died, and his mother married General Aupick, afterwards ambassador to Constantinople, an excellent man in every respect, but quite incapable of sympathizing with or even of understanding the love for literature that now began to manifest itself in the mind of his stepson. All possible means were tried to turn him from literature to some more lucrative and more respectable profession. Family quarrels arose over this all-important question, and young Baudelaire, who seems to have given some real cause for offence to the stepfather whose aspirations and profession he despised, was at length sent away upon a long voyage, in the hopes that the sight of strange lands and new faces would perhaps cause him to forget the ambitions his relatives could but consider as foolish and idealistic. He sailed the Indian Seas; visited the islands of Mauritius, Bourbon, Madagascar, and Ceylon; saw the yellow waters of the sacred Ganges; stored up the memory of tropical sounds and colors and odors for use later on; and returned to Paris shortly after his twenty-first, birthday, more than ever determined to be a man of letters.

His parents were in despair; no doubt quite rightly so from their point of view. Théophile Gautier, perhaps remembering the many disappointments and martyrdoms of his own sad life, defends the attitude of General Aupick in a passage where he poignantly describes the hopelessness of the profession of letters. The future author of *The Flowers of Evil*, however, was now his own master and in a position, so far as monetary matters were concerned, to follow out his own whim. He took apartments in the Hôtel Pimodan, a kind of literary lodging-house where all Bohemia met; and where Gautier and Boissard were also at that period installed. Then began that life of uninterrupted labor and meditation that has given to France her most characteristic literature, for these poems of Baudelaire's are not only original in themselves but have been the cause of originality in others; they are the root of modern French literature and much of the best English literature; they were the origin of that new method in poetry that gave Mallarme and Verlaine to France; Yeats and some others to England. It was in the Hôtel Pimodan that Baudelaire and Gautier first met and formed one of those unfading friendships not so rare among men of letters as among men of the world; there also the "Hashish-Eaters" held the stances that have since become famous in the history of literature. Hashish and opium, indeed, contribute not a little to the odor of the strange *Flowers of Evil*; as also, perhaps, they contributed to Baudelaire's death from the terrible malady known as general paralysis, for he was a man who could not resist a so easy path into the world of *macabre* visions. I shall return to this question again; there is internal evidence in his writings that shows he made good literary use of these opiate-born dreams which in the end dragged him into their own abyss.

It was in 1849, when Baudelaire was twenty-eight years of age, that he made the acquaintance of the already famous Théophile Gautier, from whose admirable essay I shall presently translate a passage giving us an excellent pen-sketch of the famous poet and cynic—for Baudelaire was a cynic: he had not in the least degree the rapt expression and vague personality usually supposed to be characteristic of the poetic mood. "He recalls," wrote M. Dulamon, who knew him well, "one of those beautiful Abbés of the eighteenth century, so correct in their doctrine, so indulgent in their commerce with life—the Abbé de Bernis, for example. At the same time, he writes better verse, and would not have demanded at Rome the destruction of the Order of Jesuits."

That was Baudelaire exactly, suave and polished, filled with skeptical faith, cynical with the terrible cynicism of the scholar who is acutely conscious of all the morbid and gloomy secrets hidden beneath the fair exteriors of the world. Gautier, in the passage I have already mentioned, emphasizes both his reserve and his cynicism: "Contrary to the somewhat loose manners of artists generally, Baudelaire prided himself upon observing the most rigid *convenances*; his courtesy, indeed, was excessive to the point of seeming affected. He measured his sentences, using only the most carefully chosen terms, and pronounced certain words in a particular manner, as though he wished to underline them and give them a mysterious importance. He had italics and capital letters in his voice. Exaggeration, much in honor at Pimodan's, he disdained as being theatrical and gross; though he himself affected paradox and excess. With a very simple, very natural, and perfectly detached air, as though retailing, *à la Prudhomme*, a newspaper paragraph about the mildness or rigor of the weather, he would advance some satanically monstrous axiom, or uphold with the coolness of ice some theory of a mathematical extravagance; for he always followed a rigorous plan in the development of his follies. His spirit was neither in words nor traits; he saw things from a particular point of view, so that their outlines were changed, as objects when one gets a bird's-eye view of them; he perceived analogies inappreciable to others, and you were struck by their fantastic logic. His rare gestures were slow and sober; he never threw his arms about, for he held southern gesticulation in horror; British coolness seemed to him to be good taste. One might describe him as a dandy who had strayed into Bohemia; though still preserving his rank, and that cult of self which characterizes a man imbued with the principles of Brummel." At this time Baudelaire was practically unknown outside his own circle of friends, writers themselves; and it was not until eight years later, in 1857, when he published his *Flowers of Evil*, that he became famous.

Infamous would perhaps be a better word to describe the kind of fame he at first obtained, for every Philistine in France joined in the cry against a poet who dared to remind his readers that the grave awaits even the rich; who dared to choose the materials of his art from among the objects of death and decay; who exposed the moldering secrecies of the grave, and painted, in the phosphorescent colors of corruption, frescoes of death and horror; who desecrated love in the sonnet entitled "Causerie":

> "You are a sky of autumn, pale and rose!
> But all the sea of sadness in my blood
> Surges, and ebbing, leaves my lip morose
> Salt with the memory of the bitter flood.
>
> In vain your hand glides my faint bosom o'er;
> That which you seek, beloved, is desecrate
> By woman's tooth and talon: ah! no more
> Seek in me for a heart which those dogs ate!
>
> It is a ruin where the jackals rest,
> And rend and tear and glut themselves and slay!
> —A perfume swims about your naked breast,
> Beauty, hard scourge of spirits, have your way!
> With flame-like eyes that at bright feasts have flared
> Burn up these tatters that the beasts have spared!"

We can recall nothing like it in the literary history of our own country; the sensation caused by the appearance of the first series of Mr. Swinburne's *Poems and Ballads* was mild in comparison; just as Mr. Swinburne's poems were but wan derivatives from Baudelaire—at least as far as ideas are concerned; I say nothing about their beauty of expression or almost absolute mastery of technique—for it is quite obvious that the English poet was indebted to Baudelaire for all the bizarre and satanic elements in his work; as Baudelaire was indebted to Poe. Mr. Swinburne, however, is wild where Baudelaire is grave; and where Baudelaire compresses some perverse and morbid image into a single unforgettable line, Mr. Swinburne beats it into a froth of many musical lovely words, until we forget the deep sea in the shining foam.

If we call to mind the reception at first given to the black-and-white work of Aubrey Beardsley, it will give some idea of the consternation caused in France by the appearance of the *Flowers of Evil*. Beardsley, indeed, resembles Baudelaire in many ways, for he achieved in art what the other achieved in literature: the apotheosis of the horrible and grotesque, the perfecting of symbols to shadow forth intellectual sin, the tearing away of the decent veil of forgetfulness that hides our own corruption from our eyes, and his one prose romance, *Under the Hill*, unhappily incomplete at his death at the age of twenty-four, beats Baudelaire on his own ground. The four or five chapters which alone remain of this incomplete romance stand alone in literature. They are the absolute attainment of what Baudelaire more or less successfully attempted—a testament of sin. Not the sin of the flesh, the gross faults of the body that are vulgarly known as sin; but sin which is a metaphysical corruption, a depravity of pure intellect, the sin of the fallen angels in hell who cover their anguish with the sound of harps and sweet odors; who are incapable of bodily impurity, and for whom spiritual purity is the only terror. And since mortality, which is the shadow of the immortal, can comprehend spiritual and abstract things only by the analogies and correspondences which exist between them and the far reflections of them that we call reality, both Baudelaire and Beardsley, as indeed all artists who speak with tongues of spiritual truth, choose more or less actual human beings to be the shadows of the divine or satanic beings they would invoke, and make them sin delicate sins of the refined bodily sense that we may get a far-off glimpse of the Evil that is not mortal but immortal, the Spiritual Evil that has set up its black throne beside the throne of Spiritual Good, and has equal share in the shaping of the world and man.

I am not sure that Baudelaire, when he wrote this sinister poetry, had any clear idea that it was his vocation to be a prophet either of good or evil. Certainly he had no thought of founding a school of poetry, and if he made any conscious effort to bring a new method into literature, it was merely because he desired to be one of the famous writers of his country. An inspired thinker, however, whether his inspiration be mighty or small, receives his thought from a profounder source than his own physical reason, and writes to the dictation of beings outside of and greater than himself. The famous Eliphas Levi, like all the mystics who came before and after him, from Basilides the Gnostic to Blake the English visionary, taught that the poet and dreamer are the mediums of the Divine Word, and sole instruments through which the gods energize in the world of material things. The writing of a great book is the casting of a pebble into the pool of human thought; it gives rise to ever-widening circles that will reach we know not whither, and begins a chain of circumstances that may end in the destruction of kingdoms and religions and the awakening of new gods. The change wrought, directly or indirectly, by *The Flowers of Evil* alone is almost too great to be properly understood. There is perhaps not a man in Europe today whose outlook on life would not have been different had *The Flowers of Evil* never been written. The first thing that happens after the publication of such a book is the theft of its ideas and the imitation of its style by the lesser writers who labor for the multitude, and so its teaching goes from book to book, from the greater to the lesser, as the divine hierarchies emanate from Divinity, until ideas that were once paradoxical, or even blasphemous and unholy, have become mere newspaper commonplaces adopted by the numberless thousands who do not think for themselves, and the world's thought is changed completely, though by infinite slow degrees. The immediate result of Baudelaire's work was the Decadent School in French literature. Then the influence spread across the Channel, and the English Aesthetes arose to preach the gospel of imagination to the unimaginative. Both Decadence and Aestheticism, as intellectual movements, have fallen into the nadir of oblivion, and the dust lies heavy upon them, but they left a little leaven to lighten the heavy inertness of correct and academic literature; and now Symbolism, a greater movement than either, is in the ascendant, giving another turn to the wheel, and to all who think deeply about such matters it seems as though Symbolist literature is to be the literature of the future. The Decadents and Aesthetes were weak because they had no banner to fight beneath, no authority to appeal to in defense of their views, no definite gospel to preach. They were by turns morbid, hysterical, foolishly blasphemous, or weakly disgusting, but never anything for long, their one desire being to produce a thrill at any cost. If the hospital failed they went to the brothel, and when even obscenity failed to stimulate the jaded palates of their generation there was still the graveyard left. A more or less successful imitation of Baudelaire's awful verses entitled "The Corpse" has been the beginning of more than one French poet's corrupt flight across the sky of literature. That Baudelaire himself was one of their company is not an accusation, for he had genius, which his imitators, English or French, have not; and his book, even apart from the fact that it made straight the way for better things, must be admitted to be a great and subtly-wrought work of art by whosoever reads it with understanding. And, moreover, his morbidness is not at all an affectation; his poems inevitably prove the writer to have been quite sincere in his perversion and in his decadence.

The Symbolist writers of today, though they are sprung from him, are greater than he because they are the prophets of a faith who believe in what they preach, They find their defense in the writings of the mystics, and their doctrines are at the root of every religion. They were held by the Gnostics and are in the books of the Kabbalists and the Magi. Blake preached them and Eliphas Levi taught them to his disciples in France, who in turn have misunderstood and perverted them, and formed strange religions and sects of Devil-worshippers. These doctrines hold that the visible world is the world of illusion, not of reality. Color and sound and perfume and all material and sensible things are but the symbols and far-off reflections of the things that are alone real. Reality is hidden away from us by the five senses and the gates of death; and Reason, the blind and laborious servant of the physical brain, deludes us into believing that we can know anything of truth through the medium of the senses. It is through the imagination alone that man can obtain spiritual revelation, for imagination is the one window in the prison-house of the flesh through which the soul can see the proud images of eternity. And Blake, who is the authority of all English Symbolist writers, long since formulated their creed in words that have been quoted again and again, and must still be quoted by all who write in defense of modern art:—"*The world of imagination is the world of Eternity. It is the divine bosom into which we shall all go after the death of the vegetated body. This world of imagination is infinite and eternal, whereat the world of generation, or vegetation, is finite and temporal. There exist in that eternal world the permanent realities of everything which we see reflected in this vegetable glass of nature.*"

In spite of the cry against *Flowers of Evil*, Baudelaire did not lack defenders among literary men themselves; and many enthusiastic articles were written in praise of his book. Thierry not unjustly compared him to Dante, to which Barbey d'Aurevilly replied, "Baudelaire comes from hell, Dante, only went there"; adding at the finish of his article: "After the *Flowers of Evil* there are only two possible ways for the poet who made them blossom: either to blow out his brains or become a Christian." Baudelaire did neither. And Victor Hugo, after reading the two poems, "The Seven Old Men" and "The Little Old Women," wrote to Baudelaire. "You have dowered the heaven of art with, one knows not what deathly gleam," he said in his letter; "you have created a new shudder." The phrase became famous, and for many years after this the creation of a new shudder was the ambition of every young French writer worth his salt.

When the first great wave of public astonishment had broken and ebbed, Baudelaire's work began to be appreciated by others than merely literary men, by all in fact who cared for careful art and subtle thinking, and before long he was admitted to be the greatest after Hugo who had written French verse. He was famous and he was unhappy. Neither glory, nor love, nor friendship—and he knew them all—could minister to the disease of that fierce mind, seeking it knew not what and never finding it; seeking it, unhappily, in the strangest excesses. He took opium to quiet his nerves when they trembled, for something to do when they did not, and made immoderate use of hashish to produce visions and heighten his fantasy. His life was a haunted weariness. Thomas de Quincey's *Confessions of an English Opium-Eater* seems to have fascinated him to a great extent, for besides imitating the vices of the author, he wrote, in imitation of his book, *The Artificial Paradises*, a monograph on the effects of opium and hashish, partly original, partly a mere translation from the *Confessions*.

He remembered his visions and sensations as an eater of drugs and made literary use of them. Among the "Poems in Prose," will be found one entitled "The Double Chamber," almost certainly written under the influence of opium, and the last verse of "The Temptation"—

> "O mystic metamorphosis!
>   My senses into one sense flow—
> Her voice makes perfume when she speaks,
>   Her breath is music faint and low!"

as well as the last six lines of that profound sonnet "Correspondences"—

> "Some perfumes are as fragrant as a child,
> Sweet as the sound of hautboys, meadow-green;
> Others, corrupted, rich, exultant, wild,
> Have all the expansion of things infinite:
> As amber, incense, musk, and benzoin,
> Which sing the sense's and the soul's delight,"

are certainly memories of a sensation he experienced under the influence of hashish, as recorded in *The Artificial Paradises*, where he has this curious passage:—"The senses become extraordinarily acute and fine. The eyes pierce Infinity. The ear seizes the most unseizable sounds in the midst of the shrillest noises. Hallucinations commence External objects take on monstrous appearances and show themselves under forms hitherto unknown. . . . The most singular equivocations, the most inexplicable transposition of ideas, take place. *Sounds are perceived to have a color, and color becomes musical.*" Baudelaire need not have gone to hashish to discover this. The mystics of all times have taught that sounds in gross matter produce color in subtle matter; and all who are subject to any visionary condition know that when in trance colors will produce words of a language whose meaning is forgotten as soon as one awakes to normal life; but I do not think Baudelaire was a visionary. His work shows too precise a method, and a too ordered appreciation of the artificial in beauty. There again he is comparable to Aubrey Beardsley, for I have read somewhere that when Beardsley was asked if ever he saw visions, he replied, "I do not permit myself to see them, except upon paper." The whole question of the color of sound is one of supreme interest to the poet, but it is too difficult and abstract a question to be written of here. A famous sonnet by Rimbaud on the color of the vowels has founded a school of symbolists in France. I will content myself with quoting that—in the original, since it loses too much by translation:

"A noir, E blanc, I rouge, U vert, O bleu, voyelles,
Je dirai quelque jour vos naissances latentes,
A, noir corset velu des mouches éclatantes
Qui bourdonnent autour des puanteurs cruelles,
Golfes d'ombres; E, candeurs des vapeurs et des tentes,
Lances des glaciers fiers, rois blancs, frissons d'ombrelles;
I, poupre, sang crache, rire des lèvres belles
Dans la colère ou les ivresses pénitentes;
U, cycles, vibrements divins des mers virides,
Paix des pâtis semés d'animaux, paix des rides
Que l'alchimie imprime aux grands fronts studieux.
O, suprême clairon, plein de strideurs étranges,
Silences traverses des mondes et des anges.
—O l'Omega, rayon violet de ses yeux."

It is to be hoped that opium and hashish rendered Baudelaire somewhat less unhappy during his life, for they certainly contributed to hasten his death. Always of an extremely neurotic temperament, he began to break down beneath his excesses, and shortly after the publication of *The Artificial Paradises*, which shows a considerable deterioration in his style, he removed from Paris to Brussels in the hope of building up his health by the change. At Brussels he grew worse. His speech began to fail; he was unable to pronounce certain words and stumbled over others. Hallucinations commenced, no longer the hallucinations of hashish; and his disease, rapidly establishing itself, was recognized as "general paralysis of the insane." Gautier tells how the news of his death came to Paris while he yet lived. It was false news, but prematurely true. Baudelaire lingered on for another three months; motionless and inert, his eyes the only part of him alive; unable to speak or even to write, and so died.

He left, besides *The Flowers of Evil* and *Little Poems in Prose* (his masterpieces), several volumes of critical essays, published under the titles of *Aesthetic Curiosities and Romantic Art*; *The Artificial Paradises*, and his translations of the works of Edgar Allan Poe—admirable pieces of work by which Poe actually gains.

III

Baudelaire's love of the artificial has been insisted upon by all who have studied his work, but to my mind never sufficiently insisted upon, for it was the foundation of his method. He wrote many arguments in favor of the artificial, and elaborated them into a kind of paradoxical philosophy of art. His hatred of nature and purely natural things was but a perverted form of the religious ecstasy that made the old monk pull his cowl about his eyes when he left his cell in the month of May lest he should see the blossoming trees, and his mind be turned towards the beautiful delusions of the world. The Egyptians and the earliest of the Christians looked upon nature not as the work of the good and benevolent spirit who is the father of our souls, but as the work of the rebellious "gods of generation," who fashion beautiful things to capture the heart of man and bind his soul to earth. Blake, whom I have already quoted, hated nature in the same fashion, and held death to be the one way of escape from "the delusions of goddess Nature and her laws." Baudelaire's revolt against external things was more a revolt of the intellect than of the imagination; and he expresses it, not by desiring that the things of nature should be swept away to make room for the things of the spirit, but that they should be so changed by art that they cease to be natural. As he was of all poets the most intensely modern, holding that "modernity is one-half of art," the other half being something "eternal and immutable," he preferred, unlike Blake and his modern followers, to express himself in quite modern terms, and so wrote his famous and much misunderstood *Eloge du Maquillage* to defend his views. As was usual with him, he pushed his ideas to their extreme logical sequence, and the casual reader who picks up that extraordinary essay is in consequence quite misled as to the writer's intention.

It seems scarcely necessary at this time of day to assert that the *Eloge du Maquillage* is something more than a mere *Praise of Cosmetics*, written by a man who wished to shock his readers. It is the part expression of a theory of art, and if it is paradoxical and far-fetched it is because Baudelaire wrote at a time when French literature, in the words of M. Asselineau, "was dying of correctness," and needed very vigorous treatment indeed. If the *Eloge du Maquillage* had been more restrained in manner, if it had not been something so entirely contrary to all accepted ideas of the well-regulated citizen who never thinks a thought that somebody else has not put into his head, it might have been passed over without notice. It was written to initiate the profane; to make them think, at least; and not to raise a smile among the initiated. And moreover, it was in a manner a defense of his own work that had met with so much hatred and opposition.

He begins by attempting to prove that Nature is innately and fundamentally wrong and wicked. "The greater number of errors relative to the beautiful date from the eighteenth century's false conceptions of morality. Nature was regarded in those times as the base, source, and type of all possible good and beauty. . . . If, however, we consent to refer simply to the visible facts, . . . we see that Nature teaches nothing, or almost nothing. That is to say, she *forces* man to sleep, to drink, to eat, and to protect himself, well or ill, against the hostilities of the atmosphere. It is she also who moves him to kill and eat or imprison and torture his kind; for, as soon as we leave the region of necessities and needs to enter into that of luxuries and pleasures, we see that Nature is no better than a counselor to crime. . . . Religion commands us to nourish our poor and infirm parents; Nature (the voice of our own interest) commands us to do away with them. Pass in review, analyze all that is natural, all the actions and desires of the natural man, and you will find nothing but what is horrible. All beautiful and noble things are the result of calculation. Crime, the taste for which the human animal absorbs before birth, is originally natural. Virtue, on the contrary, is *artificial*, supernatural, since there has been a necessity in all ages and among all nations for gods and prophets to preach virtue to humanity; since man alone would have been unable to discover it. Evil is done without effort, *naturally* and by fatality; good is always the product of an art."

So far the argument is straightforward and expresses what many must have thought, but Baudelaire, remembering that exaggeration is the best way of impressing one's ideas upon the unimaginative, immediately carries his argument from the moral order to the order of the beautiful, and applies it there. The result is strange enough. "I am thus led to regard personal adornment as one of the signs of the primitive nobility of the human soul. The races that our confused and perverted civilization, with a fatuity and pride entirely laughable, treats as savages, understand as does the child the high spirituality of the toilet. The savage and the child, by their naïve love of all brilliant things, of glittering plumage and shining stuffs, and the superlative majesty of artificial forms, bear witness to their distaste for reality, and so prove, unknown to themselves, the immateriality of their souls."

Thus, with some appearance of logic, he carries his argument a step farther, and this immediately brings him to the bizarre conclusion that the more beautiful a woman naturally is, the more she should hide her natural beauty beneath the artificial charm of rouge and powder. "She performs a duty in attempting to appear magical and supernatural. She is an idol who must adorn herself to be adored." Powder and rouge and kohl, all the little artifices that shock respectability, have for their end "the creation of an abstract unity in the grain and color of the skin." This unity brings the human being nearer to the condition of a statue— that is to say, "a divine and superior being." Red and black are the symbols of "an excessive and supernatural life." A touch of kohl "lends to the eye a more decided appearance of a window opened upon infinity"; and rouge augments the brilliance of the eye, "and adds to a beautiful feminine face the mysterious passion of the priestess." But artifice cannot make ugliness any the less ugly, nor help age to rival youth. "Who dare assign to art the sterile function of imitating nature?" Deception, if it is to have any charm, must be obvious and unashamed; it must be displayed "if not with affectation, at least with a kind of candor."

Such theories as these, if they are sincerely held, necessarily lead the theorist into the strangest bypaths of literature. Baudelaire, like many another writers whose business is with verse, pondered so long upon the musical and rhythmical value of words that at times words became meaningless to him. He thought his own language too simple to express the complexities of poetic reverie, and dreamed of writing his poems in Latin. Not, however, in the Latin of classical times; that was too robust, too natural, too "brutal and purely epidermic," to use an expression of his own; but in the corrupt Latin of the Byzantine decadence, which he considered as "the supreme sigh of a strong being already transformed and prepared for the spiritual life."

One of these Latin poems has appeared in all editions of *The Flowers of Evil*. Though dozens as good are to be found in the Breviary of the Roman Church, "Franciscan Meae Laudes" is one example of Baudelaire's many successful steps in the wrong direction.

IV

In almost every line of *The Flowers of Evil* one can trace the influence of Edgar Allan Poe, and in the many places where Baudelaire has attained a pure imaginative beauty as in "The Sadness of the Moon" or "Music" or "The Death of Lovers," it is a beauty that would have pleased the author of *Tales of the Grotesque and Arabesque*. Another kind of beauty, the beauty of death—for in Baudelaire's crucible everything is melted into loveliness—is even more directly traceable to Poe. In spite of the sonnet "Correspondences," and in spite of his Symbolist followers of the present day, Baudelaire himself made but an imperfect use of such symbols as he had; and these he found ready to his hand in the works of the American poet. The Tomb, the symbol of death or of an intellectual darkness inhabited by the Worm, who is remorse; the Abyss, which is the despair into which the mortal part of man's mind plunges when brought into contact with dead and perishing substances; all these are borrowed from Poe. The Worm, who "devours with a kiss," occasionally becomes Time devouring life, or the Demon, "the obscure Enemy who gnaws the heart"; and when it is none of these it is the Serpent, as in that somber poem "To a Madonna"—the Serpent beneath the feet of conquering purity. Baudelaire's imagination, however, which continually ran upon *macabre* images, loved remorse more than peace, and loved the Serpent more than the purity that would slay it, so he destroys purity with "Seven Knives" which are "the Seven Deadly Sins," that the Serpent may live to prey upon a heart that finds no beauty in peace. Even Love is evil, for his "ancient arrows" are "crime, horror, folly," and the god Eros becomes a demon lying in wait:

> "Let us love gently. Love, from his retreat
> Ambushed and shadowy, bends his fatal bow,
> And I too well his ancient arrows know:
> Crime, Horror, Folly. . . ."

Gautier pretends that the poet preserved his ideal under the form of "the adorable phantom of La Beatrix, the ideal ever desired, never attained, the divine and superior beauty incarnated in an ethereal woman, spiritualized, made of light and flame and perfume, a vapor, a dream, a reflection of the seraphical world"; but when Baudelaire has a vision of this same Beatrice he sees her as one of a crowd of "cruel and curious demons" who mock at his sorrow, and she, too, mocks him, and caresses the demons who are his spiritual foes.

Baudelaire was too deeply in love with the artificial to care overmuch for the symbols he could have found among natural objects. Only once in *The Flowers of Evil* does he look upon the Moon with the eyes of a mystic; and that is when he remembers that all people of imagination are under the Moon's influence, and makes his poet hide her iridescent tear in his heart, "far from the eyes of the Sun," for the Sun is lord of material labors and therefore hostile to the dreams and reveries that are the activity of the poet. He sought more for bizarre analogies and striking metaphors than for true symbols or correspondences. He is happiest when comparing the vault of the heaven to "the lighted ceiling of a music hall," or "the black lid of the mighty pot where the human generations boil"; and when he thinks of the unfortunate and unhappy folk of the world, he does not see any hope for them in any future state; he sees, simply, "God's awful claw" stretched out to tear them. He offers pity, but no comfort.

Sometimes he has a vision of a beauty unmingled with any malevolence; but it is always evoked by sensuous and material things; perfume or music; and always it is a sorrowful loveliness he mourns or praises. Perhaps of all his poems "The Balcony" is most full of that tender and reverential melancholy we look for in a poem of love; but even it tells of a passion that has faded out of heart and mind and become beautiful only with its passing away, and not of an existing love. The other love poems—if indeed such a name can be given to "A Madrigal of Sorrow," "The Eyes of Beauty," "The Remorse of the Dead," and the like—are nothing but terrible confessions of satiety, or cruelty, or terror. I have translated "The Corpse," his most famous and most infamous poem, partly because it shows him at his worst as the others in the volume at his best, partly because it is something of the nature of a literary curiosity. A poem like "The Corpse," which is simply an example of what may happen if any writer pushes his theories to the extreme, does not at all detract, be it said, from

Baudelaire's delicate genius; for though he may not be quite worthy of a place by Dante, he has written poems that Dante might have been proud to write, and he is worthy to be set among the very greatest of the moderns, alongside Hugo and Verlaine. Read the sonnet entitled "Beauty" and you will see how he has invoked in fourteen lines the image of a goddess, mysterious and immortal; as fair as that Aphrodite who cast the shadow of her loveliness upon the Golden Age; as terrible as Pallas, "the warrior maid invincible." And as Minerva loved mortality in the person of Ulysses, so Baudelaire's personification of Beauty loves the poets who pray before her and gaze into her eternal eyes, watching the rising and setting of their visionary Star in those placid mirrors.

The explanation of most of Baudelaire's morbid imaginings is this, that he was a man haunted by terrible dream-like memories; chief among them the memory that the loveliness he had adored in woman— the curve of a perfect cheek, the lifting of a perfect arm in some gesture of imperial indolence, the fall of a curl across a pale brow, all the minute and unforgettable things that give immortality to some movement of existence—all these, and the woman and her lover, must pass away from Time and Space; and he, unhappily, knew nothing of the philosophy that teaches us how all objects and events, even the most trivial—a woman's gesture, a rose, a sigh, a fading flame, the sound that trembles on a lute-string—find a place in Eternity when they pass from the recognition of our senses. If he believed in the deathlessness of man's personality he gained no comfort from his belief. He mourned the body's decay; he was not concerned with the soul; and no heaven less palpable than Mohammed's could have had any reality in his imagination.

His prose is as distinguished in its manner as his verse. I think it was Professor Saintsbury who first brought *The Little Poems in Prose*, before the notice of English readers in an essay written many years ago. I am writing this in France, far from the possibility of consulting any English books, but if my memory serves me rightly he considered the prose of these prose poems to be as perfect as literature can be. I think he said, "they go as far as prose can go." They need no other introduction than themselves, for they are perfect of their kind, and not different in thought from the more elaborately wrought poems of *The Flowers of Evil*. Some of them, as for instance "Every Man His Chimera," are as classical and as universally true as the myths and symbolisms of the Old Testament; and all of them, I think, are worthy of a place in that book the Archangel of the Presence will consult when all is weighed in the balance —the book written by man himself, the record of his deep and shallow imaginings. Baudelaire wrote them, he said, because he had dreamed, "in his days of ambition," "of a miracle of poetical prose, musical without rhythm and without rhyme." His attitude of mind was always so natural to him that he never thought it necessary to make any excuse for the spirit of his art or the drear philosophy he preached; unless a short notice printed in the first edition of his poems, but withdrawn from the second edition, explaining that "faithful to his dolorous programme, the author of *The Flowers of Evil*, as a perfect comedian, has had to mould his spirit to all sophisms as to all corruptions," can be considered as an excuse. From whatever point of view we regard him: whether we praise his art and blame his philosophy, or blame his art and praise his philosophy, he is as difficult to analyze as he is difficult to give a place to, for we have none with whom to compare him, or very few, too few to be of service to the critic. His art is like the pearl, a beautiful product of disease, and to blame it is like blaming the pearl.

He looked upon life very much as Poe, whom he so admired, looked upon it: with the eye of a sensitive spectator in some gloomy vault of the Spanish Inquisition, where beauty was upon the rack; he was horrified, but unable to turn from a sight that fascinated him by its very terror. His moments of inspiration are haunted by the consciousness that evil beings, clothed with horror as with a shroud, are ever lingering about the temple of life and awaiting an opportunity to enter. He was like a man who awakens trembling from a nightmare, afraid of the darkness, and unable to believe the dawn may be less hopeless than the midnight. Perhaps he was haunted, as many artists and all mystics, by a fear of madness and of the unseen world of evil shapes that sanity hides from us and madness reveals. Is there a man, is there a writer, especially, who has not at times been conscious of a vague and terrible fear that the whole world of visible nature is but a comfortable illusion that may fade away in a moment and leave him face to face with the horror that has visited him in dreams? The old occult writers held that the evil thoughts of others beget phantoms in the air that can make themselves bodies out of our fear, and haunt even our waking moments. These were the shapes of terror that haunted Baudelaire. Shelley, too, writes of them with as profound a knowledge as the magical writer of the Middle Ages. They come to haunt his Prometheus.

> "Blackening the birth of day with countless wings,
> And hollow underneath, like death."

They are the elemental beings who dwell beside the soul of the dreamer and the poet, "like a vain loud multitude"; turning life into death and all beautiful thoughts into poems like *The Flowers of Evil*, or into tales like the satanic reveries of Edgar Poe.

"We are the ministers of pain, and fear,
And disappointment, and mistrust, and hate,
And clinging crime; and as lean dogs pursue'

Through wood and lake some struck and sobbing fawn,
We track all things that weep, and bleed, and live,
When the great King betrays them to our will."

And every man gives them of the substance of his imagination to clothe them in prophetic shapes that are the images of his destiny:

"From our victim's destined agony
The shade which is our form invests us round,
Else we are shapeless as our mother Night."

The greatest of all poets conquer their dreams; others, who are great, but not of the greatest, are conquered by them, and Baudelaire was one of these. There is a passage in the works of Edgar Allan Poe that Baudelaire may well have pondered as he labored at his translation, for it reveals the secret of his life: "There are moments when, even to the sober eye of reason, the world of our sad humanity may assume the semblance of a hell; but the imagination of man is no Carathis to explore with impunity its every cavern. Alas! the grim legion of sepulchral terrors cannot be regarded as altogether fanciful; but, like the demons in whose company Afrasiab made his voyage down the Oxus, they must sleep or they will devour us—they must be suffered to slumber or we perish."

FRANK PEARCE STURM

1919.

The Flowers of Evil

DEDICACE

Au poète impeccable
Au parfait magicien ès lettres françaises
A mon très-cher et très-vénéré
Maître et ami
Théophile Gautier
Avec les sentiments
De la plus profonde humilité
Je dédie
Ces fleurs maladives
C.B.

DEDICATION

To the impeccable poet
To the perfect magician of French letters
To my very dear and very revered
Master and friend
Théophile Gautier
With sentiments
Of the most profound humility
I dedicate
These unhealthy flowers

AU LECTEUR

La sottise, l'erreur, le péché, la lésine,
Occupent nos esprits et travaillent nos corps,
Et nous alimentons nos aimables remords,
Comme les mendiants nourrissent leur vermine.

Nos péchés sont têtus, nos repentirs sont lâches;
Nous nous faisons payer grassement nos aveux,
Et nous rentrons gaiement dans le chemin bourbeux,
Croyant par de vils pleurs laver toutes nos taches.

Sur l'oreiller du mal c'est Satan Trismégiste
Qui berce longuement notre esprit enchanté,
Et le riche métal de notre volonté
Est tout vaporisé par ce savant chimiste.

C'est le Diable qui tient les fils qui nous remuent!
Aux objets répugnants nous trouvons des appas;
Chaque jour vers l'Enfer nous descendons d'un pas,
Sans horreur, à travers des ténèbres qui puent.

Ainsi qu'un débauché pauvre qui baise et mange
Le sein martyrisé d'une antique catin,
Nous volons au passage un plaisir clandestin
Que nous pressons bien fort comme une vieille orange.

Serré, fourmillant, comme un million d'helminthes,
Dans nos cerveaux ribote un peuple de Démons,
Et, quand nous respirons, la Mort dans nos poumons
Descend, fleuve invisible, avec de sourdes plaintes.

Si le viol, le poison, le poignard, l'incendie,
N'ont pas encor brodé de leurs plaisants dessins
Le canevas banal de nos piteux destins,
C'est que notre âme, hélas! n'est pas assez hardie.

Mais parmi les chacals, les panthères, les lices,
Les singes, les scorpions, les vautours, les serpents,
Les monstres glapissants, hurlants, grognants, rampants,
Dans la ménagerie infâme de nos vices,

Il en est un plus laid, plus méchant, plus immonde!
Quoiqu'il ne pousse ni grands gestes ni grands cris,
Il ferait volontiers de la terre un débris
Et dans un bâillement avalerait le monde;

C'est l'Ennui! L'oeil chargé d'un pleur involontaire,
Il rêve d'échafauds en fumant son houka.
Tu le connais, lecteur, ce monstre délicat,
—Hypocrite lecteur,—mon semblable,—mon frère!

TO THE READER

Folly, error, sin, avarice
Occupy our minds and labor our bodies,
And we feed our pleasant remorse
As beggars nourish their vermin.

Our sins are obstinate, our repentance is faint;
We exact a high price for our confessions,
And we gaily return to the miry path,
Believing that base tears wash away all our stains.

On the pillow of evil Satan, Trismegist,
Incessantly lulls our enchanted minds,
And the noble metal of our will
Is wholly vaporized by this wise alchemist.

The Devil holds the strings which move us!
In repugnant things we discover charms;
Every day we descend a step further toward Hell,
Without horror, through gloom that stinks.

Like a penniless rake who with kisses and bites
Tortures the breast of an old prostitute,
We steal as we pass by a clandestine pleasure
That we squeeze very hard like a dried up orange.

Serried, swarming, like a million maggots,
A legion of Demons carouses in our brains,
And when we breathe, Death, that unseen river,
Descends into our lungs with muffled wails.

If rape, poison, daggers, arson
Have not yet embroidered with their pleasing designs
The banal canvas of our pitiable lives,
It is because our souls have not enough boldness.

But among the jackals, the panthers, the bitch hounds,
The apes, the scorpions, the vultures, the serpents,
The yelping, howling, growling, crawling monsters,
In the filthy menagerie of our vices,

There is one more ugly, more wicked, more filthy!
Although he makes neither great gestures nor great cries,
He would willingly make of the earth a shambles
And, in a yawn, swallow the world;

He is Ennui!—His eye watery as though with tears,
He dreams of scaffolds as he smokes his hookah pipe.
You know him reader, that refined monster,
—Hypocritical reader,—my fellow,—my brother!

SPLEEN ET IDÉAL — SPLEEN AND IDEAL

BENEDICTION

Lorsque, par un décret des puissances suprêmes,
Le Poète apparaît en ce monde ennuyé,
Sa mère épouvantée et pleine de blasphèmes
Crispe ses poings vers Dieu, qui la prend en pitié:

—«Ah! que n'ai-je mis bas tout un noeud de vipères,
Plutôt que de nourrir cette dérision!
Maudite soit la nuit aux plaisirs éphémères
Où mon ventre a conçu mon expiation!

Puisque tu m'as choisie entre toutes les femmes
Pour être le dégoût de mon triste mari,
Et que je ne puis pas rejeter dans les flammes,
Comme un billet d'amour, ce monstre rabougri,

Je ferai rejaillir ta haine qui m'accable
Sur l'instrument maudit de tes méchancetés,
Et je tordrai si bien cet arbre misérable,
Qu'il ne pourra pousser ses boutons empestés!»

Elle ravale ainsi l'écume de sa haine,
Et, ne comprenant pas les desseins éternels,
Elle-même prépare au fond de la Géhenne
Les bûchers consacrés aux crimes maternels.

Pourtant, sous la tutelle invisible d'un Ange,
L'Enfant déshérité s'enivre de soleil
Et dans tout ce qu'il boit et dans tout ce qu'il mange
Retrouve l'ambroisie et le nectar vermeil.

Il joue avec le vent, cause avec le nuage,
Et s'enivre en chantant du chemin de la croix;
Et l'Esprit qui le suit dans son pèlerinage
Pleure de le voir gai comme un oiseau des bois.

Tous ceux qu'il veut aimer l'observent avec crainte,
Ou bien, s'enhardissant de sa tranquillité,
Cherchent à qui saura lui tirer une plainte,
Et font sur lui l'essai de leur férocité.

Dans le pain et le vin destinés à sa bouche
Ils mêlent de la cendre avec d'impurs crachats;
Avec hypocrisie ils jettent ce qu'il touche,
Et s'accusent d'avoir mis leurs pieds dans ses pas.

Sa femme va criant sur les places publiques:
«Puisqu'il me trouve assez belle pour m'adorer,
Je ferai le métier des idoles antiques,
Et comme elles je veux me faire redorer;

Et je me soûlerai de nard, d'encens, de myrrhe,
De génuflexions, de viandes et de vins,
Pour savoir si je puis dans un coeur qui m'admire
Usurper en riant les hommages divins!

Et, quand je m'ennuierai de ces farces impies,
Je poserai sur lui ma frêle et forte main;
Et mes ongles, pareils aux ongles des harpies,
Sauront jusqu'à son coeur se frayer un chemin.

Comme un tout jeune oiseau qui tremble et qui palpite,
J'arracherai ce coeur tout rouge de son sein,
Et, pour rassasier ma bête favorite
Je le lui jetterai par terre avec dédain!»

Vers le Ciel, où son oeil voit un trône splendide,
Le Poète serein lève ses bras pieux
Et les vastes éclairs de son esprit lucide
Lui dérobent l'aspect des peuples furieux:

—«Soyez béni, mon Dieu, qui donnez la souffrance
Comme un divin remède à nos impuretés
Et comme la meilleure et la plus pure essence
Qui prépare les forts aux saintes voluptés!

Je sais que vous gardez une place au Poète
Dans les rangs bienheureux des saintes Légions,
Et que vous l'invitez à l'éternelle fête
Des Trônes, des Vertus, des Dominations.

Je sais que la douleur est la noblesse unique
Où ne mordront jamais la terre et les enfers,
Et qu'il faut pour tresser ma couronne mystique
Imposer tous les temps et tous les univers.

Mais les bijoux perdus de l'antique Palmyre,
Les métaux inconnus, les perles de la mer,
Par votre main montés, ne pourraient pas suffire
A ce beau diadème éblouissant et clair;

Car il ne sera fait que de pure lumière,
Puisée au foyer saint des rayons primitifs,
Et dont les yeux mortels, dans leur splendeur entière,
Ne sont que des miroirs obscurcis et plaintifs!»

BENEDICTION

When, after a decree of the supreme powers,
The Poet is brought forth in this wearisome world,
His mother terrified and full of blasphemies
Raises her clenched fist to God, who pities her:

—"Ah! would that I had spawned a whole knot of vipers
Rather than to have fed this derisive object!
Accursed be the night of ephemeral joy
When my belly conceived this, my expiation!

Since of all women You have chosen me
To be repugnant to my sorry spouse,
And since I cannot cast this misshapen monster
Into the flames, like an old love letter,

I shall spew the hatred with which you crush me down
On the cursed instrument of your malevolence,
And twist so hard this wretched tree
That it cannot put forth its pestilential buds!"

Thus she gulps down the froth of her hatred,
And not understanding the eternal designs,
Herself prepares deep down in Gehenna
The pyre reserved for a mother's crimes.

However, protected by an unseen Angel,
The outcast child is enrapt by the sun,
And in all that he eats, in everything he drinks,
He finds sweet ambrosia and rubiate nectar.

He cavorts with the wind, converses with the clouds,
And singing, transported, goes the way of the cross;
And the Angel who follows him on pilgrimage
Weeps to see him as carefree as a bird.

All those whom he would love watch him with fear,
Or, emboldened by his tranquility,
Emulously attempt to wring a groan from him
And test on him their inhumanity.

With the bread and the wine intended for his mouth
They mix ashes and foul spittle,
And, hypocrites, cast away what he touches
And feel guilty if they have trod in his footprints.

His wife goes about the market-places
Crying: "Since he finds me fair enough to adore,
I shall imitate the idols of old,
And like them I want to be regilded;

I shall get drunk with spikenard, incense, myrrh,
And with genuflections, viands and wine,
To see if laughingly I can usurp
In an admiring heart the homage due to God!

And when I tire of these impious jokes,
I shall lay upon him my strong, my dainty hand;
And my nails, like harpies' talons,
Will cut a path straight to his heart.

That heart which flutters like a fledgling bird
I'll tear, all bloody, from his breast,
And scornfully I'll throw it in the dust
To sate the hunger of my favorite hound!"

To Heav'n, where his eye sees a radiant throne,
Piously, the Poet, serene, raises his arms,
And the dazzling brightness of his illumined mind
Hides from his sight the raging mob:

—"Praise be to You, O God, who send us suffering
As a divine remedy for our impurities
And as the best and the purest essence
To prepare the strong for holy ecstasies!

I know that you reserve a place for the Poet
Within the blessed ranks of the holy Legions,
And that you invite him to the eternal feast
Of the Thrones, the Virtues, and the Dominations.

I know that suffering is the sole nobility
Which earth and hell shall never mar,
And that to weave my mystic crown,
You must tax every age and every universe.

But the lost jewels of ancient Palmyra,
The unfound metals, the pearls of the sea,
Set by Your own hand, would not be adequate
For that diadem of dazzling splendor,

For that crown will be made of nothing but pure light
Drawn from the holy source of primal rays,
Whereof our mortal eyes, in their fullest brightness,
Are no more than tarnished, mournful mirrors!"

L'ALBATROS

Souvent, pour s'amuser, les hommes d'équipage
Prennent des albatros, vastes oiseaux des mers,
Qui suivent, indolents compagnons de voyage,
Le navire glissant sur les gouffres amers.

À peine les ont-ils déposés sur les planches,
Que ces rois de l'azur, maladroits et honteux,
Laissent piteusement leurs grandes ailes blanches
Comme des avirons traîner à côté d'eux.

Ce voyageur ailé, comme il est gauche et veule!
Lui, naguère si beau, qu'il est comique et laid!
L'un agace son bec avec un brûle-gueule,
L'autre mime, en boitant, l'infirme qui volait!

Le Poète est semblable au prince des nuées
Qui hante la tempête et se rit de l'archer;
Exilé sur le sol au milieu des huées,
Ses ailes de géant l'empêchent de marcher.

THE ALBATROSS

Often, to amuse themselves, the men of a crew
Catch albatrosses, those vast sea birds
That indolently follow a ship
As it glides over the deep, briny sea.

Scarcely have they placed them on the deck
Than these kings of the sky, clumsy, ashamed,
Pathetically let their great white wings
Drag beside them like oars.

That winged voyager, how weak and gauche he is,
So beautiful before, now comic and ugly!
One man worries his beak with a stubby clay pipe;
Another limps, mimics the cripple who once flew!

The poet resembles this prince of cloud and sky
Who frequents the tempest and laughs at the bowman;
When exiled on the earth, the butt of hoots and jeers,
His giant wings prevent him from walking.

ÉLEVATION

Au-dessus des étangs, au-dessus des vallées,
Des montagnes, des bois, des nuages, des mers,
Par delà le soleil, par delà les éthers,
Par delà les confins des sphères étoilées,

Mon esprit, tu te meus avec agilité,
Et, comme un bon nageur qui se pâme dans l'onde,
Tu sillonnes gaiement l'immensité profonde
Avec une indicible et mâle volupté.

Envole-toi bien loin de ces miasmes morbides;
Va te purifier dans l'air supérieur,
Et bois, comme une pure et divine liqueur,
Le feu clair qui remplit les espaces limpides.

Derrière les ennuis et les vastes chagrins
Qui chargent de leur poids l'existence brumeuse,
Heureux celui qui peut d'une aile vigoureuse
S'élancer vers les champs lumineux et sereins;

Celui dont les pensers, comme des alouettes,
Vers les cieux le matin prennent un libre essor,
—Qui plane sur la vie, et comprend sans effort
Le langage des fleurs et des choses muettes!

ELEVATION

Above the lakes, above the vales,
The mountains and the woods, the clouds, the seas,
Beyond the sun, beyond the ether,
Beyond the confines of the starry spheres,

My soul, you move with ease,
And like a strong swimmer in rapture in the wave
You wing your way blithely through boundless space
With virile joy unspeakable.

Fly far, far away from this baneful miasma
And purify yourself in the celestial air,
Drink the ethereal fire of those limpid regions
As you would the purest of heavenly nectars.

Beyond the vast sorrows and all the vexations
That weigh upon our lives and obscure our vision,
Happy is he who can with his vigorous wing
Soar up towards those fields luminous and serene,

He whose thoughts, like skylarks,
Toward the morning sky take flight
—Who hovers over life and understands with ease
The language of flowers and silent things!

CORRESPONDANCES

La Nature est un temple où de vivants piliers
Laissent parfois sortir de confuses paroles;
L'homme y passe à travers des forêts de symboles
Qui l'observent avec des regards familiers.

Comme de longs échos qui de loin se confondent
Dans une ténébreuse et profonde unité,
Vaste comme la nuit et comme la clarté,
Les parfums, les couleurs et les sons se répondent.

II est des parfums frais comme des chairs d'enfants,
Doux comme les hautbois, verts comme les prairies,
—Et d'autres, corrompus, riches et triomphants,

Ayant l'expansion des choses infinies,
Comme l'ambre, le musc, le benjoin et l'encens,
Qui chantent les transports de l'esprit et des sens.

CORRESPONDENCES

Nature is a temple in which living pillars
Sometimes give voice to confused words;
Man passes there through forests of symbols
Which look at him with understanding eyes.

Like prolonged echoes mingling in the distance
In a deep and tenebrous unity,
Vast as the dark of night and as the light of day,
Perfumes, sounds, and colors correspond.

There are perfumes as cool as the flesh of children,
Sweet as oboes, green as meadows
—And others are corrupt, and rich, triumphant,

With power to expand into infinity,
Like amber and incense, musk, benzoin,
That sing the ecstasy of the soul and senses.

J'AIME LE SOUVENIR DE CES EPOQUES NUES

J'aime le souvenir de ces époques nues,
Dont Phoebus se plaisait à dorer les statues.
Alors l'homme et la femme en leur agilité
Jouissaient sans mensonge et sans anxiété,
Et, le ciel amoureux leur caressant l'échine,
Exerçaient la santé de leur noble machine.
Cybèle alors, fertile en produits généreux,
Ne trouvait point ses fils un poids trop onéreux,
Mais, louve au coeur gonflé de tendresses communes
Abreuvait l'univers à ses tétines brunes.
L'homme, élégant, robuste et fort, avait le droit
D'être fier des beautés qui le nommaient leur roi;
Fruits purs de tout outrage et vierges de gerçures,
Dont la chair lisse et ferme appelait les morsures!

Le Poète aujourd'hui, quand il veut concevoir
Ces natives grandeurs, aux lieux où se font voir
La nudité de l'homme et celle de la femme,
Sent un froid ténébreux envelopper son âme
Devant ce noir tableau plein d'épouvantement.
Ô monstruosités pleurant leur vêtement!
Ô ridicules troncs! torses dignes des masques!
Ô pauvres corps tordus, maigres, ventrus ou flasques,
Que le dieu de l'Utile, implacable et serein,
Enfants, emmaillota dans ses langes d'airain!
Et vous, femmes, hélas! pâles comme des cierges,
Que ronge et que nourrit la débauche, et vous, vierges,
Du vice maternel traînant l'hérédité
Et toutes les hideurs de la fécondité!

Nous avons, il est vrai, nations corrompues,
Aux peuples anciens des beautés inconnues:
Des visages rongés par les chancres du coeur,
Et comme qui dirait des beautés de langueur;
Mais ces inventions de nos muses tardives
N'empêcheront jamais les races maladives
De rendre à la jeunesse un hommage profond,
—À la sainte jeunesse, à l'air simple, au doux front,
À l'oeil limpide et clair ainsi qu'une eau courante,
Et qui va répandant sur tout, insouciante
Comme l'azur du ciel, les oiseaux et les fleurs,
Ses parfums, ses chansons et ses douces chaleurs!

I LOVE TO THINK OF THOSE NAKED EPOCHS

I love to think of those naked epochs
Whose statues Phoebus liked to tinge with gold.
At that time men and women, lithe and strong,
Tasted the thrill of love free from care and prudery,
And with the amorous sun caressing their loins
They gloried in the health of their noble bodies.
Then Cybele, generous with her fruits,
Did not find her children too heavy a burden;
A she-wolf from whose heart flowed boundless love for all,
She fed the universe from her tawny nipples.
Man, graceful, robust, strong, was justly proud
Of the beauties who proclaimed him their king;
Fruits unblemished and free from every scar,
Whose smooth, firm flesh invited biting kisses!

Today, when the Poet wishes to imagine
This primitive grandeur, in places where
Men and women show themselves in a state of nudity,
He feels a gloomy cold enveloping his soul
Before this dark picture full of terror.
Monstrosities bewailing their clothing!
Ridiculous torsos appropriate for masks!
Poor bodies, twisted, thin, bulging or flabby,

That the god Usefulness, implacable and calm,
Wrapped up at tender age in swaddling clothes of brass!
And you, women, alas! pale as candies,
Whom Debauch gnaws and feeds, and you, virgins,
Who trail the heritage of the maternal vice
And all the hideousness of fecundity!

Degenerate races, we have, it's true,
Types of beauty unknown to the ancient peoples:
Visages gnawed by cankers of the heart
And what one might say were languor's marks of beauty;
But these inventions of our backward Muses
Will never prevent unhealthy races
From paying to their youth deep and sincere homage,
—To holy youth, with serene brow and guileless air,
With eyes bright and clear, like a running brook,
Which goes spreading over all things, as free from care
As the blue of the sky, the birds and the flowers,
Its perfumes, its songs and its sweet ardor!

LES PHARES

Rubens, fleuve d'oubli, jardin de la paresse,
Oreiller de chair fraîche où l'on ne peut aimer,
Mais où la vie afflue et s'agite sans cesse,
Comme l'air dans le ciel et la mer dans la mer;

Léonard de Vinci, miroir profond et sombre,
Où des anges charmants, avec un doux souris
Tout chargé de mystère, apparaissent à l'ombre
Des glaciers et des pins qui ferment leur pays;

Rembrandt, triste hôpital tout rempli de murmures,
Et d'un grand crucifix décoré seulement,
Où la prière en pleurs s'exhale des ordures,
Et d'un rayon d'hiver traversé brusquement;

Michel-Ange, lieu vague où l'on voit des Hercules
Se mêler à des Christs, et se lever tout droits
Des fantômes puissants qui dans les crépuscules
Déchirent leur suaire en étirant leurs doigts;

Colères de boxeur, impudences de faune,
Toi qui sus ramasser la beauté des goujats,
Grand coeur gonflé d'orgueil, homme débile et jaune,
Puget, mélancolique empereur des forçats;

Watteau, ce carnaval où bien des coeurs illustres,
Comme des papillons, errent en flamboyant,
Décors frais et légers éclairés par des lustres
Qui versent la folie à ce bal tournoyant;

Goya, cauchemar plein de choses inconnues,
De foetus qu'on fait cuire au milieu des sabbats,
De vieilles au miroir et d'enfants toutes nues,
Pour tenter les démons ajustant bien leurs bas;

Delacroix, lac de sang hanté des mauvais anges,
Ombragé par un bois de sapins toujours vert,
Où, sous un ciel chagrin, des fanfares étranges
Passent, comme un soupir étouffé de Weber;

Ces malédictions, ces blasphèmes, ces plaintes,
Ces extases, ces cris, ces pleurs, ces Te Deum,
Sont un écho redit par mille labyrinthes;
C'est pour les coeurs mortels un divin opium!

C'est un cri répété par mille sentinelles,
Un ordre renvoyé par mille porte-voix;
C'est un phare allumé sur mille citadelles,
Un appel de chasseurs perdus dans les grands bois!

Car c'est vraiment, Seigneur, le meilleur témoignage
Que nous puissions donner de notre dignité
Que cet ardent sanglot qui roule d'âge en âge
Et vient mourir au bord de votre éternité!

THE BEACONS

Rubens, river of oblivion, garden of indolence,
Pillow of cool flesh where one cannot love,
But where life moves and whirls incessantly
Like the air in the sky and the tide in the sea;

Leonardo, dark, unfathomable mirror,
In which charming angels, with sweet smiles
Full of mystery, appear in the shadow
Of the glaciers and pines that enclose their country;

Rembrandt, gloomy hospital filled with murmuring,
Ornamented only with a large crucifix,
Lit for a moment by a wintry sun,
Where from rot and ordure rise tearful prayers;

Angelo, shadowy place where Hercules' are seen
Mingling with Christs, and rising straight up,
Powerful phantoms, which in the twilights
Rend their winding-sheets with outstretched fingers;

Boxer's wrath, shamelessness of Fauns, you whose genius
Showed to us the beauty in a villain,
Great heart filled with pride, sickly, yellow man,
Puget, melancholy emperor of galley slaves;

Watteau, carnival where the loves of many famous hearts
Flutter capriciously like butterflies with gaudy wings;
Cool, airy settings where the candelabras' light
Touches with madness the couples whirling in the dance

Goya, nightmare full of unknown things,
Of fetuses roasted in the midst of witches' sabbaths,
Of old women at the mirror and of nude children,
Tightening their hose to tempt the demons;

Delacroix, lake of blood haunted by bad angels,
Shaded by a wood of fir-trees, ever green,
Where, under a gloomy sky, strange fanfares
Pass, like a stifled sigh from Weber;

These curses, these blasphemies, these lamentations,
These *Te Deums*, these ecstasies, these cries, these tears,
Are an echo repeated by a thousand labyrinths;
They are for mortal hearts a divine opium.

They are a cry passed on by a thousand sentinels,
An order re-echoed through a thousand megaphones;
They are a beacon lighted on a thousand citadels,
A call from hunters lost deep in the woods!

For truly, Lord, the clearest proofs
That we can give of our nobility,
Are these impassioned sobs that through the ages roll,
And die away upon the shore of your Eternity.

LA MUSE MALADE

Ma pauvre muse, hélas! qu'as-tu donc ce matin?
Tes yeux creux sont peuplés de visions nocturnes,
Et je vois tour à tour réfléchis sur ton teint
La folie et l'horreur, froides et taciturnes.

Le succube verdâtre et le rose lutin
T'ont-ils versé la peur et l'amour de leurs urnes?
Le cauchemar, d'un poing despotique et mutin
T'a-t-il noyée au fond d'un fabuleux Minturnes?

Je voudrais qu'exhalant l'odeur de la santé
Ton sein de pensers forts fût toujours fréquenté,
Et que ton sang chrétien coulât à flots rythmiques,

Comme les sons nombreux des syllabes antiques,
Où règnent tour à tour le père des chansons,
Phoebus, et le grand Pan, le seigneur des moissons.

THE SICK MUSE

My poor Muse, alas! what ails you today?
Your hollow eyes are full of nocturnal visions;
I see in turn reflected on your face
Horror and madness, cold and taciturn.

Have the green succubus, the rosy elf,
Poured out for you love and fear from their urns?
Has the hand of Nightmare, cruel and despotic,
Plunged you to the bottom of some weird Minturnae?

I would that your bosom, fragrant with health,
Were constantly the dwelling place of noble thoughts,
And that your Christian blood would flow in rhythmic waves

Like the measured sounds of ancient verse,
Over which reign in turn the father of all songs,
Phoebus, and the great Pan, lord of harvest.

LA MUSE VENALE

Ô muse de mon coeur, amante des palais,
Auras-tu, quand Janvier lâchera ses Borées,
Durant les noirs ennuis des neigeuses soirées,
Un tison pour chauffer tes deux pieds violets?

Ranimeras-tu donc tes épaules marbrées
Aux nocturnes rayons qui percent les volets?
Sentant ta bourse à sec autant que ton palais
Récolteras-tu l'or des voûtes azurées?

Il te faut, pour gagner ton pain de chaque soir,
Comme un enfant de choeur, jouer de l'encensoir,
Chanter des Te Deum auxquels tu ne crois guère,

Ou, saltimbanque à jeun, étaler tes appas
Et ton rire trempé de pleurs qu'on ne voit pas,
Pour faire épanouir la rate du vulgaire.

THE VENAL MUSE

Muse of my heart, you who love palaces,
When January frees his north winds, will you have,
During the black ennui of snowy evenings,
An ember to warm your two feet blue with cold?

Will you bring the warmth back to your mottled shoulders,
With the nocturnal beams that pass through the shutters?
Knowing that your purse is as dry as your palate,
Will you harvest the gold of the blue, vaulted sky?

To earn your daily bread you are obliged
To swing the censer like an altar boy,
And to sing *Te Deums* in which you don't believe,

Or, hungry mountebank, to put up for sale your charm,
Your laughter wet with tears which people do not see,
To make the vulgar herd shake with laughter.

LE MAUVAIS MOINE

Les cloîtres anciens sur leurs grandes murailles
Etalaient en tableaux la sainte Vérité,
Dont l'effet réchauffant les pieuses entrailles,
Tempérait la froideur de leur austérité.

En ces temps où du Christ florissaient les semailles,
Plus d'un illustre moine, aujourd'hui peu cité,
Prenant pour atelier le champ des funérailles,
Glorifiait la Mort avec simplicité.

—Mon âme est un tombeau que, mauvais cénobite,
Depuis l'éternité je parcours et j'habite;
Rien n'embellit les murs de ce cloître odieux.

Ô moine fainéant! quand saurai-je donc faire
Du spectacle vivant de ma triste misère
Le travail de mes mains et l'amour de mes yeux?

THE BAD MONK

Cloisters in former times portrayed on their high walls
The truths of Holy Writ with fitting pictures
Which gladdened pious hearts and lessened the coldness,
The austere appearance, of those monasteries.

In those days the sowing of Christ's Gospel flourished,
And more than one famed monk, seldom quoted today,
Taking his inspiration from the graveyard,
Glorified Death with naive simplicity.

—My soul is a tomb where, bad cenobite,
I wander and dwell eternally;
Nothing adorns the walls of that loathsome cloister.

O lazy monk! When shall I learn to make
Of the living spectacle of my bleak misery
The labor of my hands and the love of my eyes?

L'ENNEMI

Ma jeunesse ne fut qu'un ténébreux orage,
Traversé çà et là par de brillants soleils;
Le tonnerre et la pluie ont fait un tel ravage,
Qu'il reste en mon jardin bien peu de fruits vermeils.

Voilà que j'ai touché l'automne des idées,
Et qu'il faut employer la pelle et les râteaux
Pour rassembler à neuf les terres inondées,
Où l'eau creuse des trous grands comme des tombeaux.

Et qui sait si les fleurs nouvelles que je rêve
Trouveront dans ce sol lavé comme une grève
Le mystique aliment qui ferait leur vigueur?

—Ô douleur! ô douleur! Le Temps mange la vie,
Et l'obscur Ennemi qui nous ronge le coeur
Du sang que nous perdons croît et se fortifie!

THE ENEMY

My youth has been nothing but a tenebrous storm,
Pierced now and then by rays of brilliant sunshine;
Thunder and rain have wrought so much havoc
That very few ripe fruits remain in my garden.

I have already reached the autumn of the mind,
And I must set to work with the spade and the rake
To gather back the inundated soil
In which the rain digs holes as big as graves.

And who knows whether the new flowers I dream of
Will find in this earth washed bare like the strand,
The mystic aliment that would give them vigor?

Alas! Alas! Time eats away our lives,
And the hidden Enemy who gnaws at our hearts
Grows by drawing strength from the blood we lose!

LE GUIGNON

Pour soulever un poids si lourd,
Sisyphe, il faudrait ton courage!
Bien qu'on ait du coeur à l'ouvrage,
L'Art est long et le Temps est court.

Loin des sépultures célèbres,
Vers un cimetière isolé,
Mon coeur, comme un tambour voilé,
Va battant des marches funèbres.

—Maint joyau dort enseveli
Dans les ténèbres et l'oubli,
Bien loin des pioches et des sondes;

Mainte fleur épanche à regret
Son parfum doux comme un secret
Dans les solitudes profondes.

EVIL FATE

To lift a weight so heavy,
Would take your courage, Sisyphus!
Although one's heart is in the work,
Art is long and Time is short.

Far from famous sepulchers
Toward a lonely cemetery
My heart, like muffled drums,
Goes beating funeral marches.

Many a jewel lies buried
In darkness and oblivion,
Far, far away from picks and drills;

Many a flower regretfully
Exhales perfume soft as secrets
In a profound solitude.

LA VIE ANTERIEURE

J'ai longtemps habité sous de vastes portiques
Que les soleils marins teignaient de mille feux,
Et que leurs grands piliers, droits et majestueux,
Rendaient pareils, le soir, aux grottes basaltiques.

Les houles, en roulant les images des cieux,
Mêlaient d'une façon solennelle et mystique
Les tout-puissants accords de leur riche musique
Aux couleurs du couchant reflété par mes yeux.

C'est là que j'ai vécu dans les voluptés calmes,
Au milieu de l'azur, des vagues, des splendeurs
Et des esclaves nus, tout imprégnés d'odeurs,

Qui me rafraîchissaient le front avec des palmes,
Et dont l'unique soin était d'approfondir
Le secret douloureux qui me faisait languir.

MY FORMER LIFE

For a long time I dwelt under vast porticos
Which the ocean suns lit with a thousand colors,
The pillars of which, tall, straight, and majestic,
Made them, in the evening, like basaltic grottos.

The billows which cradled the image of the sky
Mingled, in a solemn, mystical way,
The omnipotent chords of their rich harmonies
With the sunsets' colors reflected in my eyes;

It was there that I lived in voluptuous calm,
In splendor, between the azure and the sea,
And I was attended by slaves, naked, perfumed,

Who fanned my brow with fronds of palms
And whose sole task it was to fathom
The dolorous secret that made me pine away.

BOHEMIENS EN VOYAGE

La tribu prophétique aux prunelles ardentes
Hier s'est mise en route, emportant ses petits
Sur son dos, ou livrant à leurs fiers appétits
Le trésor toujours prêt des mamelles pendantes.

Les hommes vont à pied sous leurs armes luisantes
Le long des chariots où les leurs sont blottis,
Promenant sur le ciel des yeux appesantis
Par le morne regret des chimères absentes.

Du fond de son réduit sablonneux, le grillon,
Les regardant passer, redouble sa chanson;
Cybèle, qui les aime, augmente ses verdures,

Fait couler le rocher et fleurir le désert
Devant ces voyageurs, pour lesquels est ouvert
L'empire familier des ténèbres futures.

GYPSIES TRAVELING

The prophetical tribe, that ardent eyed people,
Set out last night, carrying their children
On their backs, or yielding to those fierce appetites
The ever ready treasure of pendulous breasts.

The men travel on foot with their gleaming weapons
Alongside the wagons where their kin are huddled,
Surveying the heavens with eyes rendered heavy
By a mournful regret for vanished illusions.

The cricket from the depths of his sandy retreat
Watches them as they pass, and louder grows his song;
Cybele, who loves them, increases her verdure,

Makes the desert blossom, water spurt from the rock
Before these travelers for whom is opened wide
The familiar domain of the future's darkness.

L'HOMME ET LA MER

Homme libre, toujours tu chériras la mer!
La mer est ton miroir; tu contemples ton âme
Dans le déroulement infini de sa lame,
Et ton esprit n'est pas un gouffre moins amer.

Tu te plais à plonger au sein de ton image;
Tu l'embrasses des yeux et des bras, et ton coeur
Se distrait quelquefois de sa propre rumeur
Au bruit de cette plainte indomptable et sauvage.

Vous êtes tous les deux ténébreux et discrets:
Homme, nul n'a sondé le fond de tes abîmes;
Ô mer, nul ne connaît tes richesses intimes,
Tant vous êtes jaloux de garder vos secrets!

Et cependant voilà des siècles innombrables
Que vous vous combattez sans pitié ni remords,
Tellement vous aimez le carnage et la mort,
Ô lutteurs éternels, ô frères implacables!

MAN AND THE SEA

Free man, you will always cherish the sea!
The sea is your mirror; you contemplate your soul
In the infinite unrolling of its billows;
Your mind is an abyss that is no less bitter.

You like to plunge into the bosom of your image;
You embrace it with eyes and arms, and your heart
Is distracted at times from its own clamoring
By the sound of this plaint, wild and untamable.

Both of you are gloomy and reticent:
Man, no one has sounded the depths of your being;
O Sea, no person knows your most hidden riches,
So zealously do you keep your secrets!

Yet for countless ages you have fought each other
Without pity, without remorse,
So fiercely do you love carnage and death,
O eternal fighters, implacable brothers!

DON JUAN AUX ENFERS

Quand Don Juan descendit vers l'onde souterraine
Et lorsqu'il eut donné son obole à Charon,
Un sombre mendiant, l'oeil fier comme Antisthène,
D'un bras vengeur et fort saisit chaque aviron.

Montrant leurs seins pendants et leurs robes ouvertes,
Des femmes se tordaient sous le noir firmament,
Et, comme un grand troupeau de victimes offertes,
Derrière lui traînaient un long mugissement.

Sganarelle en riant lui réclamait ses gages,
Tandis que Don Luis avec un doigt tremblant
Montrait à tous les morts errant sur les rivages
Le fils audacieux qui railla son front blanc.

Frissonnant sous son deuil, la chaste et maigre Elvire,
Près de l'époux perfide et qui fut son amant,
Semblait lui réclamer un suprême sourire
Où brillât la douceur de son premier serment.

Tout droit dans son armure, un grand homme de pierre
Se tenait à la barre et coupait le flot noir;
Mais le calme héros, courbé sur sa rapière,
Regardait le sillage et ne daignait rien voir.

DON JUAN IN HADES

When Don Juan descended to the underground sea,
And when he had given his obolus to Charon,
That gloomy mendicant, with Antisthenes' proud look,
Seized the two oars with strong, revengeful hands.

Showing their pendent breasts and their unfastened gowns
Women writhed and twisted under the black heavens,
And like a great flock of sacrificial victims,
A continuous groan trailed along in the wake.

Sganarelle with a laugh was demanding his wage,
While Don Luis with a trembling finger
Was showing to the dead, wandering along the shores,
The impudent son who had mocked his white brow.

Shuddering in her grief, Elvira, chaste and thin,
Near her treacherous spouse who was once her lover,
Seemed to implore of him a final, parting smile
That would shine with the sweetness of his first promises.

Erect in his armor, a tall man carved from stone
Was standing at the helm and cutting the black flood;
But the hero unmoved, leaning on his rapier,
Kept gazing at the wake and deigned not look aside.

CHATIMENT DE L'ORGUEIL

En ces temps merveilleux où la Théologie
Fleurit avec le plus de sève et d'énergie,
On raconte qu'un jour un docteur des plus grands,
—Après avoir forcé les coeurs indifférents;
Les avoir remués dans leurs profondeurs noires;
Après avoir franchi vers les célestes gloires
Des chemins singuliers à lui-même inconnus,
Où les purs Esprits seuls peut-être étaient venus,—
Comme un homme monté trop haut, pris de panique,
S'écria, transporté d'un orgueil satanique:
«Jésus, petit Jésus! je t'ai poussé bien haut!
Mais, si j'avais voulu t'attaquer au défaut
De l'armure, ta honte égalerait ta gloire,
Et tu ne serais plus qu'un foetus dérisoire!»

Immédiatement sa raison s'en alla.
L'éclat de ce soleil d'un crêpe se voila
Tout le chaos roula dans cette intelligence,
Temple autrefois vivant, plein d'ordre et d'opulence,
Sous les plafonds duquel tant de pompe avait lui.
Le silence et la nuit s'installèrent en lui,
Comme dans un caveau dont la clef est perdue.
Dès lors il fut semblable aux bêtes de la rue,
Et, quand il s'en allait sans rien voir, à travers
Les champs, sans distinguer les étés des hivers,
Sale, inutile et laid comme une chose usée,
Il faisait des enfants la joie et la risée.

PUNISHMENT FOR PRIDE

In that marvelous time in which Theology
Flourished with the greatest energy and vigor,
It is said that one day a most learned doctor
—After winning by force the indifferent hearts,
Having stirred them in the dark depths of their being;
After crossing on the way to celestial glory,
Singular and strange roads, even to him unknown,
Which only pure Spirits, perhaps, had reached,—
Panic-stricken, like one who has clambered too high,
He cried, carried away by a satanic pride:
"Jesus, little jesus! I raised you very high!
But had I wished to attack you through the defect
In your armor, your shame would equal your glory,
And you would be no more than a despised fetus!"

At that very moment his reason departed.
A crape of mourning veiled the brilliance of that sun;
Complete chaos rolled in and filled that intellect,
A temple once alive, ordered and opulent,
Within whose walls so much pomp had glittered.
Silence and darkness took possession of it
Like a cellar to which the key is lost.

Henceforth he was like the beasts in the street,
And when he went along, seeing nothing, across
The fields, distinguishing nor summer nor winter,
Dirty, useless, ugly, like a discarded thing,
He was the laughing-stock, the joke, of the children.

LA BEAUTE

Je suis belle, ô mortels! comme un rêve de pierre,
Et mon sein, où chacun s'est meurtri tour à tour,
Est fait pour inspirer au poète un amour
Eternel et muet ainsi que la matière.

Je trône dans l'azur comme un sphinx incompris;
J'unis un coeur de neige à la blancheur des cygnes;
Je hais le mouvement qui déplace les lignes,
Et jamais je ne pleure et jamais je ne ris.

Les poètes, devant mes grandes attitudes,
Que j'ai l'air d'emprunter aux plus fiers monuments,
Consumeront leurs jours en d'austères études;

Car j'ai, pour fasciner ces dociles amants,
De purs miroirs qui font toutes choses plus belles:
Mes yeux, mes larges yeux aux clartés éternelles!

BEAUTY

I am fair, O mortals! like a dream carved in stone,
And my breast where each one in turn has bruised himself
Is made to inspire in the poet a love
As eternal and silent as matter.

On a throne in the sky, a mysterious sphinx,
I join a heart of snow to the whiteness of swans;
I hate movement for it displaces lines,
And never do I weep and never do I laugh.

Poets, before my grandiose poses,
Which I seem to assume from the proudest statues,
Will consume their lives in austere study;

For I have, to enchant those submissive lovers,
Pure mirrors that make all things more beautiful:
My eyes, my large, wide eyes of eternal brightness!

L'IDEAL

Ce ne seront jamais ces beautés de vignettes,
Produits avariés, nés d'un siècle vaurien,
Ces pieds à brodequins, ces doigts à castagnettes,
Qui sauront satisfaire un coeur comme le mien.

Je laisse à Gavarni, poète des chloroses,
Son troupeau gazouillant de beautés d'hôpital,
Car je ne puis trouver parmi ces pâles roses
Une fleur qui ressemble à mon rouge idéal.

Ce qu'il faut à ce coeur profond comme un abîme,
C'est vous, Lady Macbeth, âme puissante au crime,
Rêve d'Eschyle éclos au climat des autans;

Ou bien toi, grande Nuit, fille de Michel-Ange,
Qui tors paisiblement dans une pose étrange
Tes appas façonnés aux bouches des Titans!

THE IDEAL

It will never be the beauties that vignettes show,
Those damaged products of a good-for-nothing age,
Their feet shod with high shoes, hands holding castanets,
Who can ever satisfy any heart like mine.

I leave to Gavarni, poet of chlorosis,
His prattling troop of consumptive beauties,
For I cannot find among those pale roses
A flower that is like my red ideal.

The real need of my heart, profound as an abyss,
Is you, Lady Macbeth, soul so potent in crime,
The dream of Aeschylus, born in the land of storms;

Or you, great Night, daughter of Michelangelo,
Who calmly contort, reclining in a strange pose
Your charms molded by the mouths of Titans!

LA GEANTE

Du temps que la Nature en sa verve puissante
Concevait chaque jour des enfants monstrueux,
J'eusse aimé vivre auprès d'une jeune géante,
Comme aux pieds d'une reine un chat voluptueux.

J'eusse aimé voir son corps fleurir avec son âme
Et grandir librement dans ses terribles jeux;
Deviner si son coeur couve une sombre flamme
Aux humides brouillards qui nagent dans ses yeux;

Parcourir à loisir ses magnifiques formes;
Ramper sur le versant de ses genoux énormes,
Et parfois en été, quand les soleils malsains,

Lasse, la font s'étendre à travers la campagne,
Dormir nonchalamment à l'ombre de ses seins,
Comme un hameau paisible au pied d'une montagne.

THE GIANTESS

At the time when Nature with a lusty spirit
Was conceiving monstrous children each day,
I should have liked to live near a young giantess,
Like a voluptuous cat at the feet of a queen.

I should have liked to see her soul and body thrive
And grow without restraint in her terrible games;
To divine by the mist swimming within her eyes
If her heart harbored a smoldering flame;

To explore leisurely her magnificent form;
To crawl upon the slopes of her enormous knees,
And sometimes in summer, when the unhealthy sun

Makes her stretch out, weary, across the countryside,
To sleep nonchalantly in the shade of her breasts,
Like a peaceful hamlet below a mountainside.

LE MASQUE

Statue allégorique dans le goût de la Renaissance

À Ernest Christophe, statuaire.

Contemplons ce trésor de grâces florentines;
Dans l'ondulation de ce corps musculeux
L'Elégance et la Force abondent, soeurs divines.
Cette femme, morceau vraiment miraculeux,
Divinement robuste, adorablement mince,
Est faite pour trôner sur des lits somptueux
Et charmer les loisirs d'un pontife ou d'un prince.

—Aussi, vois ce souris fin et voluptueux
Où la Fatuité promène son extase;
Ce long regard sournois, langoureux et moqueur;
Ce visage mignard, tout encadré de gaze,
Dont chaque trait nous dit avec un air vainqueur:
«La Volupté m'appelle et l'Amour me couronne!»
À cet être doué de tant de majesté
Vois quel charme excitant la gentillesse donne!
Approchons, et tournons autour de sa beauté.

Ô blasphème de l'art! ô surprise fatale!
La femme au corps divin, promettant le bonheur,
Par le haut se termine en monstre bicéphale!

—Mais non! ce n'est qu'un masque, un décor suborneur,
Ce visage éclairé d'une exquise grimace,
Et, regarde, voici, crispée atrocement,
La véritable tête, et la sincère face
Renversée à l'abri de la face qui ment
Pauvre grande beauté! le magnifique fleuve
De tes pleurs aboutit dans mon coeur soucieux
Ton mensonge m'enivre, et mon âme s'abreuve
Aux flots que la Douleur fait jaillir de tes yeux!

—Mais pourquoi pleure-t-elle? Elle, beauté parfaite,
Qui mettrait à ses pieds le genre humain vaincu,
Quel mal mystérieux ronge son flanc d'athlète?

—Elle pleure insensé, parce qu'elle a vécu!
Et parce qu'elle vit! Mais ce qu'elle déplore
Surtout, ce qui la fait frémir jusqu'aux genoux,
C'est que demain, hélas! il faudra vivre encore!
Demain, après-demain et toujours!—comme nous!

THE MASK

Allegorical Statue in the Style of the Renaissance

To Ernest Christophe, Sculptor

Let us gaze at this gem of Florentine beauty;
In the undulation of this brawny body
Those divine sisters, Gracefulness and Strength, abound.
This woman, a truly miraculous marble,
Adorably slender, divinely robust,
Is made to be enthroned upon sumptuous beds
And to charm the leisure of a Pope or a Prince.

—And see that smile, voluptuous and delicate,
Where self-conceit displays its ecstasy;
That sly, lingering look, mocking and languorous;
That dainty face, framed in a veil of gauze,
Whose every feature says, with a triumphant air:
"Pleasure calls me and Love gives me a crown!"
To that being endowed with so much majesty

See what exciting charm is lent by prettiness!
Let us draw near, and walk around its loveliness.

O blasphemy of art! Fatal surprise!
That exquisite body, that promise of delight,
At the top turns into a two-headed monster!

Why no! it's but a mask, a lying ornament,
That visage enlivened by a dainty grimace,
And look, here is, atrociously shriveled,
The real, true head, the sincere countenance
Reversed and hidden by the lying face.
Poor glamorous beauty! the magnificent stream
Of your tears flows into my anguished heart;
Your falsehood makes me drunk and my soul slakes its thirst
At the flood from your eyes, which Suffering causes!

—But why is she weeping? She, the perfect beauty,
Who could put at her feet the conquered human race,
What secret malady gnaws at those sturdy flanks?

—She is weeping, fool, because she has lived!
And because she lives! But what she deplores
Most, what makes her shudder down to her knees,
Is that tomorrow, alas! she will still have to live!
Tomorrow, after tomorrow, always!—like us!

HYMNE A LA BEAUTE

Viens-tu du ciel profond ou sors-tu de l'abîme,
O Beauté? ton regard, infernal et divin,
Verse confusément le bienfait et le crime,
Et l'on peut pour cela te comparer au vin.

Tu contiens dans ton oeil le couchant et l'aurore;
Tu répands des parfums comme un soir orageux;
Tes baisers sont un philtre et ta bouche une amphore
Qui font le héros lâche et l'enfant courageux.

Sors-tu du gouffre noir ou descends-tu des astres?
Le Destin charmé suit tes jupons comme un chien;
Tu sèmes au hasard la joie et les désastres,
Et tu gouvernes tout et ne réponds de rien.

Tu marches sur des morts, Beauté, dont tu te moques;
De tes bijoux l'Horreur n'est pas le moins charmant,
Et le Meurtre, parmi tes plus chères breloques,
Sur ton ventre orgueilleux danse amoureusement.

L'éphémère ébloui vole vers toi, chandelle,
Crépite, flambe et dit: Bénissons ce flambeau!
L'amoureux pantelant incliné sur sa belle
A l'air d'un moribond caressant son tombeau.

Que tu viennes du ciel ou de l'enfer, qu'importe,
Ô Beauté! monstre énorme, effrayant, ingénu!
Si ton oeil, ton souris, ton pied, m'ouvrent la porte
D'un Infini que j'aime et n'ai jamais connu?

De Satan ou de Dieu, qu'importe? Ange ou Sirène,
Qu'importe, si tu rends,—fée aux yeux de velours,
Rythme, parfum, lueur, ô mon unique reine!—
L'univers moins hideux et les instants moins lourds?

HYMN TO BEAUTY

Do you come from Heaven or rise from the abyss,
Beauty? Your gaze, divine and infernal,
Pours out confusedly benevolence and crime,
And one may for that, compare you to wine.

You contain in your eyes the sunset and the dawn;
You scatter perfumes like a stormy night;
Your kisses are a philtre, your mouth an amphora,
Which make the hero weak and the child courageous.

Do you come from the stars or rise from the black pit?
Destiny, bewitched, follows your skirts like a dog;
You sow at random joy and disaster,
And you govern all things but answer for nothing.

You walk upon corpses which you mock, O Beauty!
Of your jewels Horror is not the least charming,
And Murder, among your dearest trinkets,
Dances amorously upon your proud belly.

The dazzled moth flies toward you, O candle!
Crepitates, flames and says: "Blessed be this flambeau!"
The panting lover bending o'er his fair one
Looks like a dying man caressing his own tomb,

Whether you come from heaven or from hell, who cares,
O Beauty! Huge, fearful, ingenuous monster!
If your regard, your smile, your foot, open for me
An Infinite I love but have not ever known?

From God or Satan, who cares? Angel or Siren,
Who cares, if you make,—fay with the velvet eyes,
Rhythm, perfume, glimmer; my one and only queen!
The world less hideous, the minutes less leaden?

PARFUM EXOTIQUE

Quand, les deux yeux fermés, en un soir chaud d'automne,
Je respire l'odeur de ton sein chaleureux,
Je vois se dérouler des rivages heureux
Qu'éblouissent les feux d'un soleil monotone;

Une île paresseuse où la nature donne
Des arbres singuliers et des fruits savoureux;
Des hommes dont le corps est mince et vigoureux,
Et des femmes dont l'oeil par sa franchise étonne.

Guidé par ton odeur vers de charmants climats,
Je vois un port rempli de voiles et de mâts
Encor tout fatigués par la vague marine,

Pendant que le parfum des verts tamariniers,
Qui circule dans l'air et m'enfle la narine,
Se mêle dans mon âme au chant des mariniers.

EXOTIC PERFUME

When, with both my eyes closed, on a hot autumn night,
I inhale the fragrance of your warm breast
I see happy shores spread out before me,
On which shines a dazzling and monotonous sun;

A lazy isle to which nature has given
Singular trees, savory fruits,
Men with bodies vigorous and slender,
And women in whose eyes shines a startling candor.

Guided by your fragrance to these charming countries,
I see a port filled with sails and rigging
Still utterly wearied by the waves of the sea,

While the perfume of the green tamarinds,
That permeates the air, and elates my nostrils,
Is mingled in my soul with the sailors' chanteys.

LA CHEVELURE

Ô toison, moutonnant jusque sur l'encolure!
Ô boucles! Ô parfum chargé de nonchaloir!
Extase! Pour peupler ce soir l'alcôve obscure
Des souvenirs dormant dans cette chevelure,
Je la veux agiter dans l'air comme un mouchoir!

La langoureuse Asie et la brûlante Afrique,
Tout un monde lointain, absent, presque défunt,
Vit dans tes profondeurs, forêt aromatique!
Comme d'autres esprits voguent sur la musique,
Le mien, ô mon amour! nage sur ton parfum.

J'irai là-bas où l'arbre et l'homme, pleins de sève,
Se pâment longuement sous l'ardeur des climats;
Fortes tresses, soyez la houle qui m'enlève!
Tu contiens, mer d'ébène, un éblouissant rêve
De voiles, de rameurs, de flammes et de mâts:

Un port retentissant où mon âme peut boire
À grands flots le parfum, le son et la couleur
Où les vaisseaux, glissant dans l'or et dans la moire
Ouvrent leurs vastes bras pour embrasser la gloire
D'un ciel pur où frémit l'éternelle chaleur.

Je plongerai ma tête amoureuse d'ivresse
Dans ce noir océan où l'autre est enfermé;
Et mon esprit subtil que le roulis caresse
Saura vous retrouver, ô féconde paresse,
Infinis bercements du loisir embaumé!

Cheveux bleus, pavillon de ténèbres tendues
Vous me rendez l'azur du ciel immense et rond;
Sur les bords duvetés de vos mèches tordues
Je m'enivre ardemment des senteurs confondues
De l'huile de coco, du musc et du goudron.

Longtemps! toujours! ma main dans ta crinière lourde
Sèmera le rubis, la perle et le saphir,
Afin qu'à mon désir tu ne sois jamais sourde!
N'es-tu pas l'oasis où je rêve, et la gourde
Où je hume à longs traits le vin du souvenir?

HEAD OF HAIR

O fleecy hair, falling in curls to the shoulders!
O black locks! O perfume laden with nonchalance!
Ecstasy! To people the dark alcove tonight
With memories sleeping in that thick head of hair.
I would like to shake it in the air like a scarf!

Sweltering Africa and languorous Asia,
A whole far-away world, absent, almost defunct,
Dwells in your depths, aromatic forest!
While other spirits glide on the wings of music,
Mine, O my love! floats upon your perfume.

I shall go there, where trees and men, full of vigor,
Are plunged in a deep swoon by the heat of the land;
Heady tresses be the billows that carry me away!
Ebony sea, you hold a dazzling dream
Of rigging, of rowers, of pennons and of masts:

A clamorous harbor where my spirit can drink
In great draughts the perfume, the sound and the color;
Where the vessels gliding through the gold and the moire
Open wide their vast arms to embrace the glory
Of a clear sky shimmering with everlasting heat.

I shall bury my head enamored with rapture
In this black sea where the other is imprisoned;
And my subtle spirit caressed by the rolling
Will find you once again, O fruitful indolence,
Endless lulling of sweet-scented leisure!

Blue-black hair, pavilion hung with shadows,
You give back to me the blue of the vast round sky;
In the downy edges of your curling tresses
I ardently get drunk with the mingled odors
Of oil of coconut, of musk and tar.

A long time! Forever! my hand in your thick mane
Will scatter sapphires, rubies and pearls,
So that you will never be deaf to my desire!
Aren't you the oasis of which I dream, the gourd
From which I drink deeply, the wine of memory?

JE T'ADORE A L'EGAL DE LA VOUTE NOCTURNE

Je t'adore à l'égal de la voûte nocturne,
Ô vase de tristesse, ô grande taciturne,
Et t'aime d'autant plus, belle, que tu me fuis,
Et que tu me parais, ornement de mes nuits,
Plus ironiquement accumuler les lieues
Qui séparent mes bras des immensités bleues.

Je m'avance à l'attaque, et je grimpe aux assauts,
Comme après un cadavre un choeur de vermisseaux,
Et je chéris, ô bête implacable et cruelle!
Jusqu'à cette froideur par où tu m'es plus belle!

I ADORE YOU AS MUCH AS THE NOCTURNAL VAULT...

I adore you as much as the nocturnal vault,
O vase of sadness, most taciturn one,
I love you all the more because you flee from me,
And because you appear, ornament of my nights,
More ironically to multiply the leagues
That separate my arms from the blue infinite.

I advance to attack, and I climb to assault,
Like a swarm of maggots after a cadaver,
And I cherish, implacable and cruel beast,
Even that coldness which makes you more beautiful.

TU METTRAIS L'UNIVERS ENTIER DANS TA RUELLE

Tu mettrais l'univers entier dans ta ruelle,
Femme impure! L'ennui rend ton âme cruelle.
Pour exercer tes dents à ce jeu singulier,
Il te faut chaque jour un coeur au râtelier.
Tes yeux, illuminés ainsi que des boutiques
Et des ifs flamboyants dans les fêtes publiques,
Usent insolemment d'un pouvoir emprunté,
Sans connaître jamais la loi de leur beauté.

Machine aveugle et sourde, en cruautés féconde!
Salutaire instrument, buveur du sang du monde,
Comment n'as-tu pas honte et comment n'as-tu pas
Devant tous les miroirs vu pâlir tes appas?
La grandeur de ce mal où tu te crois savante
Ne t'a donc jamais fait reculer d'épouvante,
Quand la nature, grande en ses desseins cachés
De toi se sert, ô femme, ô reine des péchés,
—De toi, vil animal,—pour pétrir un génie?

Ô fangeuse grandeur! sublime ignominie!

YOU WOULD TAKE THE WHOLE WORLD TO BED WITH YOU

You would take the whole world to bed with you,
Impure woman! Ennui makes your soul cruel;
To exercise your teeth at this singular game,
You need a new heart in the rack each day.
Your eyes, brilliant as shop windows
Or as blazing lamp-stands at public festivals,
Insolently use a borrowed power
Without ever knowing the law of their beauty.

Blind, deaf machine, fecund in cruelties!
Remedial instrument, drinker of the world's blood,
Why are you not ashamed and why have you not seen
In every looking-glass how your charms are fading?
Why have you never shrunk at the enormity
Of this evil at which you think you are expert,
When Nature, resourceful in her hidden designs,
Makes use of you, woman, O queen of sin,
Of you, vile animal,—to fashion a genius?

O foul magnificence! Sublime ignominy!

SED NON SATIATA

Bizarre déité, brune comme les nuits,
Au parfum mélangé de musc et de havane,
Oeuvre de quelque obi, le Faust de la savane,
Sorcière au flanc d'ébène, enfant des noirs minuits,

Je préfère au constance, à l'opium, au nuits,
L'élixir de ta bouche où l'amour se pavane;
Quand vers toi mes désirs partent en caravane,
Tes yeux sont la citerne où boivent mes ennuis.

Par ces deux grands yeux noirs, soupiraux de ton âme,
Ô démon sans pitié! verse-moi moins de flamme;
Je ne suis pas le Styx pour t'embrasser neuf fois,

Hélas! et je ne puis, Mégère libertine,
Pour briser ton courage et te mettre aux abois,
Dans l'enfer de ton lit devenir Proserpine!

UNSLAKEABLE LUST

Singular deity, brown as the nights,
Scented with the perfume of Havana and musk,
Work of some obeah, Faust of the savanna,
Witch with ebony flanks, child of the black midnight,

I prefer to *constance,* to opium, to *nuits,*
The nectar of your mouth upon which love parades;
When toward you my desires set out in caravan,
Your eyes are the cistern that gives drink to my cares.

Through those two great black eyes, the outlets of your soul,
O pitiless demon! pour upon me less flame;
I'm not the River Styx to embrace you nine times,

Alas! and I cannot, licentious Megaera,
To break your spirit and bring you to bay
In the hell of your bed turn into Proserpine!

AVEC SES VETEMENTS ONDOYANTS ET NACRES

Avec ses vêtements ondoyants et nacrés,
Même quand elle marche on croirait qu'elle danse,
Comme ces longs serpents que les jongleurs sacrés
Au bout de leurs bâtons agitent en cadence.

Comme le sable morne et l'azur des déserts,
Insensibles tous deux à l'humaine souffrance
Comme les longs réseaux de la houle des mers
Elle se développe avec indifférence.

Ses yeux polis sont faits de minéraux charmants,
Et dans cette nature étrange et symbolique
Où l'ange inviolé se mêle au sphinx antique,

Où tout n'est qu'or, acier, lumière et diamants,
Resplendit à jamais, comme un astre inutile,
La froide majesté de la femme stérile.

WITH HER PEARLY, UNDULATING DRESSES

With her pearly, undulating dresses,
Even when she's walking, she seems to be dancing
Like those long snakes which the holy fakirs
Set swaying in cadence on the end of their staffs.

Like the dull sand and the blue of deserts,
Both of them unfeeling toward human suffering,
Like the long web of the ocean's billows,
She unfurls herself with unconcern.

Her glossy eyes are made of charming minerals
And in that nature, symbolic and strange,
Where pure angel is united with ancient sphinx,

Where everything is gold, steel, light and diamonds,
There glitters forever, like a useless star,
The frigid majesty of the sterile woman.

LE SERPENT QUI DANSE

Que j'aime voir, chère indolente,
De ton corps si beau,
Comme une étoffe vacillante,
Miroiter la peau!

Sur ta chevelure profonde
Aux âcres parfums,
Mer odorante et vagabonde
Aux flots bleus et bruns,

Comme un navire qui s'éveille
Au vent du matin,
Mon âme rêveuse appareille
Pour un ciel lointain.

Tes yeux, où rien ne se révèle
De doux ni d'amer,
Sont deux bijoux froids où se mêle
L'or avec le fer.

À te voir marcher en cadence,
Belle d'abandon,
On dirait un serpent qui danse
Au bout d'un bâton.

Sous le fardeau de ta paresse
Ta tête d'enfant
Se balance avec la mollesse
D'un jeune éléphant,

Et ton corps se penche et s'allonge
Comme un fin vaisseau
Qui roule bord sur bord et plonge
Ses vergues dans l'eau.

Comme un flot grossi par la fonte
Des glaciers grondants,
Quand l'eau de ta bouche remonte
Au bord de tes dents,

Je crois boire un vin de Bohême,
Amer et vainqueur,
Un ciel liquide qui parsème
D'étoiles mon coeur!

THE DANCING SERPENT

Indolent darling, how I love
To see the skin
Of your body so beautiful
Shimmer like silk!

Upon your heavy head of hair
With its acrid scents,
Adventurous, odorant sea
With blue and brown waves,

Like a vessel that awakens
To the morning wind,
My dreamy soul sets sail
For a distant sky.

Your eyes where nothing is revealed
Of bitter or sweet,
Are two cold jewels where are mingled
Iron and gold.

To see you walking in cadence
With fine abandon,
One would say a snake which dances
On the end of a staff.

Under the weight of indolence
Your child-like head sways
Gently to and fro like the head
Of a young elephant,

And your body stretches and leans
Like a slender ship
That rolls from side to side and dips
Its yards in the sea.

Like a stream swollen by the thaw
Of rumbling glaciers,
When the water of your mouth rises
To the edge of your teeth,

It seems I drink Bohemian wine,
Bitter and conquering,
A liquid sky that scatters
Stars in my heart!

UNE CHAROGNE

Rappelez-vous l'objet que nous vîmes, mon âme,
Ce beau matin d'été si doux:
Au détour d'un sentier une charogne infâme
Sur un lit semé de cailloux,

Les jambes en l'air, comme une femme lubrique,
Brûlante et suant les poisons,
Ouvrait d'une façon nonchalante et cynique
Son ventre plein d'exhalaisons.

Le soleil rayonnait sur cette pourriture,
Comme afin de la cuire à point,
Et de rendre au centuple à la grande Nature
Tout ce qu'ensemble elle avait joint;

Et le ciel regardait la carcasse superbe
Comme une fleur s'épanouir.
La puanteur était si forte, que sur l'herbe
Vous crûtes vous évanouir.

Les mouches bourdonnaient sur ce ventre putride,
D'où sortaient de noirs bataillons
De larves, qui coulaient comme un épais liquide
Le long de ces vivants haillons.

Tout cela descendait, montait comme une vague
Ou s'élançait en pétillant;
On eût dit que le corps, enflé d'un souffle vague,
Vivait en se multipliant.

Et ce monde rendait une étrange musique,
Comme l'eau courante et le vent,
Ou le grain qu'un vanneur d'un mouvement rythmique
Agite et tourne dans son van.

Les formes s'effaçaient et n'étaient plus qu'un rêve,
Une ébauche lente à venir
Sur la toile oubliée, et que l'artiste achève
Seulement par le souvenir.

Derrière les rochers une chienne inquiète
Nous regardait d'un oeil fâché,
Epiant le moment de reprendre au squelette
Le morceau qu'elle avait lâché.

—Et pourtant vous serez semblable à cette ordure,
À cette horrible infection,
Etoile de mes yeux, soleil de ma nature,
Vous, mon ange et ma passion!

Oui! telle vous serez, ô la reine des grâces,
Apres les derniers sacrements,
Quand vous irez, sous l'herbe et les floraisons grasses,
Moisir parmi les ossements.

Alors, ô ma beauté! dites à la vermine
Qui vous mangera de baisers,
Que j'ai gardé la forme et l'essence divine
De mes amours décomposés!

A CARCASS

My love, do you recall the object which we saw,
That fair, sweet, summer morn!
At a turn in the path a foul carcass
On a gravel strewn bed,

Its legs raised in the air, like a lustful woman,
Burning and dripping with poisons,
Displayed in a shameless, nonchalant way
Its belly, swollen with gases.

The sun shone down upon that putrescence,
As if to roast it to a turn,
And to give back a hundredfold to great Nature
The elements she had combined;

And the sky was watching that superb cadaver
Blossom like a flower.
So frightful was the stench that you believed
You'd faint away upon the grass.

The blow-flies were buzzing round that putrid belly,
From which came forth black battalions
Of maggots, which oozed out like a heavy liquid
All along those living tatters.

All this was descending and rising like a wave,
Or poured out with a crackling sound;
One would have said the body, swollen with a vague breath,
Lived by multiplication.

And this world gave forth singular music,
Like running water or the wind,
Or the grain that winnowers with a rhythmic motion
Shake in their winnowing baskets.

The forms disappeared and were no more than a dream,
A sketch that slowly falls
Upon the forgotten canvas, that the artist
Completes from memory alone.

Crouched behind the boulders, an anxious dog
Watched us with angry eye,
Waiting for the moment to take back from the carcass
The morsel he had left.

—And yet you will be like this corruption,
Like this horrible infection,
Star of my eyes, sunlight of my being,
You, my angel and my passion!

Yes! thus will you be, queen of the Graces,
After the last sacraments,
When you go beneath grass and luxuriant flowers,
To molder among the bones of the dead.

Then, O my beauty! say to the worms who will
Devour you with kisses,
That I have kept the form and the divine essence
Of my decomposed love!

DE PROFUNDIS CLAMAVI

J'implore ta pitié, Toi, l'unique que j'aime,
Du fond du gouffre obscur où mon coeur est tombé.
C'est un univers morne à l'horizon plombé,
Où nagent dans la nuit l'horreur et le blasphème;

Un soleil sans chaleur plane au-dessus six mois,
Et les six autres mois la nuit couvre la terre;
C'est un pays plus nu que la terre polaire
—Ni bêtes, ni ruisseaux, ni verdure, ni bois!

Or il n'est pas d'horreur au monde qui surpasse
La froide cruauté de ce soleil de glace
Et cette immense nuit semblable au vieux Chaos;

Je jalouse le sort des plus vils animaux
Qui peuvent se plonger dans un sommeil stupide,
Tant l'écheveau du temps lentement se dévide!

OUT OF THE DEPTHS HAVE I CRIED

I beg pity of Thee, the only one I love,
From the depths of the dark pit where my heart has fallen,
It's a gloomy world with a leaden horizon,
Where through the night swim horror and blasphemy;

A frigid sun floats overhead six months,
And the other six months darkness covers the land;
It's a land more bleak than the polar wastes
—Neither beasts, nor streams, nor verdure, nor woods!

But no horror in the world can surpass
The cold cruelty of that glacial sun
And this vast night which is like old Chaos;

I envy the lot of the lowest animals
Who are able to sink into a stupid sleep,
So slowly does the skein of time unwind!

LE VAMPIRE

Toi qui, comme un coup de couteau,
Dans mon coeur plaintif es entrée;
Toi qui, forte comme un troupeau
De démons, vins, folle et parée,

De mon esprit humilié
Faire ton lit et ton domaine;
—Infâme à qui je suis lié
Comme le forçat à la chaîne,

Comme au jeu le joueur têtu,
Comme à la bouteille l'ivrogne,
Comme aux vermines la charogne
—Maudite, maudite sois-tu!

J'ai prié le glaive rapide
De conquérir ma liberté,
Et j'ai dit au poison perfide
De secourir ma lâcheté.

Hélas! le poison et le glaive
M'ont pris en dédain et m'ont dit:
«Tu n'es pas digne qu'on t'enlève
À ton esclavage maudit,

Imbécile!—de son empire
Si nos efforts te délivraient,
Tes baisers ressusciteraient
Le cadavre de ton vampire!»

THE VAMPIRE

You who, like the stab of a knife,
Entered my plaintive heart;
You who, strong as a herd
Of demons, came, ardent and adorned,

To make your bed and your domain
Of my humiliated mind
—Infamous bitch to whom I'm bound
Like the convict to his chain,

Like the stubborn gambler to the game,
Like the drunkard to his wine,
Like the maggots to the corpse,
—Accurst, accurst be you!

I begged the swift poniard
To gain for me my liberty,
I asked perfidious poison
To give aid to my cowardice.

Alas! both poison and the knife
Contemptuously said to me:
"You do not deserve to be freed
From your accursed slavery,

Fool!—if from her domination
Our efforts could deliver you,
Your kisses would resuscitate
The cadaver of your vampire!"

UNE NUIT QUE J'ETAIS PRES D'UNE AFFREUSE JUIVE

Une nuit que j'étais près d'une affreuse Juive,
Comme au long d'un cadavre un cadavre étendu,
Je me pris à songer près de ce corps vendu
À la triste beauté dont mon désir se prive.

Je me représentai sa majesté native,
Son regard de vigueur et de grâces armé,
Ses cheveux qui lui font un casque parfumé,
Et dont le souvenir pour l'amour me ravive.

Car j'eusse avec ferveur baisé ton noble corps,
Et depuis tes pieds frais jusqu'à tes noires tresses
Déroulé le trésor des profondes caresses,

Si, quelque soir, d'un pleur obtenu sans effort
Tu pouvais seulement, ô reine des cruelles!
Obscurcir la splendeur de tes froides prunelles.

ONE NIGHT I LAY WITH A FRIGHTFUL JEWESS

One night I lay with a frightful Jewess,
Like a cadaver stretched out beside a cadaver,
And I began to muse, by that peddled body,
About the sad beauty my desire forgoes.

I pictured to myself her native majesty,
Her gaze with power and with grace endowed,
The hair which forms for her a perfumed casque,
And whose souvenir awakens love's desire.

For I would fervently have kissed your fair body
And spread out the treasure of soulful caresses
From your cool feet up to your tresses black,

If, some night, with a tear evoked without effort
You could only, queen of cruel women!
Soften the brilliancy of your cold eyes.

REMORDS POSTHUME

Lorsque tu dormiras, ma belle ténébreuse,
Au fond d'un monument construit en marbre noir,
Et lorsque tu n'auras pour alcôve et manoir
Qu'un caveau pluvieux et qu'une fosse creuse;

Quand la pierre, opprimant ta poitrine peureuse
Et tes flancs qu'assouplit un charmant nonchaloir,
Empêchera ton coeur de battre et de vouloir,
Et tes pieds de courir leur course aventureuse,

Le tombeau, confident de mon rêve infini
(Car le tombeau toujours comprendra le poète),
Durant ces grandes nuits d'où le somme est banni,

Te dira: «Que vous sert, courtisane imparfaite,
De n'avoir pas connu ce que pleurent les morts?»
—Et le ver rongera ta peau comme un remords.

POSTHUMOUS REMORSE

When you will sleep, O dusky beauty mine,
Beneath a monument fashioned of black marble,
When you will have for bedroom and mansion
Only a rain-swept vault and a hollow grave,

When the slab of stone, oppressing your frightened breast
And your flanks now supple with charming nonchalance,
Will keep your heart from beating, from wishing,
And your feet from running their adventurous course,

The tomb, confidant of my infinite dreams
(For the tomb will always understand the poet)
Through those long nights from which all sleep is banned, will say:

"What does it profit you, imperfect courtesan,
Not to have known why the dead weep?"
—And like remorse the worm will gnaw your skin.

LE CHAT

Viens, mon beau chat, sur mon coeur amoureux;
Retiens les griffes de ta patte,
Et laisse-moi plonger dans tes beaux yeux,
Mêlés de métal et d'agate.

Lorsque mes doigts caressent à loisir
Ta tête et ton dos élastique,
Et que ma main s'enivre du plaisir
De palper ton corps électrique,

Je vois ma femme en esprit. Son regard,
Comme le tien, aimable bête
Profond et froid, coupe et fend comme un dard,

Et, des pieds jusques à la tête,
Un air subtil, un dangereux parfum
Nagent autour de son corps brun.

THE CAT

Come, superb cat, to my amorous heart;
Hold back the talons of your paws,
Let me gaze into your beautiful eyes
Of metal and agate.

When my fingers leisurely caress you,
Your head and your elastic back,
And when my hand tingles with the pleasure
Of feeling your electric body,

In spirit I see my woman. Her gaze
Like your own, amiable beast,
Profound and cold, cuts and cleaves like a dart,

And, from her head down to her feet,
A subtle air, a dangerous perfume
Floats about her dusky body.

DUELLUM

Deux guerriers ont couru l'un sur l'autre, leurs armes
Ont éclaboussé l'air de lueurs et de sang.
Ces jeux, ces cliquetis du fer sont les vacarmes
D'une jeunesse en proie à l'amour vagissant.

Les glaives sont brisés! comme notre jeunesse,
Ma chère! Mais les dents, les ongles acérés,
Vengent bientôt l'épée et la dague traîtresse.
—Ô fureur des coeurs mûrs par l'amour ulcérés!

Dans le ravin hanté des chats-pards et des onces
Nos héros, s'étreignant méchamment, ont roulé,
Et leur peau fleurira l'aridité des ronces.

—Ce gouffre, c'est l'enfer, de nos amis peuplé!
Roulons-y sans remords, amazone inhumaine,
Afin d'éterniser l'ardeur de notre haine!

THE DUEL

Two warriors rushed upon each other; their arms
Spattered the air with sparks and blood.
This fencing, this clashing of steel, are the uproar
Of youth when it becomes a prey to puling love.

The blades are broken! like our youth
My darling! But the teeth, the steely fingernails,
Soon avenge the sword and the treacherous dagger.
—O Fury of mature hearts embittered by love!

In the ravine haunted by lynxes and panthers,
Our heroes viciously clasping each other, rolled,
And their skin will put blooms on the barren brambles.

This abyss, it is hell, thronged with our friends!
Let us roll there without remorse, cruel amazon,
So the ardor of our hatred will be immortalized!

LE BALCON

Mère des souvenirs, maîtresse des maîtresses,
Ô toi, tous mes plaisirs! ô toi, tous mes devoirs!
Tu te rappelleras la beauté des caresses,
La douceur du foyer et le charme des soirs,
Mère des souvenirs, maîtresse des maîtresses!

Les soirs illuminés par l'ardeur du charbon,
Et les soirs au balcon, voilés de vapeurs roses.
Que ton sein m'était doux! que ton coeur m'était bon!
Nous avons dit souvent d'impérissables choses
Les soirs illuminés par l'ardeur du charbon.

Que les soleils sont beaux dans les chaudes soirées!
Que l'espace est profond! que le coeur est puissant!
En me penchant vers toi, reine des adorées,
Je croyais respirer le parfum de ton sang.
Que les soleils sont beaux dans les chaudes soirées!

La nuit s'épaississait ainsi qu'une cloison,
Et mes yeux dans le noir devinaient tes prunelles,
Et je buvais ton souffle, ô douceur! ô poison!
Et tes pieds s'endormaient dans mes mains fraternelles.
La nuit s'épaississait ainsi qu'une cloison.

Je sais l'art d'évoquer les minutes heureuses,
Et revis mon passé blotti dans tes genoux.
Car à quoi bon chercher tes beautés langoureuses
Ailleurs qu'en ton cher corps et qu'en ton coeur si doux?
Je sais l'art d'évoquer les minutes heureuses!

Ces serments, ces parfums, ces baisers infinis,
Renaîtront-ils d'un gouffre interdit à nos sondes,
Comme montent au ciel les soleils rajeunis
Après s'être lavés au fond des mers profondes?
—Ô serments! ô parfums! ô baisers infinis!

THE BALCONY

Mother of memories, mistress of mistresses,
O you, all my pleasure, O you, all my duty!
You'll remember the sweetness of our caresses,
The peace of the fireside, the charm of the evenings.
Mother of memories, mistress of mistresses!

The evenings lighted by the glow of the coals,
The evenings on the balcony, veiled with rose mist;
How soft your breast was to me! how kind was your heart!
We often said imperishable things,
The evenings lighted by the glow of the coals.

How splendid the sunsets are on warm evenings!
How deep space is! how potent is the heart!
In bending over you, queen of adored women,
I thought I breathed the perfume in your blood.
How splendid the sunsets are on warm evenings!

The night was growing dense like an encircling wall,
My eyes in the darkness felt the fire of your gaze
And I drank in your breath, O sweetness, O poison!
And your feet nestled soft in my brotherly hands.
The night was growing dense like an encircling wall.

I know the art of evoking happy moments,
And live again our past, my head laid on your knees,
For what's the good of seeking your languid beauty
Elsewhere than in your dear body and gentle heart?
I know the art of evoking happy moments.

Those vows, those perfumes, those infinite kisses,
Will they be reborn from a gulf we may not sound,
As rejuvenated suns rise in the heavens
After being bathed in the depths of deep seas?
—O vows! O perfumes! O infinite kisses!

LE POSSEDE

Le soleil s'est couvert d'un crêpe. Comme lui,
Ô Lune de ma vie! emmitoufle-toi d'ombre
Dors ou fume à ton gré; sois muette, sois sombre,
Et plonge tout entière au gouffre de l'Ennui;

Je t'aime ainsi! Pourtant, si tu veux aujourd'hui,
Comme un astre éclipsé qui sort de la pénombre,
Te pavaner aux lieux que la Folie encombre
C'est bien! Charmant poignard, jaillis de ton étui!

Allume ta prunelle à la flamme des lustres!
Allume le désir dans les regards des rustres!
Tout de toi m'est plaisir, morbide ou pétulant;

Sois ce que tu voudras, nuit noire, rouge aurore;
Il n'est pas une fibre en tout mon corps tremblant
Qui ne crie: *Ô mon cher Belzébuth, je t'adore!*

THE ONE POSSESSED

The sun was covered with a crape. Like him,
Moon of my life! swathe yourself with darkness;
Sleep or smoke as you will; be silent, be somber,
And plunge your whole being into Ennui's abyss;

I love you thus! However, if today you wish,
Like an eclipsed star that leaves the half-light,
To strut in the places which Madness encumbers,
That is fine! Charming poniard spring out of your sheath!

Light your eyes at the flame of the lusters!
Kindle passion in the glances of churls!
To me you're all pleasure, morbid or petulant;

Be what you will, black night, red dawn;
There is no fiber in my whole trembling body
That does not cry: "Dear Beelzebub, I adore you!"

UN FANTOME

I. Les Ténèbres

Dans les caveaux d'insondable tristesse
Où le Destin m'a déjà relégué;
Où jamais n'entre un rayon rose et gai;
Où, seul avec la Nuit, maussade hôtesse,

Je suis comme un peintre qu'un Dieu moqueur
Condamne à peindre, hélas! sur les ténèbres;
Où, cuisinier aux appétits funèbres,
Je fais bouillir et je mange mon coeur,

Par instants brille, et s'allonge, et s'étale
Un spectre fait de grâce et de splendeur.
À sa rêveuse allure orientale,

Quand il atteint sa totale grandeur,
Je reconnais ma belle visiteuse:
C'est Elle! noire et pourtant lumineuse.

II. Le Parfum

Lecteur, as-tu quelquefois respiré
Avec ivresse et lente gourmandise
Ce grain d'encens qui remplit une église,
Ou d'un sachet le musc invétéré?

Charme profond, magique, dont nous grise
Dans le présent le passé restauré!
Ainsi l'amant sur un corps adoré
Du souvenir cueille la fleur exquise.

De ses cheveux élastiques et lourds,
Vivant sachet, encensoir de l'alcôve,
Une senteur montait, sauvage et fauve,

Et des habits, mousseline ou velours,
Tout imprégnés de sa jeunesse pure,
Se dégageait un parfum de fourrure.

III. Le Cadre

Comme un beau cadre ajoute à la peinture,
Bien qu'elle soit d'un pinceau très-vanté,
Je ne sais quoi d'étrange et d'enchanté
En l'isolant de l'immense nature,

Ainsi bijoux, meubles, métaux, dorure,
S'adaptaient juste à sa rare beauté;
Rien n'offusquait sa parfaite clarté,
Et tout semblait lui servir de bordure.

Même on eût dit parfois qu'elle croyait
Que tout voulait l'aimer; elle noyait
Sa nudité voluptueusement

Dans les baisers du satin et du linge,
Et, lente ou brusque, à chaque mouvement
Montrait la grâce enfantine du singe.

IV. Le Portrait

La Maladie et la Mort font des cendres
De tout le feu qui pour nous flamboya.
De ces grands yeux si fervents et si tendres,
De cette bouche où mon coeur se noya,

De ces baisers puissants comme un dictame,
De ces transports plus vifs que des rayons,
Que reste-t-il? C'est affreux, ô mon âme!
Rien qu'un dessin fort pâle, aux trois crayons,

Qui, comme moi, meurt dans la solitude,
Et que le Temps, injurieux vieillard,
Chaque jour frotte avec son aile rude...

Noir assassin de la Vie et de l'Art,
Tu ne tueras jamais dans ma mémoire
Celle qui fut mon plaisir et ma gloire!

A PHANTOM

I. The Darkness

In the mournful vaults of fathomless gloom
To which Fate has already banished me,
Where a bright, rosy beam never enters;
Where, alone with Night, that sullen hostess,

I'm like a painter whom a mocking God
Condemns to paint, alas! upon darkness;
Where, a cook with a woeful appetite,
I boil and I eat my own heart;

At times there shines, and lengthens, and broadens
A specter made of grace and of splendor;
By its dreamy, oriental manner,

When it attains its full stature,
I recognize my lovely visitor;
It's She! dark and yet luminous.

II. The Perfume

Reader, have you at times inhaled
With rapture and slow greediness
That grain of incense which pervades a church,
Or the inveterate musk of a sachet?

Profound, magical charm, with which the past,
Restored to life, makes us inebriate!
Thus the lover from an adored body
Plucks memory's exquisite flower.

From her tresses, heavy and elastic,
Living sachet, censer for the bedroom,
A wild and savage odor rose,

And from her clothes, of muslin or velvet,
All redolent of her youth's purity,
There emanated the odor of furs.

III. The Frame

As a lovely frame adds to a painting,
Even though it's from a master's brush,
An indefinable strangeness and charm
By isolating it from vast nature,

Thus jewels, metals, gilding, furniture,
Suited her rare beauty to perfection;
Nothing dimmed its flawless splendor;
All seemed to form for her a frame.

One would even have said that she believed
That everything wished to love her; she drowned
Her nudity voluptuously

In the kisses of the satin and linen,
And, with each movement, slow or brusque,
She showed the child-like grace of a monkey.

IV. The Portrait

Disease and Death make ashes
Of all the fire that flamed for us.
Of those wide eyes, so fervent and tender,
Of that mouth in which my heart was drowned,

Of those kisses potent as dittany,
Of those transports more vivid than sunbeams,
What remains? It is frightful, O my soul!
Nothing but a faint sketch, in three colors,

Which, like me, is dying in solitude,
And which Time, that contemptuous old man,
Grazes each day with his rough wing...

Black murderer of Life and Art,
You will never kill in my memory
The one who was my glory and my joy!

JE TE DONNE CES VERS AFIN QUE SI MON NOM

Je te donne ces vers afin que si mon nom
Aborde heureusement aux époques lointaines,
Et fait rêver un soir les cervelles humaines,
Vaisseau favorisé par un grand aquilon,

Ta mémoire, pareille aux fables incertaines,
Fatigue le lecteur ainsi qu'un tympanon,
Et par un fraternel et mystique chaînon
Reste comme pendue à mes rimes hautaines;

Être maudit à qui, de l'abîme profond
Jusqu'au plus haut du ciel, rien, hors moi, ne répond!
—Ô toi qui, comme une ombre à la trace éphémère,

Foules d'un pied léger et d'un regard serein
Les stupides mortels qui t'ont jugée amère,
Statue aux yeux de jais, grand ange au front d'airain!

I GIVE YOU THESE VERSES SO THAT IF MY NAME

I give you these verses so that if my name,
A vessel favored by a strong north wind,
Fortunately reaches the distant future's shore,
And some night sets the minds of men to dreaming,

Your memory, like fables shrouded in the past,
Will weary the reader like a dulcimer,
And by a mystical, brotherly bond
Remain suspended from my haughty verse;

Accurst being to whom, from the deep abysm
To the highest heaven, nothing responds, save me!
—O you who, like an ephemeral ghost,

Trample lightly and with a serene look
Upon the dull mortals who found you repugnant,
Jet eyed statue, tall angel with a brow of bronze!

SEMPER EADEM

«D'où vous vient, disiez-vous, cette tristesse étrange,
Montant comme la mer sur le roc noir et nu?»
—Quand notre coeur a fait une fois sa vendange
Vivre est un mal. C'est un secret de tous connu,

Une douleur très simple et non mystérieuse
Et, comme votre joie, éclatante pour tous.
Cessez donc de chercher, ô belle curieuse!
Et, bien que votre voix soit douce, taisez-vous!

Taisez-vous, ignorante! âme toujours ravie!
Bouche au rire enfantin! Plus encor que la Vie,
La Mort nous tient souvent par des liens subtils.

Laissez, laissez mon coeur s'enivrer d'un *mensonge,*
Plonger dans vos beaux yeux comme dans un beau songe
Et sommeiller longtemps à l'ombre de vos cils!

EVER THE SAME

"Whence comes to you, you asked, this singular sadness
That rises like the sea on the naked, black rock?"
—Once our heart has gathered the grapes from its vineyard,
Living is an evil. That's a secret known to all,

A simple pain, with no mystery,
As obvious to all men as your gaiety.
So abandon your search, inquisitive beauty;
And though your voice is sweet, be still!

Be silent, ignorant! ever enraptured soul!
Mouth with the child-like laugh! Still more than Life,
Death holds us frequently with subtle bonds.

Let, let my heart become drunk with a *lie;* let it
Plunge into your fair eyes as into a fair dream
And slumber long in the shadow of your lashes.

TOUT ENTIERE

Le Démon, dans ma chambre haute
Ce matin est venu me voir,
Et, tâchant à me prendre en faute
Me dit: «Je voudrais bien savoir

Parmi toutes les belles choses
Dont est fait son enchantement,
Parmi les objets noirs ou roses
Qui composent son corps charmant,

Quel est le plus doux.»—Ô mon âme!
Tu répondis à l'Abhorré:
«Puisqu'en Elle tout est dictame
Rien ne peut être préféré.

Lorsque tout me ravit, j'ignore
Si quelque chose me séduit.
Elle éblouit comme l'Aurore
Et console comme la Nuit;

Et l'harmonie est trop exquise,
Qui gouverne tout son beau corps,
Pour que l'impuissante analyse
En note les nombreux accords.

Ô métamorphose mystique
De tous mes sens fondus en un!
Son haleine fait la musique,
Comme sa voix fait le parfum!»

ALL OF HER

The Devil into my high room
This morning came to pay a call,
And trying to find me in fault
Said: "I should like to know,

Among all the beautiful things
Which make her an enchantress,
Among the objects black or rose
That compose her charming body,

Which is the sweetest."—O my soul!
You answered the loathsome Creature:
"Since in Her all is dittany,
No single thing can be preferred.

When all delights me, I don't know
If some one thing entrances me.
She dazzles like the Dawn
And consoles like the Night;

And the harmony that governs
Her whole body is too lovely
For impotent analysis
To note its numerous accords.

O mystic metamorphosis
Of all my senses joined in one!
Her breath makes music,
And her voice makes perfume!"

QUE DIRAS-TU CE SOIR, PAUVRE AME SOLITAIRE

Que diras-tu ce soir, pauvre âme solitaire,
Que diras-tu, mon coeur, coeur autrefois flétri,
À la très belle, à la très bonne, à la très chère,
Dont le regard divin t'a soudain refleuri?

—Nous mettrons notre orgueil à chanter ses louanges:
Rien ne vaut la douceur de son autorité
Sa chair spirituelle a le parfum des Anges
Et son oeil nous revêt d'un habit de clarté.

Que ce soit dans la nuit et dans la solitude
Que ce soit dans la rue et dans la multitude
Son fantôme dans l'air danse comme un flambeau.

Parfois il parle et dit: «Je suis belle, et j'ordonne
Que pour l'amour de moi vous n'aimiez que le Beau;
Je suis l'Ange gardien, la Muse et la Madone.»

WHAT WILL YOU SAY TONIGHT, POOR SOLITARY SOUL

What will you say tonight, poor solitary soul,
What will you say, my heart, heart once so withered,
To the kindest, dearest, the fairest of women,
Whose divine glance suddenly revived you?

—We shall try our pride in singing her praises:
There is nothing sweeter than to do her bidding;
Her spiritual flesh has the fragrance of Angels,
And when she looks upon us we are clothed with light.

Be it in the darkness of night, in solitude,
Or in the city street among the multitude,
Her image in the air dances like a torch flame.

Sometimes it speaks and says: "I am fair, I command
That for your love of me you love only Beauty;
I am your guardian Angel, your Muse and Madonna."

LE FLAMBEAU VIVANT

Ils marchent devant moi, ces Yeux pleins de lumières,
Qu'un Ange très savant a sans doute aimantés
Ils marchent, ces divins frères qui sont mes frères,
Secouant dans mes yeux leurs feux diamantés.

Me sauvant de tout piège et de tout péché grave,
Ils conduisent mes pas dans la route du Beau
Ils sont mes serviteurs et je suis leur esclave
Tout mon être obéit à ce vivant flambeau.

Charmants Yeux, vous brillez de la clarté mystique
Qu'ont les cierges brûlant en plein jour; le soleil
Rougit, mais n'éteint pas leur flamme fantastique;

Ils célèbrent la Mort, vous chantez le Réveil
Vous marchez en chantant le réveil de mon âme,
Astres dont nul soleil ne peut flétrir la flamme!

THE LIVING TORCH

They walk in front of me, those eyes aglow with light
Which a learned Angel has rendered magnetic;
They walk, divine brothers who are my brothers too,
Casting into my eyes diamond scintillations.

They save me from all snares and from all grievous sin;
They guide my steps along the pathway of Beauty;
They are my servitors, I am their humble slave;
My whole being obeys this living torch.

Bewitching eyes, you shine like mystical candles
That burn in broad daylight; the sun
Reddens, but does not quench their eerie flame;

While they celebrate Death, you sing the Awakening;
You walk, singing the awakening of my soul,
Bright stars whose flame no sun can pale!

REVERSIBILITE

Ange plein de gaieté, connaissez-vous l'angoisse,
La honte, les remords, les sanglots, les ennuis,
Et les vagues terreurs de ces affreuses nuits
Qui compriment le coeur comme un papier qu'on froisse?
Ange plein de gaieté, connaissez-vous l'angoisse?

Ange plein de bonté, connaissez-vous la haine,
Les poings crispés dans l'ombre et les larmes de fiel,
Quand la Vengeance bat son infernal rappel,
Et de nos facultés se fait le capitaine?
Ange plein de bonté connaissez-vous la haine?

Ange plein de santé, connaissez-vous les Fièvres,
Qui, le long des grands murs de l'hospice blafard,
Comme des exilés, s'en vont d'un pied traînard,
Cherchant le soleil rare et remuant les lèvres?
Ange plein de santé, connaissez-vous les Fièvres?

Ange plein de beauté, connaissez-vous les rides,
Et la peur de vieillir, et ce hideux tourment
De lire la secrète horreur du dévouement
Dans des yeux où longtemps burent nos yeux avide!
Ange plein de beauté, connaissez-vous les rides?

Ange plein de bonheur, de joie et de lumières,
David mourant aurait demandé la santé
Aux émanations de ton corps enchanté;
Mais de toi je n'implore, ange, que tes prières,
Ange plein de bonheur, de joie et de lumières!

REVERSIBILITY

Angel full of gaiety, do you know anguish,
Shame, remorse, sobs, vexations,
And the vague terrors of those frightful nights
That compress the heart like a paper one crumples?
Angel full of gaiety, do you know anguish?

Angel full of kindness, do you know hatred,
The clenched fists in the darkness and the tears of gall,
When Vengeance beats out his hellish call to arms,
And makes himself the captain of our faculties?
Angel full of kindness, do you know hatred?

Angel full of health, do you know Fever,
Walking like an exile, moving with dragging steps,
Along the high, wan walls of the charity ward,
And with muttering lips seeking the rare sunlight?
Angel full of health, do you know Fever?

Angel full of beauty, do you know wrinkles,
The fear of growing old, and the hideous torment
Of reading in the eyes of her he once adored
Horror at seeing love turning to devotion?
Angel full of beauty, do you know wrinkles?

Angel full of happiness, of joy and of light,
David on his death-bed would have appealed for health
To the emanations of your enchanted flesh;
But of you, angel, I beg only prayers,
Angel full of happiness, of joy and of light!

CONFESSION

Une fois, une seule, aimable et douce femme,
À mon bras votre bras poli
S'appuya (sur le fond ténébreux de mon âme
Ce souvenir n'est point pâli);

Il était tard; ainsi qu'une médaille neuve
La pleine lune s'étalait,
Et la solennité de la nuit, comme un fleuve,
Sur Paris dormant ruisselait.

Et le long des maisons, sous les portes cochères,
Des chats passaient furtivement
L'oreille au guet, ou bien, comme des ombres chères,
Nous accompagnaient lentement.

Tout à coup, au milieu de l'intimité libre
Eclose à la pâle clarté
De vous, riche et sonore instrument où ne vibre
Que la radieuse gaieté,

De vous, claire et joyeuse ainsi qu'une fanfare
Dans le matin étincelant
Une note plaintive, une note bizarre
S'échappa, tout en chancelant

Comme une enfant chétive, horrible, sombre, immonde,
Dont sa famille rougirait,
Et qu'elle aurait longtemps, pour la cacher au monde,
Dans un caveau mise au secret.

Pauvre ange, elle chantait, votre note criarde:
«Que rien ici-bas n'est certain,
Et que toujours, avec quelque soin qu'il se farde,
Se trahit l'égoïsme humain;

Que c'est un dur métier que d'être belle femme,
Et que c'est le travail banal
De la danseuse folle et froide qui se pâme
Dans son sourire machinal;

Que bâtir sur les coeurs est une chose sotte;
Que tout craque, amour et beauté,
Jusqu'à ce que l'Oubli les jette dans sa hotte
Pour les rendre à l'Eternité!»

J'ai souvent évoqué cette lune enchantée,
Ce silence et cette langueur,
Et cette confidence horrible chuchotée
Au confessionnal du coeur.

CONFESSION

One time, once only, sweet, amiable woman,
On my arm your smooth arm
Rested (on the tenebrous background of my soul
That memory is not faded);

It was late; like a newly struck medal
The full moon spread its rays,
And the solemnity of the night streamed
Like a river over sleeping Paris.

And along the houses, under the porte-cocheres,
Cats passed by furtively,
With ears pricked up, or else, like beloved shades,
Slowly escorted us.

Suddenly, in the midst of that frank intimacy
Born in the pale moonlight,
From you, sonorous, rich instrument which vibrates
Only with radiant gaiety,

From you, clear and joyful as a fanfare
In the glistening morning light,
A plaintive note, a bizarre note
Escaped, faltering

Like a puny, filthy, sullen, horrible child,
Who would make his family blush,
And whom they have hidden for a long time
In a secret cellar.

Poor angel, it sang, your discordant note:
"That naught is certain here below,
That always, though it paint its face with utmost care
Man's selfishness reveals itself,

That it's a hard calling to be a lovely woman,
And that it is the banal task
Of the cold and silly danseuse who faints away
With a mechanical smile,

That to build on hearts is a foolish thing,
That all things break, love, and beauty,
Till Oblivion tosses them into his dosser
To give them back to Eternity!"

I've often evoked that enchanted moon,
The silence and the languidness,
And that horrible confidence whispered
In the heart's confessional.

L'AUBE SPIRITUELLE

Quand chez les débauchés l'aube blanche et vermeille
Entre en société de l'Idéal rongeur,
Par l'opération d'un mystère vengeur
Dans la brute assoupie un ange se réveille.

Des Cieux Spirituels l'inaccessible azur,
Pour l'homme terrassé qui rêve encore et souffre,
S'ouvre et s'enfonce avec l'attirance du gouffre.
Ainsi, chère Déesse, Etre lucide et pur,

Sur les débris fumeux des stupides orgies
Ton souvenir plus clair, plus rose, plus charmant,
À mes yeux agrandis voltige incessamment.

Le soleil a noirci la flamme des bougies;
Ainsi, toujours vainqueur, ton fantôme est pareil,
Ame resplendissante, à l'immortel soleil!

SPIRITUAL DAWN

When debauchees are roused by the white, rosy dawn,
Escorted by the Ideal which gnaws at their hearts
Through the action of a mysterious, vengeful law,
In the somnolent brute an Angel awakens.

The inaccessible blue of Spiritual Heavens,
For the man thrown to earth who suffers and still dreams,
Opens and yawns with the lure of the abyss.
Thus, dear Goddess, Being, lucid and pure,

Over the smoking ruins of stupid orgies,
Your memory, clearer, more rosy, more charming,
Hovers incessantly before my widened eyes.

The sunlight has darkened the flame of the candles;
Thus, ever triumphant, resplendent soul!
Your phantom is like the immortal sun!

HARMONIE DU SOIR

Voici venir les temps où vibrant sur sa tige
Chaque fleur s'évapore ainsi qu'un encensoir;
Les sons et les parfums tournent dans l'air du soir;
Valse mélancolique et langoureux vertige!

Chaque fleur s'évapore ainsi qu'un encensoir;
Le violon frémit comme un coeur qu'on afflige;
Valse mélancolique et langoureux vertige!
Le ciel est triste et beau comme un grand reposoir.

Le violon frémit comme un coeur qu'on afflige,
Un coeur tendre, qui hait le néant vaste et noir!
Le ciel est triste et beau comme un grand reposoir;
Le soleil s'est noyé dans son sang qui se fige.

Un coeur tendre, qui hait le néant vaste et noir,
Du passé lumineux recueille tout vestige!
Le soleil s'est noyé dans son sang qui se fige...
Ton souvenir en moi luit comme un ostensoir!

EVENING HARMONY

The season is at hand when swaying on its stem
Every flower exhales perfume like a censer;
Sounds and perfumes turn in the evening air;
Melancholy waltz and languid vertigo!

Every flower exhales perfume like a censer;
The violin quivers like a tormented heart;
Melancholy waltz and languid vertigo!
The sky is sad and beautiful like an immense altar.

The violin quivers like a tormented heart,
A tender heart, that hates the vast, black void!
The sky is sad and beautiful like an immense altar;
The sun has drowned in his blood which congeals...

A tender heart that hates the vast, black void
Gathers up every shred of the luminous past!
The sun has drowned in his blood which congeals...
Your memory in me glitters like a monstrance!

LE FLACON

Il est de forts parfums pour qui toute matière
Est poreuse. On dirait qu'ils pénètrent le verre.
En ouvrant un coffret venu de l'Orient
Dont la serrure grince et rechigne en criant,

Ou dans une maison déserte quelque armoire
Pleine de l'âcre odeur des temps, poudreuse et noire,
Parfois on trouve un vieux flacon qui se souvient,
D'où jaillit toute vive une âme qui revient.

Mille pensers dormaient, chrysalides funèbres,
Frémissant doucement dans les lourdes ténèbres,
Qui dégagent leur aile et prennent leur essor,
Teintés d'azur, glacés de rose, lamés d'or.

Voilà le souvenir enivrant qui voltige
Dans l'air troublé; les yeux se ferment; le Vertige
Saisit l'âme vaincue et la pousse à deux mains
Vers un gouffre obscurci de miasmes humains;

Il la terrasse au bord d'un gouffre séculaire,
Où, Lazare odorant déchirant son suaire,
Se meut dans son réveil le cadavre spectral
D'un vieil amour ranci, charmant et sépulcral.

Ainsi, quand je serai perdu dans la mémoire
Des hommes, dans le coin d'une sinistre armoire
Quand on m'aura jeté, vieux flacon désolé,
Décrépit, poudreux, sale, abject, visqueux, fêlé,

Je serai ton cercueil, aimable pestilence!
Le témoin de ta force et de ta virulence,
Cher poison préparé par les anges! liqueur
Qui me ronge, ô la vie et la mort de mon coeur!

THE PERFUME FLASK

There are strong perfumes for which all matter
Is porous. One would say they go through glass.
On opening a coffer that has come from the East,
Whose creaking lock resists and grates,

Or in a deserted house, some cabinet
Full of the Past's acrid odor, dusty and black,
Sometimes one finds an antique phial which remembers,
Whence gushes forth a living soul returned to life.

Many thoughts were sleeping, death-like chrysalides,
Quivering softly in the heavy shadows,
That free their wings and rise in flight,
Tinged with azure, glazed with rose, spangled with gold.

That is the bewitching souvenir which flutters
In the troubled air; the eyes close; Dizziness
Seizes the vanquished soul, pushes it with both hands
Toward a darkened abyss of human pollution:

He throws it down at the edge of an ancient abyss,
Where, like stinking Lazarus tearing wide his shroud,
There moves as it wakes up, the ghostly cadaver
Of a rancid old love, charming and sepulchral.

Thus, when I'll be lost to the memory
Of men, when I shall be tossed into the corner
Of a dismal wardrobe, a desolate old phial,
Decrepit, cracked, slimy, dirty, dusty, abject,

Delightful pestilence! I shall be your coffin,
The witness of your strength and of your virulence,
Beloved poison prepared by the angels! Liqueur
That consumes me, O the life and death of my heart!

LE POISON

Le vin sait revêtir le plus sordide bouge
D'un luxe miraculeux,
Et fait surgir plus d'un portique fabuleux
Dans l'or de sa vapeur rouge,
Comme un soleil couchant dans un ciel nébuleux.

L'opium agrandit ce qui n'a pas de bornes,
Allonge l'illimité,
Approfondit le temps, creuse la volupté,
Et de plaisirs noirs et mornes
Remplit l'âme au delà de sa capacité.

Tout cela ne vaut pas le poison qui découle
De tes yeux, de tes yeux verts,
Lacs où mon âme tremble et se voit à l'envers...
Mes songes viennent en foule
Pour se désaltérer à ces gouffres amers.

Tout cela ne vaut pas le terrible prodige
De ta salive qui mord,
Qui plonge dans l'oubli mon âme sans remords,
Et charriant le vertige,
La roule défaillante aux rives de la mort!

POISON

Wine knows how to adorn the most sordid hovel
With marvelous luxury
And make more than one fabulous portal appear
In the gold of its red mist
Like a sun setting in a cloudy sky.

Opium magnifies that which is limitless,
Lengthens the unlimited,
Makes time deeper, hollows out voluptuousness,
And with dark, gloomy pleasures
Fills the soul beyond its capacity.

All that is not equal to the poison which flows
From your eyes, from your green eyes,
Lakes where my soul trembles and sees its evil side...
My dreams come in multitude
To slake their thirst in those bitter gulfs.

All that is not equal to the awful wonder
Of your biting saliva,
Charged with madness, that plunges my remorseless soul
Into oblivion
And rolls it in a swoon to the shores of death.

CIEL BROUILLE

On dirait ton regard d'une vapeur couvert;
Ton oeil mystérieux (est-il bleu, gris ou vert?)
Alternativement tendre, rêveur, cruel,
Réfléchit l'indolence et la pâleur du ciel.

Tu rappelles ces jours blancs, tièdes et voilés,
Qui font se fondre en pleurs les coeurs ensorcelés,
Quand, agités d'un mal inconnu qui les tord,
Les nerfs trop éveillés raillent l'esprit qui dort.

Tu ressembles parfois à ces beaux horizons
Qu'allument les soleils des brumeuses saisons...
Comme tu resplendis, paysage mouillé
Qu'enflamment les rayons tombant d'un ciel brouillé!

Ô femme dangereuse, ô séduisants climats!
Adorerai-je aussi ta neige et vos frimas,
Et saurai-je tirer de l'implacable hiver
Des plaisirs plus aigus que la glace et le fer?

CLOUDY SKY

One would say that your gaze was veiled with mist;
Your mysterious eyes (are they blue, gray or green?)
Alternately tender, dreamy, cruel,
Reflect the indolence and pallor of the sky.

You call to mind those days, white, soft, and mild,
That make enchanted hearts burst into tears,
When, shaken by a mysterious, wracking pain,
The nerves, too wide-awake, jeer at the sleeping mind.

You resemble at times those gorgeous horizons
That the sun sets ablaze in the seasons of mist...
How resplendent you are, landscape drenched with rain,
Aflame with rays that fall from a cloudy sky!

O dangerous woman, O alluring climates!
Will I also adore your snow and your hoar-frost,
And can I draw from your implacable winter
Pleasures keener than iron or ice?

LE CHAT

I

Dans ma cervelle se promène,
Ainsi qu'en son appartement,
Un beau chat, fort, doux et charmant.
Quand il miaule, on l'entend à peine,

Tant son timbre est tendre et discret;
Mais que sa voix s'apaise ou gronde,
Elle est toujours riche et profonde.
C'est là son charme et son secret.

Cette voix, qui perle et qui filtre
Dans mon fonds le plus ténébreux,
Me remplit comme un vers nombreux
Et me réjouit comme un philtre.

Elle endort les plus cruels maux
Et contient toutes les extases;
Pour dire les plus longues phrases,
Elle n'a pas besoin de mots.

Non, il n'est pas d'archet qui morde
Sur mon coeur, parfait instrument,
Et fasse plus royalement
Chanter sa plus vibrante corde,

Que ta voix, chat mystérieux,
Chat séraphique, chat étrange,
En qui tout est, comme en un ange,
Aussi subtil qu'harmonieux!

II

De sa fourrure blonde et brune
Sort un parfum si doux, qu'un soir
J'en fus embaumé, pour l'avoir
Caressée une fois, rien qu'une.

C'est l'esprit familier du lieu;
Il juge, il préside, il inspire
Toutes choses dans son empire;
peut-être est-il fée, est-il dieu?

Quand mes yeux, vers ce chat que j'aime
Tirés comme par un aimant,
Se retournent docilement
Et que je regarde en moi-même,

Je vois avec étonnement
Le feu de ses prunelles pâles,
Clairs fanaux, vivantes opales
Qui me contemplent fixement.

THE CAT

I

In my brain there walks about,
As though he were in his own home,
A lovely cat, strong, sweet, charming.
When he mews, one scarcely hears him,

His tone is so discreet and soft;
But purring or growling, his voice
Is always deep and rich;
That is his charm and secret.

That voice forms into drops, trickles
Into the depths of my being,
Fills me like harmonious verse
And gladdens me like a philtre.

It lulls to sleep the sharpest pains,
Contains all ecstasies;
To say the longest sentences,
It has no need of words,

No, there's no bow that plays upon
My heart, that perfect instrument,
And makes its most vibrant chord
Sing more gloriously

Than your voice, mysterious cat,
Seraphic cat, singular cat,
In whom, as in angels, all is
As subtle as harmonious!

II

From his brown and yellow fur
Comes such sweet fragrance that one night
I was perfumed with it because
I caressed him once, once only.

A familiar figure in the place,
He presides, judges, inspires
Everything within his province;
Perhaps he is a fay, a god?

When my gaze, drawn as by a magnet,
Turns in a docile way
Toward that cat whom I love,
And when I look within myself,

I see with amazement
The fire of his pale pupils,
Clear signal-lights, living opals,
That contemplate me fixedly.

LE BEAU NAVIRE

Je veux te raconter, ô molle enchanteresse!
Les diverses beautés qui parent ta jeunesse;
Je veux te peindre ta beauté,
Où l'enfance s'allie à la maturité.

Quand tu vas balayant l'air de ta jupe large,
Tu fais l'effet d'un beau vaisseau qui prend le large,
Chargé de toile, et va roulant
Suivant un rythme doux, et paresseux, et lent.

Sur ton cou large et rond, sur tes épaules grasses,
Ta tête se pavane avec d'étranges grâces;
D'un air placide et triomphant
Tu passes ton chemin, majestueuse enfant.

Je veux te raconter, ô molle enchanteresse!
Les diverses beautés qui parent ta jeunesse;
Je veux te peindre ta beauté,
Où l'enfance s'allie à la maturité.

Ta gorge qui s'avance et qui pousse la moire,
Ta gorge triomphante est une belle armoire
Dont les panneaux bombés et clairs
Comme les boucliers accrochent des éclairs;

Boucliers provoquants, armés de pointes roses!
Armoire à doux secrets, pleine de bonnes choses,
De vins, de parfums, de liqueurs
Qui feraient délirer les cerveaux et les coeurs!

Quand tu vas balayant l'air de ta jupe large
Tu fais l'effet d'un beau vaisseau qui prend le large,
Chargé de toile, et va roulant
Suivant un rythme doux, et paresseux, et lent.

Tes nobles jambes, sous les volants qu'elles chassent,
Tourmentent les désirs obscurs et les agacent,
Comme deux sorcières qui font
Tourner un philtre noir dans un vase profond.

Tes bras, qui se joueraient des précoces hercules,
Sont des boas luisants les solides émules,
Faits pour serrer obstinément,
Comme pour l'imprimer dans ton coeur, ton amant.

Sur ton cou large et rond, sur tes épaules grasses,
Ta tête se pavane avec d'étranges grâces;
D'un air placide et triomphant
Tu passes ton chemin, majestueuse enfant.

THE BEAUTIFUL SHIP

I want to name for you, indolent sorceress!
The divers marks of beauty which adorn your youth;
I want to describe your beauty,
In which are blended childhood and maturity.

When you go sweeping by in your full, flowing skirts,
You resemble a trim ship as it puts to sea
Under full sail and goes rolling
Lazily, to a slow and easy rhythm.

On your large, round neck, on your plump shoulders,
Your head moves proudly and with a strange grace;
With a placid, triumphant air
You go your way, majestic child.

I want to name for you, indolent sorceress!
The divers marks of beauty which adorn your youth;
I want to describe your beauty,
In which are blended childhood and maturity.

Your exuberant breast which swells your silken gown,
Your triumphant breast is a lovely cabinet
Whose panels, round and bright,
Catch each flash of light like bucklers,

Exciting bucklers, armed with rosy points!
Cabinet of sweet secrets, crowded with good things,
With wines, with perfumes, with liqueurs
That would make delirious the minds and hearts of men!

When you go sweeping by in your full, flowing skirts,
You resemble a trim ship as it puts to sea
Under full sail and goes rolling
Lazily, to a slow and easy rhythm.

Your shapely legs beneath the flounces they pursue
Arouse and torment obscure desires
Like two sorceresses who stir
A black philtre in a deep vessel.

Your arms which would scorn precocious Hercules
Are the worthy rivals of glistening boas,
Made to clasp stubbornly
Your lover, as if to imprint him on your heart.

On your large, round neck, on your plump shoulders,
Your head moves proudly and with a strange grace;
With a placid, triumphant air
You go your way, majestic child.

L'INVITATION AU VOYAGE

Mon enfant, ma soeur,
Songe à la douceur
D'aller là-bas vivre ensemble!
Aimer à loisir,
Aimer et mourir
Au pays qui te ressemble!
Les soleils mouillés

De ces ciels brouillés
Pour mon esprit ont les charmes
Si mystérieux
De tes traîtres yeux,
Brillant à travers leurs larmes.

Là, tout n'est qu'ordre et beauté,
Luxe, calme et volupté.

Des meubles luisants,
Polis par les ans,
Décoreraient notre chambre;
Les plus rares fleurs
Mêlant leurs odeurs
Aux vagues senteurs de l'ambre,
Les riches plafonds,
Les miroirs profonds,
La splendeur orientale,
Tout y parlerait
À l'âme en secret
Sa douce langue natale.

Là, tout n'est qu'ordre et beauté,
Luxe, calme et volupté.

Vois sur ces canaux
Dormir ces vaisseaux
Dont l'humeur est vagabonde;
C'est pour assouvir
Ton moindre désir
Qu'ils viennent du bout du monde.
—Les soleils couchants
Revêtent les champs,
Les canaux, la ville entière,
D'hyacinthe et d'or;
Le monde s'endort
Dans une chaude lumière.

Là, tout n'est qu'ordre et beauté,
Luxe, calme et volupté.

INVITATION TO THE VOYAGE

My child, my sister,
Think of the rapture
Of living together there!
Of loving at will,
Of loving till death,
In the land that is like you!
The misty sunlight
Of those cloudy skies
Has for my spirit the charms,
So mysterious,
Of your treacherous eyes,
Shining brightly through their tears.

There all is order and beauty,
Luxury, peace, and pleasure.

Gleaming furniture,
Polished by the years,
Will ornament our bedroom;
The rarest flowers
Mingling their fragrance
With the faint scent of amber,
The ornate ceilings,
The limpid mirrors,
The oriental splendor,
All would whisper there
Secretly to the soul
In its soft, native language.

There all is order and beauty,
Luxury, peace, and pleasure.

See on the canals
Those vessels sleeping.
Their mood is adventurous;
It's to satisfy
Your slightest desire
That they come from the ends of the earth.
—The setting suns
Adorn the fields,
The canals, the whole city,
With hyacinth and gold;

The world falls asleep
In a warm glow of light.

There all is order and beauty,
Luxury, peace, and pleasure.

L'IRREPARABLE

Pouvons-nous étouffer le vieux, le long Remords,
Qui vit, s'agite et se tortille
Et se nourrit de nous comme le ver des morts,
Comme du chêne la chenille?
Pouvons-nous étouffer l'implacable Remords?

Dans quel philtre, dans quel vin, dans quelle tisane,
Noierons-nous ce vieil ennemi,
Destructeur et gourmand comme la courtisane,
Patient comme la fourmi?
Dans quel philtre?—dans quel vin?—dans quelle tisane?

Dis-le, belle sorcière, oh! dis, si tu le sais,
À cet esprit comblé d'angoisse
Et pareil au mourant qu'écrasent les blessés,
Que le sabot du cheval froisse,
Dis-le, belle sorcière, oh! dis, si tu le sais,

À cet agonisant que le loup déjà flaire
Et que surveille le corbeau,
À ce soldat brisé! s'il faut qu'il désespère
D'avoir sa croix et son tombeau;
Ce pauvre agonisant que déjà le loup flaire!

Peut-on illuminer un ciel bourbeux et noir?
Peut-on déchirer des ténèbres
Plus denses que la poix, sans matin et sans soir,
Sans astres, sans éclairs funèbres?
Peut-on illuminer un ciel bourbeux et noir?

L'Espérance qui brille aux carreaux de l'Auberge
Est soufflée, est morte à jamais!
Sans lune et sans rayons, trouver où l'on héberge
Les martyrs d'un chemin mauvais!
Le Diable a tout éteint aux carreaux de l'Auberge!

Adorable sorcière, aimes-tu les damnés?
Dis, connais-tu l'irrémissible?
Connais-tu le Remords, aux traits empoisonnés,
À qui notre coeur sert de cible?
Adorable sorcière, aimes-tu les damnés?

L'Irréparable ronge avec sa dent maudite
Notre âme, piteux monument,
Et souvent il attaque ainsi que le termite,
Par la base le bâtiment.
L'Irréparable ronge avec sa dent maudite!

—J'ai vu parfois, au fond d'un théâtre banal
Qu'enflammait l'orchestre sonore,
Une fée allumer dans un ciel infernal
Une miraculeuse aurore;
J'ai vu parfois au fond d'un théâtre banal

Un être, qui n'était que lumière, or et gaze,
Terrasser l'énorme Satan;
Mais mon coeur, que jamais ne visite l'extase,
Est un théâtre où l'on attend
Toujours. toujours en vain, l'Etre aux ailes de gaze!

THE IRREPARABLE

Can we stifle the old, the lingering Remorse,
That lives, quivers and writhes,
And feeds on us like the worm on the dead,
Like the grub on the oak?
Can we stifle implacable Remorse?

In what philtre, in what potion, what wine,
Shall we drown this old enemy,
Destructive and greedy as a harlot,
Patient as the ant?
In what philtre, in what potion, what wine?

Tell it, fair sorceress, O! tell it, if you know,
To this spirit filled with anguish,
So like a dying man crushed beneath the wounded,
Who is struck by the horses' shoes;
Tell it, fair sorceress, O! tell it, if you know,

To this dying man whom the wolf already scents
And whom the crow watches,
To this broken soldier! if he must despair
Of having his cross and his grave,
This poor, dying man whom the wolf already scents!

Can one illuminate a black and miry sky?
Can one tear asunder darkness
Thicker than pitch, without morning, without evening,
Without stars, without ominous lightning?
Can one illuminate a black and miry sky?

Hope that shines in the windows of the Inn
Is snuffed out, dead forever!
Without the moon, without light, to find where they lodge
The martyrs of an evil road!
The Devil has put out all the lights at the Inn!

Adorable sorceress, do you love the damned?
Say, do you know the irremissible?
Do you know Remorse, with the poisoned darts,
For whom our hearts serve as targets?
Adorable sorceress, do you love the damned?

The Irreparable gnaws with his accurst teeth
Our soul, pitiful monument,
And often he attacks like the termite
The foundations of the building.
The Irreparable gnaws with his accurst teeth!

—Sometimes I have seen at the back of a trite stage
Enlivened by a deep-toned orchestra,
A fairy set ablaze a miraculous dawn
In an infernal sky;
Sometimes I have been at the back of a trite stage

A being who was only light, gold and gauze,
Throw down the enormous Satan;
But my heart, which rapture never visits,
Is a playhouse where one awaits
Always, always in vain, the Being with gauze wings!

CAUSERIE

Vous êtes un beau ciel d'automne, clair et rose!
Mais la tristesse en moi monte comme la mer,
Et laisse, en refluant, sur ma lèvre morose
Le souvenir cuisant de son limon amer.

—Ta main se glisse en vain sur mon sein qui se pâme;
Ce qu'elle cherche, amie, est un lieu saccagé
Par la griffe et la dent féroce de la femme.
Ne cherchez plus mon coeur; les bêtes l'ont mangé.

Mon coeur est un palais flétri par la cohue;
On s'y soûle, on s'y tue, on s'y prend aux cheveux!
—Un parfum nage autour de votre gorge nue!...

Ô Beauté, dur fléau des âmes, tu le veux!
Avec tes yeux de feu, brillants comme des fêtes,
Calcine ces lambeaux qu'ont épargnés les bêtes!

CONVERSATION

You are a lovely autumn sky, clear and rosy!
But sadness rises in me like the sea,
And as it ebbs, leaves on my sullen lips
The burning memory of its bitter slime.

—In vain does your hand slip over my swooning breast;
What it seeks, darling, is a place plundered
By the claws and the ferocious teeth of woman.
Seek my heart no longer; the beasts have eaten it.

My heart is a palace polluted by the mob;
They get drunk there, kill, tear each other's hair!
—A perfume floats about your naked breast!...

O Beauty, ruthless scourge of souls, you desire it!
With the fire of your eyes, brilliant as festivals,
Bum these tatters which the beasts spared!

CHANT D'AUTOMNE

I

Bientôt nous plongerons dans les froides ténèbres;
Adieu, vive clarté de nos étés trop courts!
J'entends déjà tomber avec des chocs funèbres
Le bois retentissant sur le pavé des cours.

Tout l'hiver va rentrer dans mon être: colère,
Haine, frissons, horreur, labeur dur et forcé,
Et, comme le soleil dans son enfer polaire,
Mon coeur ne sera plus qu'un bloc rouge et glacé.

J'écoute en frémissant chaque bûche qui tombe
L'échafaud qu'on bâtit n'a pas d'écho plus sourd.
Mon esprit est pareil à la tour qui succombe
Sous les coups du bélier infatigable et lourd.

Il me semble, bercé par ce choc monotone,
Qu'on cloue en grande hâte un cercueil quelque part.
Pour qui?—C'était hier l'été; voici l'automne!
Ce bruit mystérieux sonne comme un départ.

II

J'aime de vos longs yeux la lumière verdâtre,
Douce beauté, mais tout aujourd'hui m'est amer,
Et rien, ni votre amour, ni le boudoir, ni l'âtre,
Ne me vaut le soleil rayonnant sur la mer.

Et pourtant aimez-moi, tendre coeur! soyez mère,
Même pour un ingrat, même pour un méchant;
Amante ou soeur, soyez la douceur éphémère
D'un glorieux automne ou d'un soleil couchant.

Courte tâche! La tombe attend; elle est avide!
Ah! laissez-moi, mon front posé sur vos genoux,
Goûter, en regrettant l'été blanc et torride,
De l'arrière-saison le rayon jaune et doux!

SONG OF AUTUMN

I

Soon we shall plunge into the cold darkness;
Farewell, vivid brightness of our short-lived summers!
Already I hear the dismal sound of firewood
Falling with a clatter on the courtyard pavements.

All winter will possess my being: wrath,
Hate, horror, shivering, hard, forced labor,
And, like the sun in his polar Hades,
My heart will be no more than a frozen red block.

All atremble I listen to each falling log;
The building of a scaffold has no duller sound.
My spirit resembles the tower which crumbles
Under the tireless blows of the battering ram.

It seems to me, lulled by these monotonous shocks,
That somewhere they're nailing a coffin, in great haste.
For whom?—Yesterday was summer; here is autumn
That mysterious noise sounds like a departure.

II

I love the greenish light of your long eyes,
Sweet beauty, but today all to me is bitter;
Nothing, neither your love, your boudoir, nor your hearth
Is worth as much as the sunlight on the sea.

Yet, love me, tender heart! be a mother,
Even to an ingrate, even to a scapegrace;
Mistress or sister, be the fleeting sweetness
Of a gorgeous autumn or of a setting sun.

Short task! The tomb awaits; it is avid!
Ah! let me, with my head bowed on your knees,
Taste the sweet, yellow rays of the end of autumn,
While I mourn for the white, torrid summer!

À UNE MADONE

Ex-voto dans le goût espagnol

Je veux bâtir pour toi, Madone, ma maîtresse,
Un autel souterrain au fond de ma détresse,
Et creuser dans le coin le plus noir de mon coeur,
Loin du désir mondain et du regard moqueur,
Une niche, d'azur et d'or tout émaillée,
Où tu te dresseras, Statue émerveillée.
Avec mes Vers polis, treillis d'un pur métal
Savamment constellé de rimes de cristal
Je ferai pour ta tête une énorme Couronne;
Et dans ma Jalousie, ô mortelle Madone
Je saurai te tailler un Manteau, de façon
Barbare, roide et lourd, et doublé de soupçon,
Qui, comme une guérite, enfermera tes charmes,
Non de Perles brodé, mais de toutes mes Larmes!
Ta Robe, ce sera mon Désir, frémissant,
Onduleux, mon Désir qui monte et qui descend,
Aux pointes se balance, aux vallons se repose,
Et revêt d'un baiser tout ton corps blanc et rose.
Je te ferai de mon Respect de beaux Souliers
De satin, par tes pieds divins humiliés,
Qui, les emprisonnant dans une molle étreinte
Comme un moule fidèle en garderont l'empreinte.
Si je ne puis, malgré tout mon art diligent
Pour Marchepied tailler une Lune d'argent
Je mettrai le Serpent qui me mord les entrailles
Sous tes talons, afin que tu foules et railles
Reine victorieuse et féconde en rachats
Ce monstre tout gonflé de haine et de crachats.
Tu verras mes Pensers, rangés comme les Cierges
Devant l'autel fleuri de la Reine des Vierges
Etoilant de reflets le plafond peint en bleu,
Te regarder toujours avec des yeux de feu;
Et comme tout en moi te chérit et t'admire,
Tout se fera Benjoin, Encens, Oliban, Myrrhe,
Et sans cesse vers toi, sommet blanc et neigeux,
En Vapeurs montera mon Esprit orageux.

Enfin, pour compléter ton rôle de Marie,
Et pour mêler l'amour avec la barbarie,
Volupté noire! des sept Péchés capitaux,
Bourreau plein de remords, je ferai sept Couteaux
Bien affilés, et comme un jongleur insensible,
Prenant le plus profond de ton amour pour cible,
Je les planterai tous dans ton Coeur pantelant,
Dans ton Coeur sanglotant, dans ton Coeur ruisselant!

TO A MADONNA

Votive Offering in the Spanish Style

I want to build for you, Madonna, my mistress,
An underground altar in the depths of my grief
And carve out in the darkest corner of my heart,
Far from worldly desires and mocking looks,
A niche, all enameled with azure and with gold,
Where you shall stand, amazed Statue;
With my polished Verses as a trellis of pure metal
Studded cunningly with rhymes of crystal,
I shall make for your head an immense Crown,
And from my Jealousy, O mortal Madonna,
I shall know how to cut a cloak in a fashion,
Barbaric, heavy, and stiff, lined with suspicion,
Which, like a sentry-box, will enclose your charms;
Embroidered not with Pearls, but with all of my Tears!
Your Gown will be my Desire, quivering,
Undulant, my Desire which rises and which falls,
Balances on the crests, reposes in the troughs,
And clothes with a kiss your white and rose body.
Of my Self-respect I shall make you Slippers
Of satin which, humbled by your divine feet,
Will imprison them in a gentle embrace,
And assume their form like a faithful mold;

If I can't, in spite of all my painstaking art,
Carve a Moon of silver for your Pedestal,
I shall put the Serpent which is eating my heart
Under your heels, so that you may trample and mock,
Triumphant queen, fecund in redemptions,
That monster all swollen with hatred and spittle.
You will see my Thoughts like Candles in rows
Before the flower-decked altar of the Queen of Virgins,

Starring with their reflections the azure ceiling,
And watching you always with eyes of fire.
And since my whole being admires and loves you,
All will become Storax, Benzoin, Frankincense, Myrrh,
And ceaselessly toward you, white, snowy pinnacle,
My turbulent spirit will rise like a vapor.

Finally, to complete your role of Mary,
And to mix love with inhumanity,
Infamous pleasure! of the seven deadly sins,
I, torturer full of remorse, shall make seven
Well sharpened Daggers and, like a callous juggler,
Taking your deepest love for a target,
I shall plant them all in your panting Heart,
In your sobbing Heart, in your bleeding Heart!

CHANSON D'APRES-MIDI

Quoique tes sourcils méchants
Te donnent un air étrange
Qui n'est pas celui d'un ange,
Sorcière aux yeux alléchants,

Je t'adore, ô ma frivole,
Ma terrible passion!
Avec la dévotion
Du prêtre pour son idole.

Le désert et la forêt
Embaument tes tresses rudes,
Ta tête a les attitudes
De l'énigme et du secret.

Sur ta chair le parfum rôde
Comme autour d'un encensoir;
Tu charmes comme le soir
Nymphe ténébreuse et chaude.

Ah! les philtres les plus forts
Ne valent pas ta paresse,
Et tu connais la caresse
Qui fait revivre les morts!

Tes hanches sont amoureuses
De ton dos et de tes seins,
Et tu ravis les coussins
Par tes poses langoureuses.

Quelquefois, pour apaiser
Ta rage mystérieuse,
Tu prodigues, sérieuse,
La morsure et le baiser;

Tu me déchires, ma brune,
Avec un rire moqueur,
Et puis tu mets sur mon coeur
Ton oeil doux comme la lune.

Sous tes souliers de satin,
Sous tes charmants pieds de soie
Moi, je mets ma grande joie,
Mon génie et mon destin,

Mon âme par toi guérie,
Par toi, lumière et couleur!
Explosion de chaleur
Dans ma noire Sibérie!

AFTERNOON SONG

Though your mischievous eyebrows
Give you a singular air,
Not that of an angel,
Sorceress with Siren's eyes,

I adore you, my madcap,
My ineffable passion!
With the pious devotion
Of a priest for his idol.

Your stiff tresses are scented
With the desert and forest,
Your head assumes the poses
Of the enigma and key.

Perfume lingers about your flesh
Like incense about a censer;
You charm like the evening,
Tenebrous, passionate nymph.

Ah! the most potent philtres
Are weaker than your languor,
And you know the caresses
That make the dead live again!

Your haunches are enamored
Of your back and your bosom
And you delight the cushions
With your languorous poses.

Sometimes, to alleviate
Your mysterious passion,
You lavish, resolutely,
Your bites and your kisses;

You tear me open, dark beauty,
With derisive laughter,
And then look at my heart
With eyes as soft as moonlight

Under your satin slippers,
Under your dear silken feet,
I place all my happiness,
My genius and destiny,

My soul brought to life by you
By your clear light and color,
Explosion of heat
In my dark Siberia!

SISINA

Imaginez Diane en galant équipage,
Parcourant les forêts ou battant les halliers,
Cheveux et gorge au vent, s'enivrant de tapage,
Superbe et défiant les meilleurs cavaliers!

Avez-vous vu Théroigne, amante du carnage,
Excitant à l'assaut un peuple sans souliers,
La joue et l'oeil en feu, jouant son personnage,
Et montant, sabre au poing, les royaux escaliers?

Telle la Sisina! Mais la douce guerrière
À l'âme charitable autant que meurtrière;
Son courage, affolé de poudre et de tambours,

Devant les suppliants sait mettre bas les armes,
Et son coeur, ravagé par la flamme, a toujours,
Pour qui s'en montre digne, un réservoir de larmes.

SISINA

Imagine Diana in elegant attire,
Roaming through the forest, or beating the thickets,
Hair flying in the wind, breast bare, drunk with the noise,
Superb, defying the finest horsemen!

Have you seen Théroigne that lover of carnage,
Urging a barefoot mob on to attack,
Her eyes and cheeks aflame, playing her role,
And climbing, sword in hand, the royal staircase?

That is Sisina! But the sweet amazon's soul
Is as charitable as it is murderous;
Her courage, exalted by powder and by drums,

Before suppliants, knows how to lay down its arms,
And her heart, ravaged by love, has always,
For him who is worthy, a reservoir of tears.

FRANCISCAE MEAE LAUDES

Novis te cantabo chordis,
O novelletum quod ludis
In solitudine cordis.

Esto sertis implicata,
Ô femina delicata
Per quam solvuntur peccata!

Sicut beneficum Lethe,
Hauriam oscula de te,
Quae imbuta es magnete.

Quum vitiorum tempegtas
Turbabat omnes semitas,
Apparuisti, Deitas,

Velut stella salutaris
In naufragiis amaris.....
Suspendam cor tuis aris!

Piscina plena virtutis,
Fons æternæ juventutis
Labris vocem redde mutis!

Quod erat spurcum, cremasti;
Quod rudius, exaequasti;
Quod debile, confirmasti.

In fame mea taberna
In nocte mea lucerna,
Recte me semper guberna.

Adde nunc vires viribus,
Dulce balneum suavibus
Unguentatum odoribus!

Meos circa lumbos mica,
O castitatis lorica,
Aqua tincta seraphica;

Patera gemmis corusca,
Panis salsus, mollis esca,
Divinum vinum, Francisca!

IN PRAISE OF MY FRANCES

I'll sing to you on a new note,
O young hind that gambols gaily
In the solitude of my heart.

Be adorned with wreaths of flowers,
O delightful woman
By whom our sins are washed away!

As from a benign Lethe,
I shall drink kisses from you,
Who were given a magnet's strength.

When a tempest of vices
Was sweeping down on every path,
You appeared, O divinity!

Like the star of salvation
Above a disastrous shipwreck...
I shall place my heart on your altar!

Reservoir full of virtue,
Fountain of eternal youth,
Restore the voice to my mute lips!

You have burned that which was filthy,
Made smooth that which was rough,
Strengthened that which was weak.

In my hunger you are the inn,
In the darkness my lamp,
Lead me always on virtue's path.

Add your strength now to my strength,
Sweet bath scented
With pleasant perfumes!

Shine forth from my loins,
O cuirass of chastity,
That was dipped in seraphic water,

Cup glittering with precious stones,
Bread seasoned with salt, delectable dish,
Heavenly wine—My Frances.

À UNE DAME CREOLE

Au pays parfumé que le soleil caresse,
J'ai connu, sous un dais d'arbres tout empourprés
Et de palmiers d'où pleut sur les yeux la paresse,
Une dame créole aux charmes ignorés.

Son teint est pâle et chaud; la brune enchanteresse
A dans le cou des airs noblement maniérés;
Grande et svelte en marchant comme une chasseresse,
Son sourire est tranquille et ses yeux assurés.

Si vous alliez, Madame, au vrai pays de gloire,
Sur les bords de la Seine ou de la verte Loire,
Belle digne d'orner les antiques manoirs,

Vous feriez, à l'abri des ombreuses retraites
Germer mille sonnets dans le coeur des poètes,
Que vos grands yeux rendraient plus soumis que vos noirs.

TO A CREOLE LADY

In the perfumed country which the sun caresses,
I knew, under a canopy of crimson trees
And palms from which indolence rains into your eyes,
A Creole lady whose charms were unknown.

Her complexion is pale and warm; the dark enchantress
Affects a noble air with the movements of her neck.
Tall and slender, she walks like a huntress;
Her smile is calm and her eye confident.

If you went, Madame, to the true land of glory,
On the banks of the Seine or along the green Loire,
Beauty fit to ornament those ancient manors,

You'd make, in the shelter of those shady retreats,
A thousand sonnets grow in the hearts of poets,
Whom your large eyes would make more subject than your slaves.

MOESTA ET ERRABUNDA

Dis-moi ton coeur parfois s'envole-t-il, Agathe,
Loin du noir océan de l'immonde cité
Vers un autre océan où la splendeur éclate,
Bleu, clair, profond, ainsi que la virginité?
Dis-moi, ton coeur parfois s'envole-t-il, Agathe?

La mer la vaste mer, console nos labeurs!
Quel démon a doté la mer, rauque chanteuse
Qu'accompagne l'immense orgue des vents grondeurs,
De cette fonction sublime de berceuse?
La mer, la vaste mer, console nos labeurs!

Emporte-moi wagon! enlève-moi, frégate!
Loin! loin! ici la boue est faite de nos pleurs!
—Est-il vrai que parfois le triste coeur d'Agathe
Dise: Loin des remords, des crimes, des douleurs,
Emporte-moi, wagon, enlève-moi, frégate?

Comme vous êtes loin, paradis parfumé,
Où sous un clair azur tout n'est qu'amour et joie,
Où tout ce que l'on aime est digne d'être aimé,
Où dans la volupté pure le coeur se noie!
Comme vous êtes loin, paradis parfumé!

Mais le vert paradis des amours enfantines,
Les courses, les chansons, les baisers, les bouquets,
Les violons vibrant derrière les collines,
Avec les brocs de vin, le soir, dans les bosquets,
—Mais le vert paradis des amours enfantines,

L'innocent paradis, plein de plaisirs furtifs,
Est-il déjà plus loin que l'Inde et que la Chine?
Peut-on le rappeler avec des cris plaintifs,
Et l'animer encor d'une voix argentine,
L'innocent paradis plein de plaisirs furtifs?

GRIEVING AND WANDERING

Tell me, does your heart sometimes fly away, Agatha,
Far from the black ocean of the filthy city,
Toward another ocean where splendor glitters,
Blue, clear, profound, as is virginity?
Tell me, does your heart sometimes fly away, Agatha?

The sea, the boundless sea, consoles us for our toil!
What demon endowed the sea, that raucous singer,
Whose accompanist is the roaring wind,
With the sublime function of cradle-rocker?
The sea, the boundless sea, consoles us for our toil!

Take me away, carriage! Carry me off, frigate!
Far, far away! Here the mud is made with our tears!
—Is it true that sometimes the sad heart of Agatha
Says: Far from crimes, from remorse, from sorrow,
Take me away, carriage, carry me off, frigate?

How far away you are, O perfumed Paradise,
Where under clear blue sky there's only love and joy,
Where all that one loves is worthy of love,
Where the heart is drowned in sheer enjoyment!
How far away you are, O perfumed Paradise!

But the green Paradise of childhood loves
The outings, the singing, the kisses, the bouquets,
The violins vibrating behind the hills,
And the evenings in the woods, with jugs of wine
—But the green Paradise of childhood loves,

That sinless Paradise, full of furtive pleasures,
Is it farther off now than India and China?
Can one call it back with plaintive cries,
And animate it still with a silvery voice,
That sinless Paradise full of furtive pleasures?

LE REVENANT

Comme les anges à l'oeil fauve,
Je reviendrai dans ton alcôve
Et vers toi glisserai sans bruit
Avec les ombres de la nuit;

Et je te donnerai, ma brune,
Des baisers froids comme la lune
Et des caresses de serpent
Autour d'une fosse rampant.

Quand viendra le matin livide,
Tu trouveras ma place vide,
Où jusqu'au soir il fera froid.

Comme d'autres par la tendresse,
Sur ta vie et sur ta jeunesse,
Moi, je veux régner par l'effroi.

THE GHOST

Like angels with wild beast's eyes
I shall return to your bedroom
And silently glide toward you
With the shadows of the night;

And, dark beauty, I shall give you
Kisses cold as the moon
And the caresses of a snake
That crawls around a grave.

When the livid morning comes,
You'll find my place empty,
And it will be cold there till night.

I wish to hold sway over
Your life and youth by fear,
As others do by tenderness.

SONNET D'AUTOMNE

Ils me disent, tes yeux, clairs comme le cristal:
«Pour toi, bizarre amant, quel est donc mon mérite?»
—Sois charmante et tais-toi! Mon coeur, que tout irrite,
Excepté la candeur de l'antique animal,

Ne veut pas te montrer son secret infernal,
Berceuse dont la main aux longs sommeils m'invite,
Ni sa noire légende avec la flamme écrite.
Je hais la passion et l'esprit me fait mal!

Aimons-nous doucement. L'Amour dans sa guérite,
Ténébreux, embusqué, bande son arc fatal.
Je connais les engins de son vieil arsenal:

Crime, horreur et folie!—Ô pâle marguerite!
Comme moi n'es-tu pas un soleil automnal,
Ô ma si blanche, ô ma si froide Marguerite?

AUTUMN SONNET

They say to me, your eyes, clear as crystal:
"For you, bizarre lover, what is my merit then?"
—Be charming and be still! My heart, which all things irk,
Except the candor of the animals of old,

Does not wish to reveal its black secret to you,
Whose lulling hands invite me to long sleep,
Nor its somber legend written with flame.
I hate passion; intelligence makes me suffer!

Let us love each other sweetly. Tenebrous Love,
Ambushed in his shelter, stretches his fatal bow.
I know all the weapons of his old arsenal:

Crime, horror, and madness!—pale marguerite!
Are you not, like me, an autumnal sun,
O my Marguerite, so white and so cold?

TRISTESSES DE LA LUNE

Ce soir, la lune rêve avec plus de paresse;
Ainsi qu'une beauté, sur de nombreux coussins,
Qui d'une main distraite et légère caresse
Avant de s'endormir le contour de ses seins,

Sur le dos satiné des molles avalanches,
Mourante, elle se livre aux longues pâmoisons,
Et promène ses yeux sur les visions blanches
Qui montent dans l'azur comme des floraisons.

Quand parfois sur ce globe, en sa langueur oisive,
Elle laisse filer une larme furtive,
Un poète pieux, ennemi du sommeil,

Dans le creux de sa main prend cette larme pâle,
Aux reflets irisés comme un fragment d'opale,
Et la met dans son coeur loin des yeux du soleil.

SADNESS OF THE MOON

Tonight the moon dreams with more indolence,
Like a lovely woman on a bed of cushions
Who fondles with a light and listless hand
The contour of her breasts before falling asleep;

On the satiny back of the billowing clouds,
Languishing, she lets herself fall into long swoons
And casts her eyes over the white phantoms
That rise in the azure like blossoming flowers.

When, in her lazy listlessness,
She sometimes sheds a furtive tear upon this globe,
A pious poet, enemy of sleep,

In the hollow of his hand catches this pale tear,
With the iridescent reflections of opal,
And hides it in his heart afar from the sun's eyes.

LES CHATS

Les amoureux fervents et les savants austères
Aiment également, dans leur mûre saison,
Les chats puissants et doux, orgueil de la maison,
Qui comme eux sont frileux et comme eux sédentaires.

Amis de la science et de la volupté
Ils cherchent le silence et l'horreur des ténèbres;
L'Erèbe les eût pris pour ses coursiers funèbres,
S'ils pouvaient au servage incliner leur fierté.

Ils prennent en songeant les nobles attitudes
Des grands sphinx allongés au fond des solitudes,
Qui semblent s'endormir dans un rêve sans fin;

Leurs reins féconds sont pleins d'étincelles magiques,
Et des parcelles d'or, ainsi qu'un sable fin,
Etoilent vaguement leurs prunelles mystiques.

CATS

Both ardent lovers and austere scholars
Love in their mature years
The strong and gentle cats, pride of the house,
Who like them are sedentary and sensitive to cold.

Friends of learning and sensual pleasure,
They seek the silence and the horror of darkness;
Erebus would have used them as his gloomy steeds:
If their pride could let them stoop to bondage.

When they dream, they assume the noble attitudes
Of the mighty sphinxes stretched out in solitude,
Who seem to fall into a sleep of endless dreams;

Their fertile loins are full of magic sparks,
And particles of gold, like fine grains of sand,
Spangle dimly their mystic eyes.

LES HIBOUX

Sous les ifs noirs qui les abritent
Les hiboux se tiennent rangés
Ainsi que des dieux étrangers
Dardant leur oeil rouge. Ils méditent.

Sans remuer ils se tiendront
Jusqu'à l'heure mélancolique
Où, poussant le soleil oblique,
Les ténèbres s'établiront.

Leur attitude au sage enseigne
Qu'il faut en ce monde qu'il craigne
Le tumulte et le mouvement;

L'homme ivre d'une ombre qui passe
Porte toujours le châtiment
D'avoir voulu changer de place.

OWLS

Under the dark yews which shade them,
The owls are perched in rows,
Like so many strange gods,
Darting their red eyes. They meditate.

Without budging they will remain
Till that melancholy hour
When, pushing back the slanting sun,
Darkness will take up its abode.

Their attitude teaches the wise
That in this world one must fear
Movement and commotion;

Man, enraptured by a passing shadow,
Forever bears the punishment
Of having tried to change his place.

LA PIPE

Je suis la pipe d'un auteur;
On voit, à contempler ma mine
D'Abyssinienne ou de Cafrine,
Que mon maître est un grand fumeur.

Quand il est comblé de douleur,
Je fume comme la chaumine
Où se prépare la cuisine
Pour le retour du laboureur.

J'enlace et je berce son âme
Dans le réseau mobile et bleu
Qui monte de ma bouche en feu,

Et je roule un puissant dictame
Qui charme son coeur et guérit
De ses fatigues son esprit.

THE PIPE

I am the pipe of an author;
One sees by my color,
Abyssinian or Kaffir,
That my master's a great smoker.

When he is laden with sorrow,
I smoke like a cottage
Where they are preparing dinner
For the return of the ploughman.

I clasp and lull his soul
In the wavy blue web
That rises from my fiery mouth.

I give forth clouds of dittany
That warm his heart and cure
His mind of its fatigue.

LA MUSIQUE

La musique souvent me prend comme une mer!
Vers ma pâle étoile,
Sous un plafond de brume ou dans un vaste éther,
Je mets à la voile;

La poitrine en avant et les poumons gonflés
Comme de la toile
J'escalade le dos des flots amoncelés
Que la nuit me voile;

Je sens vibrer en moi toutes les passions
D'un vaisseau qui souffre;
Le bon vent, la tempête et ses convulsions

Sur l'immense gouffre
Me bercent. D'autres fois, calme plat, grand miroir
De mon désespoir!

MUSIC

Music often transports me like a sea!
Toward my pale star,
Under a ceiling of fog or a vast ether,
I get under sail;

My chest thrust out and my lungs filled
Like the canvas,
I scale the slopes of wave on wave
That the night obscures;

I feel vibrating within me all the passions
Of ships in distress;
The good wind and the tempest with its convulsions

Over the vast gulf
Cradle me. At other times, dead calm, great mirror
Of my despair!

SEPULTURE

Si par une nuit lourde et sombre
Un bon chrétien, par charité,
Derrière quelque vieux décombre
Enterre votre corps vanté,

À l'heure où les chastes étoiles
Ferment leurs yeux appesantis,
L'araignée y fera ses toiles,
Et la vipère ses petits;

Vous entendrez toute l'année
Sur votre tête condamnée
Les cris lamentables des loups

Et des sorcières faméliques,
Les ébats des vieillards lubriques
Et les complots des noirs filous.

SEPULCHER

If on a dismal, sultry night
Some good Christian, through charity,
Will bury your vaunted body
Behind the ruins of a building

At the hour when the chaste stars
Close their eyes, heavy with sleep,
The spider will make his webs there,
And the viper his progeny;

You will hear all year long
Above your damned head
The mournful cries of wolves

And of the half-starved witches,
The frolics of lustful old men
And the plots of vicious robbers.

UNE GRAVURE FANTASTIQUE

Ce spectre singulier n'a pour toute toilette,
Grotesquement campé sur son front de squelette,
Qu'un diadème affreux sentant le carnaval.
Sans éperons, sans fouet, il essouffle un cheval,
Fantôme comme lui, rosse apocalyptique,
Qui bave des naseaux comme un épileptique.
Au travers de l'espace ils s'enfoncent tous deux,
Et foulent l'infini d'un sabot hasardeux.
Le cavalier promène un sabre qui flamboie
Sur les foules sans nom que sa monture broie,
Et parcourt, comme un prince inspectant sa maison,
Le cimetière immense et froid, sans horizon,
Où gisent, aux lueurs d'un soleil blanc et terne,
Les peuples de l'histoire ancienne et moderne.

A FANTASTIC PRINT

That strange specter wears nothing more
Than a diadem, atrocious and tawdry,
Grotesquely fixed on his skeleton brow.
Without spurs, without whip, he winds a horse,
A phantom like himself, an apocalyptic steed

That foams at the nostrils like an epileptic.
Both of them are plunging through space
And trampling on the infinite with daring feet.
The horseman is waving a flaming sword
Over the nameless crowds who are crushed by his mount
And examines like a prince inspecting his house,
The graveyard, immense and cold, with no horizon,
Where lie, in the glimmer of a white, lifeless sun,
The races of history, ancient and modern.

LE MORT JOYEUX

Dans une terre grasse et pleine d'escargots
Je veux creuser moi-même une fosse profonde,
Où je puisse à loisir étaler mes vieux os
Et dormir dans l'oubli comme un requin dans l'onde.

Je hais les testaments et je hais les tombeaux;
Plutôt que d'implorer une larme du monde,
Vivant, j'aimerais mieux inviter les corbeaux
À saigner tous les bouts de ma carcasse immonde.

Ô vers! noirs compagnons sans oreille et sans yeux,
Voyez venir à vous un mort libre et joyeux;
Philosophes viveurs, fils de la pourriture,

À travers ma ruine allez donc sans remords,
Et dites-moi s'il est encor quelque torture
Pour ce vieux corps sans âme et mort parmi les morts!

THE JOYFUL CORPSE

In a rich, heavy soil, infested with snails,
I wish to dig my own grave, wide and deep,
Where I can at leisure stretch out my old bones
And sleep in oblivion like a shark in the wave.

I have a hatred for testaments and for tombs;
Rather than implore a tear of the world,
I'd sooner, while alive, invite the crows
To drain the blood from my filthy carcass.

O worms! black companions with neither eyes nor ears,
See a dead man, joyous and free, approaching you;
Wanton philosophers, children of putrescence,

Go through my ruin then, without remorse,
And tell me if there still remains any torture
For this old soulless body, dead among the dead!

LE TONNEAU DE LA HAINE

La Haine est le tonneau des pâles Danaïdes;
La Vengeance éperdue aux bras rouges et forts
À beau précipiter dans ses ténèbres vides
De grands seaux pleins du sang et des larmes des morts,

Le Démon fait des trous secrets à ces abîmes,
Par où fuiraient mille ans de sueurs et d'efforts,
Quand même elle saurait ranimer ses victimes,
Et pour les pressurer ressusciter leurs corps.

La Haine est un ivrogne au fond d'une taverne,
Qui sent toujours la soif naître de la liqueur
Et se multiplier comme l'hydre de Lerne.

—Mais les buveurs heureux connaissent leur vainqueur,
Et la Haine est vouée à ce sort lamentable
De ne pouvoir jamais s'endormir sous la table.

HATRED'S CASK

Hatred is the cask of the pale Danaides;
Bewildered Vengeance with arms red and strong
Vainly pours into its empty darkness
Great pailfuls of the blood and the tears of the dead;

The Demon makes secret holes in this abyss,
Whence would escape a thousand years of sweat and strain,
Even if she could revive her victims,
Could restore their bodies, to squeeze them dry once more.

Hatred is a drunkard in a tavern,
Who feels his thirst grow greater with each drink
And multiply itself like the Lernaean hydra.

—While fortunate drinkers know they can be conquered,
Hatred is condemned to this lamentable fate,
That she can never fall asleep beneath the table.

LA CLOCHE FELEE

Il est amer et doux, pendant les nuits d'hiver,
D'écouter, près du feu qui palpite et qui fume,
Les souvenirs lointains lentement s'élever
Au bruit des carillons qui chantent dans la brume.

Bienheureuse la cloche au gosier vigoureux
Qui, malgré sa vieillesse, alerte et bien portante,
Jette fidèlement son cri religieux,
Ainsi qu'un vieux soldat qui veille sous la tente!

Moi, mon âme est fêlée, et lorsqu'en ses ennuis
Elle veut de ses chants peupler l'air froid des nuits,
Il arrive souvent que sa voix affaiblie

Semble le râle épais d'un blessé qu'on oublie
Au bord d'un lac de sang, sous un grand tas de morts
Et qui meurt, sans bouger, dans d'immenses efforts.

THE FLAWED BELL

It is bitter and sweet on winter nights
To listen by the fire that smokes and palpitates,
To distant souvenirs that rise up slowly
At the sound of the chimes that sing in the fog.

Happy is the bell which in spite of age
Is vigilant and healthy, and with lusty throat
Faithfully sounds its religious call,
Like an old soldier watching from his tent!

I, my soul is flawed, and when, a prey to ennui,
She wishes to fill the cold night air with her songs,
It often happens that her weakened voice

Resembles the death rattle of a wounded man,
Forgotten beneath a heap of dead, by a lake of blood,
Who dies without moving, striving desperately.

SPLEEN I

Pluviôse, irrité contre la ville entière,
De son urne à grands flots verse un froid ténébreux
Aux pâles habitants du voisin cimetière
Et la mortalité sur les faubourgs brumeux.

Mon chat sur le carreau cherchant une litière
Agite sans repos son corps maigre et galeux;
L'âme d'un vieux poète erre dans la gouttière
Avec la triste voix d'un fantôme frileux.

Le bourdon se lamente, et la bûche enfumée
Accompagne en fausset la pendule enrhumée
Cependant qu'en un jeu plein de sales parfums,

Héritage fatal d'une vieille hydropique,
Le beau valet de coeur et la dame de pique
Causent sinistrement de leurs amours défunts.

SPLEEN I

January, irritated with the whole city,
Pours from his urn great waves of gloomy cold
On the pale occupants of the nearby graveyard
And death upon the foggy slums.

My cat seeking a bed on the tiled floor
Shakes his thin, mangy body ceaselessly;
The soul of an old poet wanders in the rain-pipe
With the sad voice of a shivering ghost.

The great bell whines, the smoking log
Accompanies in falsetto the snuffling clock,
While in a deck of cards reeking of filthy scents,

My mortal heritage from some dropsical old woman,
The handsome knave of hearts and the queen of spades
Converse sinisterly of their dead love affair.

SPLEEN II

J'ai plus de souvenirs que si j'avais mille ans.

Un gros meuble à tiroirs encombré de bilans,
De vers, de billets doux, de procès, de romances,
Avec de lourds cheveux roulés dans des quittances,
Cache moins de secrets que mon triste cerveau.
C'est une pyramide, un immense caveau,
Qui contient plus de morts que la fosse commune.
—Je suis un cimetière abhorré de la lune,
Où comme des remords se traînent de longs vers
Qui s'acharnent toujours sur mes morts les plus chers.
Je suis un vieux boudoir plein de roses fanées,
Où gît tout un fouillis de modes surannées,
Où les pastels plaintifs et les pâles Boucher
Seuls, respirent l'odeur d'un flacon débouché.

Rien n'égale en longueur les boiteuses journées,
Quand sous les lourds flocons des neigeuses années
L'ennui, fruit de la morne incuriosité,
Prend les proportions de l'immortalité.
—Désormais tu n'es plus, ô matière vivante!
Qu'un granit entouré d'une vague épouvante,
Assoupi dans le fond d'un Sahara brumeux;
Un vieux sphinx ignoré du monde insoucieux,
Oublié sur la carte, et dont l'humeur farouche
Ne chante qu'aux rayons du soleil qui se couche.

SPLEEN II

I have more memories than if I'd lived a thousand years.

A heavy chest of drawers cluttered with balance-sheets,
Processes, love-letters, verses, ballads,
And heavy locks of hair enveloped in receipts,
Hides fewer secrets than my gloomy brain.
It is a pyramid, a vast burial vault
Which contains more corpses than potter's field.
—I am a cemetery abhorred by the moon,
In which long worms crawl like remorse
And constantly harass my dearest dead.
I am an old boudoir full of withered roses,
Where lies a whole litter of old-fashioned dresses,

Where the plaintive pastels and the pale Bouchers,
Alone, breathe in the fragrance from an opened phial.

Nothing is so long as those limping days,
When under the heavy flakes of snowy years
Ennui, the fruit of dismal apathy,
Becomes as large as immortality.
—Henceforth you are no more, O living matter!
Than a block of granite surrounded by vague terrors,
Dozing in the depths of a hazy Sahara
An old sphinx ignored by a heedless world,
Omitted from the map, whose savage nature
Sings only in the rays of a setting sun.

SPLEEN III

Je suis comme le roi d'un pays pluvieux,
Riche, mais impuissant, jeune et pourtant très vieux,
Qui, de ses précepteurs méprisant les courbettes,
S'ennuie avec ses chiens comme avec d'autres bêtes.
Rien ne peut l'égayer, ni gibier, ni faucon,
Ni son peuple mourant en face du balcon.
Du bouffon favori la grotesque ballade
Ne distrait plus le front de ce cruel malade;
Son lit fleurdelisé se transforme en tombeau,
Et les dames d'atour, pour qui tout prince est beau,
Ne savent plus trouver d'impudique toilette
Pour tirer un souris de ce jeune squelette.
Le savant qui lui fait de l'or n'a jamais pu
De son être extirper l'élément corrompu,
Et dans ces bains de sang qui des Romains nous viennent,
Et dont sur leurs vieux jours les puissants se souviennent,
Il n'a su réchauffer ce cadavre hébété
Où coule au lieu de sang l'eau verte du Léthé

SPLEEN III

I am like the king of a rainy land,
Wealthy but powerless, both young and very old,
Who contemns the fawning manners of his tutors
And is bored with his dogs and other animals.
Nothing can cheer him, neither the chase nor falcons,
Nor his people dying before his balcony.
The ludicrous ballads of his favorite clown
No longer smooth the brow of this cruel invalid;

His bed, adorned with fleurs-de-lis, becomes a grave;
The lady's maids, to whom every prince is handsome,
No longer can find gowns shameless enough
To wring a smile from this young skeleton.
The alchemist who makes his gold was never able
To extract from him the tainted element,
And in those baths of blood come down from Roman times,
And which in their old age the powerful recall,
He failed to warm this dazed cadaver in whose veins
Flows the green water of Lethe in place of blood.

SPLEEN IV

Quand le ciel bas et lourd pèse comme un couvercle
Sur l'esprit gémissant en proie aux longs ennuis,
Et que de l'horizon embrassant tout le cercle
Il nous verse un jour noir plus triste que les nuits;

Quand la terre est changée en un cachot humide,
Où l'Espérance, comme une chauve-souris,
S'en va battant les murs de son aile timide
Et se cognant la tête à des plafonds pourris;

Quand la pluie étalant ses immenses traînées
D'une vaste prison imite les barreaux,
Et qu'un peuple muet d'infâmes araignées
Vient tendre ses filets au fond de nos cerveaux,

Des cloches tout à coup sautent avec furie
Et lancent vers le ciel un affreux hurlement,
Ainsi que des esprits errants et sans patrie
Qui se mettent à geindre opiniâtrement.

—Et de longs corbillards, sans tambours ni musique,
Défilent lentement dans mon âme; l'Espoir,
Vaincu, pleure, et l'Angoisse atroce, despotique,
Sur mon crâne incliné plante son drapeau noir.

SPLEEN IV

When the low, heavy sky weighs like a lid
On the groaning spirit, victim of long ennui,
And from the all-encircling horizon
Spreads over us a day gloomier than the night;

When the earth is changed into a humid dungeon,
In which Hope like a bat
Goes beating the walls with her timid wings
And knocking her head against the rotten ceiling;

When the rain stretching out its endless train
Imitates the bars of a vast prison
And a silent horde of loathsome spiders
Comes to spin their webs in the depths of our brains,

All at once the bells leap with rage
And hurl a frightful roar at heaven,
Even as wandering spirits with no country
Burst into a stubborn, whimpering cry.

—And without drums or music, long hearses
Pass by slowly in my soul; Hope, vanquished,
Weeps, and atrocious, despotic Anguish
On my bowed skull plants her black flag.

OBSESSION

Grands bois, vous m'effrayez comme des cathédrales;
Vous hurlez comme l'orgue; et dans nos coeurs maudits,
Chambres d'éternel deuil où vibrent de vieux râles,
Répondent les échos de vos *De profundis.*

Je te hais, Océan! tes bonds et tes tumultes,
Mon esprit les retrouve en lui; ce rire amer
De l'homme vaincu, plein de sanglots et d'insultes,
Je l'entends dans le rire énorme de la mer

Comme tu me plairais, ô nuit! sans ces étoiles
Dont la lumière parle un langage connu!
Car je cherche le vide, et le noir, et le nu!

Mais les ténèbres sont elles-mêmes des toiles
Où vivent, jaillissant de mon oeil par milliers,
Des êtres disparus aux regards familiers.

OBSESSION

Great woods, you frighten me like cathedrals;
You roar like the organ; and in our cursed hearts,
Rooms of endless mourning where old death-rattles sound,
Respond the echoes of your De profundis.

I hate you, Ocean! your bounding and your tumult,
My mind finds them within itself; that bitter laugh
Of the vanquished man, full of sobs and insults,
I hear it in the immense laughter of the sea.

How I would like you, Night! without those stars
Whose light speaks a language I know!
For I seek emptiness, darkness, and nudity!

But the darkness is itself a canvas
Upon which live, springing from my eyes by thousands,
Beings with understanding looks, who have vanished.

LE GOUT DU NEANT

Morne esprit, autrefois amoureux de la lutte,
L'Espoir, dont l'éperon attisait ton ardeur,
Ne veut plus t'enfourcher! Couche-toi sans pudeur,
Vieux cheval dont le pied à chaque obstacle butte.

Résigne-toi, mon coeur; dors ton sommeil de brute.

Esprit vaincu, fourbu! Pour toi, vieux maraudeur,
L'amour n'a plus de goût, non plus que la dispute;
Adieu donc, chants du cuivre et soupirs de la flûte!
Plaisirs, ne tentez plus un coeur sombre et boudeur!

Le Printemps adorable a perdu son odeur!

Et le Temps m'engloutit minute par minute,
Comme la neige immense un corps pris de roideur;
—Je contemple d'en haut le globe en sa rondeur
Et je n'y cherche plus l'abri d'une cahute.

Avalanche, veux-tu m'emporter dans ta chute?

THE DESIRE FOR ANNIHILATION

Dejected soul, once anxious for the strife,
Hope, whose spur fanned your ardor into flame,
No longer wishes to mount you! Lie down shamelessly,
Old horse who stumbles over every rut.

Resign yourself, my heart; sleep your brutish sleep.

Conquered, foundered spirit! For you, old jade,
Love has no more relish, no more than war;
Farewell then, songs of the brass and sighs of the flute!
Pleasure, tempt no more a dark, sullen heart!

Adorable spring has lost its fragrance!

And Time engulfs me minute by minute,
As the immense snow a stiffening corpse;
I survey from above the roundness of the globe
And I no longer seek there the shelter of a hut.

Avalanche, will you sweep me along in your fall?

ALCHIMIE DE LA DOULEUR

L'un t'éclaire avec son ardeur,
L'autre en toi met son deuil, Nature!
Ce qui dit à l'un: Sépulture!
Dit à l'autre: Vie et splendeur!

Hermès inconnu qui m'assistes
Et qui toujours m'intimidas,
Tu me rends l'égal de Midas,
Le plus triste des alchimistes;

Par toi je change l'or en fer
Et le paradis en enfer;
Dans le suaire des nuages

Je découvre un cadavre cher,
Et sur les célestes rivages
Je bâtis de grands sarcophages.

THE ALCHEMY OF SORROW

One man lights you with his ardor,
Another puts you in mourning, Nature!
That which says to one: sepulcher!
Says to another: life! glory!

You have always frightened me,
Hermes the unknown, you who help me.
You make me the peer of Midas,
The saddest of all alchemists;

Through you I change gold to iron
And make of paradise a hell;
In the winding sheet of the clouds

I discover a beloved corpse,
And on the celestial shores
I build massive sarcophagi.

HORREUR SYMPATHIQUE

De ce ciel bizarre et livide,
Tourmenté comme ton destin,
Quels pensers dans ton âme vide
Descendent? réponds, libertin.

—Insatiablement avide
De l'obscur et de l'incertain,
Je ne geindrai pas comme Ovide
Chassé du paradis latin.

Cieux déchirés comme des grèves
En vous se mire mon orgueil;
Vos vastes nuages en deuil

Sont les corbillards de mes rêves,
Et vos lueurs sont le reflet
De l'Enfer où mon coeur se plaît.

REFLECTED HORROR

From that sky, bizarre and livid,
Distorted as your destiny,
What thoughts into your empty soul
Descend? Answer me, libertine.

—Insatiably avid
For the dark and the uncertain,
I shall not whimper like Ovid
Chased from his Latin paradise.

Skies torn like the shores of the sea,
You are the mirror of my pride;
Your vast clouds in mourning

Are the black hearses of my dreams,
And your gleams are the reflection
Of the Hell which delights my heart.

L'HEAUTONTIMOROUMENOS

À J.G.F.

Je te frapperai sans colère
Et sans haine, comme un boucher,
Comme Moïse le rocher
Et je ferai de ta paupière,

Pour abreuver mon Saharah
Jaillir les eaux de la souffrance.
Mon désir gonflé d'espérance
Sur tes pleurs salés nagera

Comme un vaisseau qui prend le large,
Et dans mon coeur qu'ils soûleront
Tes chers sanglots retentiront
Comme un tambour qui bat la charge!

Ne suis-je pas un faux accord
Dans la divine symphonie,
Grâce à la vorace Ironie
Qui me secoue et qui me mord

Elle est dans ma voix, la criarde!
C'est tout mon sang ce poison noir!
Je suis le sinistre miroir
Où la mégère se regarde.

Je suis la plaie et le couteau!
Je suis le soufflet et la joue!
Je suis les membres et la roue,
Et la victime et le bourreau!

Je suis de mon coeur le vampire,
—Un de ces grands abandonnés
Au rire éternel condamnés
Et qui ne peuvent plus sourire!

THE MAN WHO TORTURES HIMSELF

To J. G. F.

I shall strike you without anger
And without hate, like a butcher,
As Moses struck the rock!
And from your eyelids I shall make

The waters of suffering gush forth
To inundate my Sahara.
My desire swollen with hope
Will float upon your salty tears

Like a vessel which puts to sea,
And in my heart that they'll make drunk
Your beloved sobs will resound
Like a drum beating the charge!

Am I not a discord
In the heavenly symphony,
Thanks to voracious Irony
Who shakes me and who bites me?

She's in my voice, the termagant!
All my blood is her black poison!
I am the sinister mirror
In which the vixen looks.

I am the wound and the dagger!
I am the blow and the cheek!
I am the members and the wheel,
Victim and executioner!

I'm the vampire of my own heart
—One of those utter derelicts
Condemned to eternal laughter,
But who can no longer smile!

L'IRREMEDIABLE

I

Une Idée, une Forme, un Etre
Parti de l'azur et tombé
Dans un Styx bourbeux et plombé
Où nul oeil du Ciel ne pénètre;

Un Ange, imprudent voyageur
Qu'a tenté l'amour du difforme,
Au fond d'un cauchemar énorme
Se débattant comme un nageur,

Et luttant, angoisses funèbres!
Contre un gigantesque remous
Qui va chantant comme les fous
Et pirouettant dans les ténèbres;

Un malheureux ensorcelé
Dans ses tâtonnements futiles
Pour fuir d'un lieu plein de reptiles,
Cherchant la lumière et la clé;

Un damné descendant sans lampe
Au bord d'un gouffre dont l'odeur
Trahit l'humide profondeur
D'éternels escaliers sans rampe,

Où veillent des monstres visqueux
Dont les larges yeux de phosphore
Font une nuit plus noire encore
Et ne rendent visibles qu'eux;

Un navire pris dans le pôle
Comme en un piège de cristal,
Cherchant par quel détroit fatal
Il est tombé dans cette geôle;

—Emblèmes nets, tableau parfait
D'une fortune irrémédiable
Qui donne à penser que le Diable
Fait toujours bien tout ce qu'il fait!

II

Tête-à-tête sombre et limpide
Qu'un coeur devenu son miroir!
Puits de Vérité, clair et noir
Où tremble une étoile livide,

Un phare ironique, infernal
Flambeau des grâces sataniques,
Soulagement et gloire uniques,
—La conscience dans le Mal!

BEYOND REDEMPTION

I

An Idea, a Form, a Being
Which left the azure sky and fell
Into a leaden, miry Styx
That no eye in Heaven can pierce;

An Angel, imprudent voyager
Tempted by love of the deformed,
In the depths of a vast nightmare
Flailing his arms like a swimmer,

And struggling, mortal agony!
Against a gigantic whirlpool
That sings constantly like madmen
And pirouettes in the darkness;

An unfortunate, enchanted,
Outstretched hands groping futilely,
Looking for the light and the key,
To flee a place filled with reptiles;

A damned soul descending endless stairs
Without banisters, without light,
On the edge of a gulf of which
The odor reveals the humid depth,

Where slimy monsters are watching,
Whose eyes, wide and phosphorescent,
Make the darkness darker still
And make visible naught but themselves;

A ship caught in the polar sea
As though in a snare of crystal,
Seeking the fatal strait through which
It came into that prison;

—Patent symbols, perfect picture
Of an irremediable fate
Which makes one think that the Devil
Always does well whatever he does!

II

Somber and limpid *tête-à-tête*—
A heart become its own mirror!
Well of Truth, clear and black,
Where a pale star flickers,

A hellish, ironic beacon,
Torch of satanical blessings,
Sole glory and only solace
—The consciousness of doing evil.

L'HORLOGE

Horloge! dieu sinistre, effrayant, impassible,
Dont le doigt nous menace et nous dit: «*Souviens-toi!*
Les vibrantes Douleurs dans ton coeur plein d'effroi
Se planteront bientôt comme dans une cible;

Le Plaisir vaporeux fuira vers l'horizon
Ainsi qu'une sylphide au fond de la coulisse;
Chaque instant te dévore un morceau du délice
À chaque homme accordé pour toute sa saison.

Trois mille six cents fois par heure, la Seconde
Chuchote: *Souviens-toi!*—Rapide, avec sa voix
D'insecte, Maintenant dit: Je suis Autrefois,
Et j'ai pompé ta vie avec ma trompe immonde!

Remember! Souviens-toi! prodigue! *Esto memor!*
(Mon gosier de métal parle toutes les langues.)
Les minutes, mortel folâtre, sont des gangues
Qu'il ne faut pas lâcher sans en extraire l'or!

Souviens-toi que le Temps est un joueur avide
Qui gagne sans tricher, à tout coup! c'est la loi.
Le jour décroît; la nuit augmente; *Souviens-toi!*
Le gouffre a toujours soif; la clepsydre se vide.

Tantôt sonnera l'heure où le divin Hasard,
Où l'auguste Vertu, ton épouse encor vierge,
Où le Repentir même (oh! la dernière auberge!),
Où tout te dira Meurs, vieux lâche! il est trop tard!»

THE CLOCK

Impassive clock! Terrifying, sinister god,
Whose finger threatens us and says: "*Remember!*
The quivering Sorrows will soon be shot
Into your fearful heart, as into a target;

Nebulous pleasure will flee toward the horizon
Like an actress who disappears into the wings;
Every instant devours a piece of the pleasure
Granted to every man for his entire season.

Three thousand six hundred times an hour, Second
Whispers: *Remember!*—Immediately
With his insect voice, Now says: I am the Past
And I have sucked out your life with my filthy trunk!

Remember! Souviens-toi, spendthrift! *Esto memor!*
(My metal throat can speak all languages.)
Minutes, blithesome mortal, are bits of ore
That you must not release without extracting the gold!

Remember, Time is a greedy player
Who wins without cheating, every round! It's the law.
The daylight wanes; the night deepens; *remember!*
The abyss thirsts always; the water-clock runs low.

Soon will sound the hour when divine Chance,
When august Virtue, your still virgin wife,
When even Repentance (the very last of inns!),
When all will say: Die, old coward! it is too late!"

TABLEAUX PARISIENS — PARISIAN SCENES

PAYSAGE

Je veux, pour composer chastement mes églogues,
Coucher auprès du ciel, comme les astrologues,
Et, voisin des clochers écouter en rêvant
Leurs hymnes solennels emportés par le vent.
Les deux mains au menton, du haut de ma mansarde,
Je verrai l'atelier qui chante et qui bavarde;
Les tuyaux, les clochers, ces mâts de la cité,
Et les grands ciels qui font rêver d'éternité.

Il est doux, à travers les brumes, de voir naître
L'étoile dans l'azur, la lampe à la fenêtre
Les fleuves de charbon monter au firmament
Et la lune verser son pâle enchantement.
Je verrai les printemps, les étés, les automnes;
Et quand viendra l'hiver aux neiges monotones,
Je fermerai partout portières et volets
Pour bâtir dans la nuit mes féeriques palais.
Alors je rêverai des horizons bleuâtres,
Des jardins, des jets d'eau pleurant dans les albâtres,
Des baisers, des oiseaux chantant soir et matin,
Et tout ce que l'Idylle a de plus enfantin.
L'Emeute, tempêtant vainement à ma vitre,
Ne fera pas lever mon front de mon pupitre;
Car je serai plongé dans cette volupté
D'évoquer le Printemps avec ma volonté,
De tirer un soleil de mon coeur, et de faire
De mes pensers brûlants une tiède atmosphère.

LANDSCAPE

I would, to compose my eclogues chastely,
Lie down close to the sky like an astrologer,
And, near the church towers, listen while I dream
To their solemn anthems borne to me by the wind.
My chin cupped in both hands, high up in my garret
I shall see the workshops where they chatter and sing,
The chimneys, the belfries, those masts of the city,
And the skies that make one dream of eternity.

It is sweet, through the mist, to see the stars
Appear in the heavens, the lamps in the windows,
The streams of smoke rise in the firmament
And the moon spread out her pale enchantment.
I shall see the springtimes, the summers, the autumns;
And when winter comes with its monotonous snow,
I shall close all the shutters and draw all the drapes
So I can build at night my fairy palaces.
Then I shall dream of pale blue horizons, gardens,
Fountains weeping into alabaster basins,
Of kisses, of birds singing morning and evening,
And of all that is most childlike in the Idyl.
Riot, storming vainly at my window,
Will not make me raise my head from my desk,
For I shall be plunged in the voluptuousness
Of evoking the Springtime with my will alone,
Of drawing forth a sun from my heart, and making
Of my burning thoughts a warm atmosphere.

LE SOLEIL

Le long du vieux faubourg, où pendent aux masures
Les persiennes, abri des secrètes luxures,
Quand le soleil cruel frappe à traits redoublés
Sur la ville et les champs, sur les toits et les blés,
Je vais m'exercer seul à ma fantasque escrime,
Flairant dans tous les coins les hasards de la rime,
Trébuchant sur les mots comme sur les pavés
Heurtant parfois des vers depuis longtemps rêvés.

Ce père nourricier, ennemi des chloroses,
Eveille dans les champs les vers comme les roses;
Il fait s'évaporer les soucis vers le ciel,
Et remplit les cerveaux et les ruches le miel.
C'est lui qui rajeunit les porteurs de béquilles
Et les rend gais et doux comme des jeunes filles,
Et commande aux moissons de croître et de mûrir
Dans le coeur immortel qui toujours veut fleurir!

Quand, ainsi qu'un poète, il descend dans les villes,
Il ennoblit le sort des choses les plus viles,
Et s'introduit en roi, sans bruit et sans valets,
Dans tous les hôpitaux et dans tous les palais.

THE SUN

Along the old street on whose cottages are hung
The slatted shutters which hide secret lecheries,
When the cruel sun strikes with increased blows
The city, the country, the roofs, and the wheat fields,
I go alone to try my fanciful fencing,
Scenting in every corner the chance of a rhyme,
Stumbling over words as over paving stones,
Colliding at times with lines dreamed of long ago.

This foster-father, enemy of chlorosis,
Makes verses bloom in the fields like roses;
He makes cares evaporate toward heaven,
And fills with honey hives and brains alike.
He rejuvenates those who go on crutches
And gives them the sweetness and gaiety of girls,
And commands crops to flourish and ripen
In those immortal hearts which ever wish to bloom!

When, like a poet, he goes down into cities,
He ennobles the fate of the lowliest things
And enters like a king, without servants or noise,
All the hospitals and all the castles.

À UNE MENDIANTE ROUSSE

Blanche fille aux cheveux roux,
Dont la robe par ses trous
Laisse voir la pauvreté
Et la beauté,

Pour moi, poète chétif,
Ton jeune corps maladif,
Plein de taches de rousseur,
À sa douceur.

Tu portes plus galamment
Qu'une reine de roman
Ses cothurnes de velours
Tes sabots lourds.

Au lieu d'un haillon trop court,
Qu'un superbe habit de cour
Traîne à plis bruyants et longs
Sur tes talons;

En place de bas troués
Que pour les yeux des roués
Sur ta jambe un poignard d'or
Reluise encor;

Que des noeuds mal attachés
Dévoilent pour nos péchés
Tes deux beaux seins, radieux
Comme des yeux;

Que pour te déshabiller
Tes bras se fassent prier
Et chassent à coups mutins
Les doigts lutins,

Perles de la plus belle eau,
Sonnets de maître Belleau
Par tes galants mis aux fers
Sans cesse offerts,

Valetaille de rimeurs
Te dédiant leurs primeurs
Et contemplant ton soulier
Sous l'escalier,

Maint page épris du hasard,
Maint seigneur et maint Ronsard
Epieraient pour le déduit
Ton frais réduit!

Tu compterais dans tes lits
Plus de baisers que de lis
Et rangerais sous tes lois
Plus d'un Valois!

—Cependant tu vas gueusant
Quelque vieux débris gisant
Au seuil de quelque Véfour
De carrefour;

Tu vas lorgnant en dessous
Des bijoux de vingt-neuf sous
Dont je ne puis, oh! Pardon!
Te faire don.

Va donc, sans autre ornement,
Parfum, perles, diamant,
Que ta maigre nudité,
Ô ma beauté!

TO AN AUBURN-HAIRED BEGGAR-MAID

Pale girl with the auburn hair,
Whose dress through its tears and holes
Reveals your poverty
And your beauty,

For me, an ailing poet,
Your body, young and sickly,
Spotted with countless freckles,
Has its sweetness.

You wear with more elegance
Your wooden clogs than the queen
In a romance her sandals
Trimmed with velvet.

Instead of a scanty rag,
Let a glittering court dress
Trail with its long, rustling folds
Over your heels;

In place of stockings with holes,
Let, for the eyes of roués,
A golden poniard glisten
In your garter;

Let ill-tied ribbons give way
And unveil, so we may sin,
Your two lovely breasts, radiant
As shining eyes;

Let your arms demand entreating
To uncover your body
And repel with saucy blows
Roguish fingers,

Pearls of the finest water,
Sonnets by Master Belleau
Constantly offered by swains
Held in love's chains,

Plebeian versifiers
Offering first books to you
And ogling your slippered foot
From under the stair;

Many a page fond of love's chance,
Many a Ronsard and lord
For amusement would spy on
Your chilly hut!

You could count in your beds
More kisses than fleurs-de-lis
And subject to your power
Many Valois!

—However, you go begging
Some moldy refuse lying
On the steps of some Véfour
At the crossroads;

You go furtively eyeing
Baubles at twenty-nine sous,
Of which I can't, oh! pardon!
Make you a gift.

Go, with no more adornment,
Perfume or pearl or diamond,
Than your slender nudity,
O my beauty!

LE CYGNE

À Victor Hugo

I

Andromaque, je pense à vous! Ce petit fleuve,
Pauvre et triste miroir où jadis resplendit
L'immense majesté de vos douleurs de veuve,
Ce Simoïs menteur qui par vos pleurs grandit,

A fécondé soudain ma mémoire fertile,
Comme je traversais le nouveau Carrousel.
Le vieux Paris n'est plus (la forme d'une ville
Change plus vite, hélas! que le coeur d'un mortel);

Je ne vois qu'en esprit tout ce camp de baraques,
Ces tas de chapiteaux ébauchés et de fûts,
Les herbes, les gros blocs verdis par l'eau des flaques,
Et, brillant aux carreaux, le bric-à-brac confus.

Là s'étalait jadis une ménagerie;
Là je vis, un matin, à l'heure où sous les cieux
Froids et clairs le Travail s'éveille, où la voirie
Pousse un sombre ouragan dans l'air silencieux,

Un cygne qui s'était évadé de sa cage,
Et, de ses pieds palmés frottant le pavé sec,
Sur le sol raboteux traînait son blanc plumage.
Près d'un ruisseau sans eau la bête ouvrant le bec

Baignait nerveusement ses ailes dans la poudre,
Et disait, le coeur plein de son beau lac natal:
«Eau, quand donc pleuvras-tu? quand tonneras-tu, foudre?»
Je vois ce malheureux, mythe étrange et fatal,

Vers le ciel quelquefois, comme l'homme d'Ovide,
Vers le ciel ironique et cruellement bleu,
Sur son cou convulsif tendant sa tête avide
Comme s'il adressait des reproches à Dieu!

II

Paris change! mais rien dans ma mélancolie
N'a bougé! palais neufs, échafaudages, blocs,
Vieux faubourgs, tout pour moi devient allégorie
Et mes chers souvenirs sont plus lourds que des rocs.

Aussi devant ce Louvre une image m'opprime:
Je pense à mon grand cygne, avec ses gestes fous,
Comme les exilés, ridicule et sublime
Et rongé d'un désir sans trêve! et puis à vous,

Andromaque, des bras d'un grand époux tombée,
Vil bétail, sous la main du superbe Pyrrhus,
Auprès d'un tombeau vide en extase courbée
Veuve d'Hector, hélas! et femme d'Hélénus!

Je pense à la négresse, amaigrie et phtisique
Piétinant dans la boue, et cherchant, l'oeil hagard,
Les cocotiers absents de la superbe Afrique
Derrière la muraille immense du brouillard;

À quiconque a perdu ce qui ne se retrouve
Jamais, jamais! à ceux qui s'abreuvent de pleurs
Et tètent la Douleur comme une bonne louve!
Aux maigres orphelins séchant comme des fleurs!

Ainsi dans la forêt où mon esprit s'exile
Un vieux Souvenir sonne à plein souffle du cor!
Je pense aux matelots oubliés dans une île,
Aux captifs, aux vaincus! ... à bien d'autres encor!

THE SWAN

To Victor Hugo

I

Andromache, I think of you!—That little stream,
That mirror, poor and sad, which glittered long ago
With the vast majesty of your widow's grieving,
That false Simois swollen by your tears,

Suddenly made fruitful my teeming memory,
As I walked across the new Carrousel.
—Old Paris is no more (the form of a city
Changes more quickly, alas! than the human heart);

I see only in memory that camp of stalls,
Those piles of shafts, of rough hewn cornices, the grass,
The huge stone blocks stained green in puddles of water,
And in the windows shine the jumbled bric-a-brac.

Once a menagerie was set up there;
There, one morning, at the hour when Labor awakens,
Beneath the clear, cold sky when the dismal hubbub
Of street-cleaners and scavengers breaks the silence,

I saw a swan that had escaped from his cage,
That stroked the dry pavement with his webbed feet
And dragged his white plumage over the uneven ground.
Beside a dry gutter the bird opened his beak,

Restlessly bathed his wings in the dust
And cried, homesick for his fair native lake:
"Rain, when will you fall? Thunder, when will you roll?"
I see that hapless bird, that strange and fatal myth,

Toward the sky at times, like the man in Ovid,
Toward the ironic, cruelly blue sky,
Stretch his avid head upon his quivering neck,
As if he were reproaching God!

II

Paris changes! but naught in my melancholy
Has stirred! New palaces, scaffolding, blocks of stone,
Old quarters, all become for me an allegory,
And my dear memories are heavier than rocks.

So, before the Louvre, an image oppresses me:
I think of my great swan with his crazy motions,
Ridiculous, sublime, like a man in exile,
Relentlessly gnawed by longing! and then of you,

Andromache, base chattel, fallen from the embrace
Of a mighty husband into the hands of proud Pyrrhus,
Standing bowed in rapture before an empty tomb,
Widow of Hector, alas! and wife of Helenus!

I think of the negress, wasted and consumptive,
Trudging through muddy streets, seeking with a fixed gaze
The absent coco-palms of splendid Africa
Behind the immense wall of mist;

Of whoever has lost that which is never found
Again! Never! Of those who deeply drink of tears
And suckle Pain as they would suck the good she-wolf!
Of the puny orphans withering like flowers!

Thus in the dim forest to which my soul withdraws,
An ancient memory sounds loud the hunting horn!
I think of the sailors forgotten on some isle,
—Of the captives, of the vanquished! ... of many others too!

LES SEPT VIEILLARDS

À Victor Hugo

Fourmillante cité, cité pleine de rêves,
Où le spectre en plein jour raccroche le passant!
Les mystères partout coulent comme des sèves
Dans les canaux étroits du colosse puissant.

Un matin, cependant que dans la triste rue
Les maisons, dont la brume allongeait la hauteur,
Simulaient les deux quais d'une rivière accrue,
Et que, décor semblable à l'âme de l'acteur,

Un brouillard sale et jaune inondait tout l'espace,
Je suivais, roidissant mes nerfs comme un héros
Et discutant avec mon âme déjà lasse,
Le faubourg secoué par les lourds tombereaux.

Tout à coup, un vieillard dont les guenilles jaunes
Imitaient la couleur de ce ciel pluvieux,
Et dont l'aspect aurait fait pleuvoir les aumônes,
Sans la méchanceté qui luisait dans ses yeux,

M'apparut. On eût dit sa prunelle trempée
Dans le fiel; son regard aiguisait les frimas,
Et sa barbe à longs poils, roide comme une épée,
Se projetait, pareille à celle de Judas.

Il n'était pas voûté, mais cassé, son échine
Faisant avec sa jambe un parfait angle droit,
Si bien que son bâton, parachevant sa mine,
Lui donnait la tournure et le pas maladroit

D'un quadrupède infirme ou d'un juif à trois pattes.
Dans la neige et la boue il allait s'empêtrant,
Comme s'il écrasait des morts sous ses savates,
Hostile à l'univers plutôt qu'indifférent.

Son pareil le suivait: barbe, oeil, dos, bâton, loques,
Nul trait ne distinguait, du même enfer venu,
Ce jumeau centenaire, et ces spectres baroques
Marchaient du même pas vers un but inconnu.

À quel complot infâme étais-je donc en butte,
Ou quel méchant hasard ainsi m'humiliait?
Car je comptai sept fois, de minute en minute,
Ce sinistre vieillard qui se multipliait!

Que celui-là qui rit de mon inquiétude
Et qui n'est pas saisi d'un frisson fraternel
Songe bien que malgré tant de décrépitude
Ces sept monstres hideux avaient l'air éternel!

Aurais-je, sans mourir, contemplé le huitième,
Sosie inexorable, ironique et fatal
Dégoûtant Phénix, fils et père de lui-même?
—Mais je tournai le dos au cortège infernal.

Exaspéré comme un ivrogne qui voit double,
Je rentrai, je fermai ma porte, épouvanté,
Malade et morfondu, l'esprit fiévreux et trouble,
Blessé par le mystère et par l'absurdité!

Vainement ma raison voulait prendre la barre;
La tempête en jouant déroutait ses efforts,
Et mon âme dansait, dansait, vieille gabarre
Sans mâts, sur une mer monstrueuse et sans bords!

THE SEVEN OLD MEN

To Victor Hugo

Teeming, swarming city, city full of dreams,
Where specters in broad day accost the passer-by!
Everywhere mysteries flow like the sap in a tree
Through the narrow canals of the mighty giant.

One morning, while in a gloomy street the houses,
Whose height was increased by the mist, simulated
The quais of a swollen river, and while
—A setting that was like the actor's soul—

A dirty yellow fog inundated all space,
I was following, steeling my nerves like a hero,
Arid arguing with my already weary soul,
A squalid street shaken by the heavy dump-carts.

Suddenly an old man whose tattered yellow clothes
Were of the same color as the rainy heavens,
And whose aspect would have brought him showers of alms
If his eyes had not gleamed with so much wickedness,

Appeared to me. One would have said his eyes were drenched
With gall; his look sharpened the winter's chill,
And his long shaggy beard, like that of Judas,
Projected from his chin as stiffly as a sword.

He was not bent over, but broken; his back-bone
Made with his legs a perfect right angle,
So that his stick, completing the picture,
Gave him the appearance and clumsy gait

Of a lame quadruped or a three-legged Jew.
He went hobbling along in the snow and the mud
As if he were crushing the dead under his shoes;
Hostile, rather than indifferent to the world,

His likeness followed him: beard, eye, back, stick, tatters,
No mark distinguished this centenarian twin,
Who came from the same hell, and these baroque specters
Were walking with the same gait toward an unknown goal.

Of what infamous plot was I then the object,
Or what evil chance humiliated me thus?
For I counted seven times in as many minutes
That sinister old man who multiplied himself!

Let him who laughs at my disquietude,
And who is not seized with a fraternal shudder,
Realize that in spite of such decrepitude
Those hideous monsters had an eternal look!

Could I, without dying, have regarded the eighth,
Unrelenting Sosia, ironic and fatal,
Disgusting Phoenix, son and father of himself?
—But I turned my back on that hellish procession.

Exasperated like a drunk who sees double,
I went home; I locked the door, terrified,
Chilled to the bone and ill, my mind fevered, confused,
Hurt by that mysterious and absurd happening!

Vainly my reason tried to take the helm;
The frolicsome tempest baffled all its efforts,
And my soul, old sailing barge without masts,
Kept dancing, dancing, on a monstrous, shoreless sea!

LES PETITES VIEILLES

À Victor Hugo

I

Dans les plis sinueux des vieilles capitales,
Où tout, même l'horreur, tourne aux enchantements,
Je guette, obéissant à mes humeurs fatales,
Des êtres singuliers, décrépits et charmants.

Ces monstres disloqués furent jadis des femmes,
Eponine ou Laïs! Monstres brisés, bossus
Ou tordus, aimons-les! ce sont encor des âmes.
Sous des jupons troués et sous de froids tissus

Ils rampent, flagellés par les bises iniques,
Frémissant au fracas roulant des omnibus,
Et serrant sur leur flanc, ainsi que des reliques,
Un petit sac brodé de fleurs ou de rébus;

Ils trottent, tout pareils à des marionnettes;
Se traînent, comme font les animaux blessés,
Ou dansent, sans vouloir danser, pauvres sonnettes
Où se pend un Démon sans pitié! Tout cassés

Qu'ils sont, ils ont des yeux perçants comme une vrille,
Luisants comme ces trous où l'eau dort dans la nuit;
Ils ont les yeux divins de la petite fille
Qui s'étonne et qui rit à tout ce qui reluit.

—Avez-vous observé que maints cercueils de vieilles
Sont presque aussi petits que celui d'un enfant?
La Mort savante met dans ces bières pareilles
Un symbole d'un goût bizarre et captivant,

Et lorsque j'entrevois un fantôme débile
Traversant de Paris le fourmillant tableau,
Il me semble toujours que cet être fragile
S'en va tout doucement vers un nouveau berceau;

À moins que, méditant sur la géométrie,
Je ne cherche, à l'aspect de ces membres discords,
Combien de fois il faut que l'ouvrier varie
La forme de la boîte où l'on met tous ces corps.

—Ces yeux sont des puits faits d'un million de larmes,
Des creusets qu'un métal refroidi pailleta...
Ces yeux mystérieux ont d'invincibles charmes
Pour celui que l'austère Infortune allaita!

II

De Frascati défunt Vestale enamourée;
Prêtresse de Thalie, hélas! dont le souffleur
Enterré sait le nom; célèbre évaporée
Que Tivoli jadis ombragea dans sa fleur,

Toutes m'enivrent; mais parmi ces êtres frêles
Il en est qui, faisant de la douleur un miel,
Ont dit au Dévouement qui leur prêtait ses ailes:
Hippogriffe puissant, mène-moi jusqu'au ciel!

L'une, par sa patrie au malheur exercée,
L'autre, que son époux surchargea de douleurs,
L'autre, par son enfant Madone transpercée,
Toutes auraient pu faire un fleuve avec leurs pleurs!

III

Ah! que j'en ai suivi de ces petites vieilles!
Une, entre autres, à l'heure où le soleil tombant
Ensanglante le ciel de blessures vermeilles,
Pensive, s'asseyait à l'écart sur un banc,

Pour entendre un de ces concerts, riches de cuivre,
Dont les soldats parfois inondent nos jardins,
Et qui, dans ces soirs d'or où l'on se sent revivre,
Versent quelque héroïsme au coeur des citadins.

Celle-là, droite encor, fière et sentant la règle,
Humait avidement ce chant vif et guerrier;
Son oeil parfois s'ouvrait comme l'oeil d'un vieil aigle;
Son front de marbre avait l'air fait pour le laurier!

IV

Telles vous cheminez, stoïques et sans plaintes,
À travers le chaos des vivantes cités,
Mères au coeur saignant, courtisanes ou saintes,
Dont autrefois les noms par tous étaient cités.

Vous qui fûtes la grâce ou qui fûtes la gloires,
Nul ne vous reconnaît! un ivrogne incivil
Vous insulte en passant d'un amour dérisoire;
Sur vos talons gambade un enfant lâche et vil.

Honteuses d'exister, ombres ratatinées,
Peureuses, le dos bas, vous côtoyez les murs;
Et nul ne vous salue, étranges destinées!
Débris d'humanité pour l'éternité mûrs!

Mais moi, moi qui de loin tendrement vous surveille,
L'oeil inquiet, fixé sur vos pas incertains,
Tout comme si j'étais votre père, ô merveille!
Je goûte à votre insu des plaisirs clandestins:

Je vois s'épanouir vos passions novices;
Sombres ou lumineux, je vis vos jours perdus;
Mon coeur multiplié jouit de tous vos vices!
Mon âme resplendit de toutes vos vertus!

Ruines! ma famille! ô cerveaux congénères!
Je vous fais chaque soir un solennel adieu!
Où serez-vous demain, Eves octogénaires,
Sur qui pèse la griffe effroyable de Dieu?

LITTLE OLD WOMEN

To Victor Hugo

I

In the sinuous folds of the old capitals,
Where all, even horror, becomes pleasant,
I watch, obedient to my fatal whims,
For singular creatures, decrepit and charming.

These disjointed monsters were women long ago,
Eponine or Lais! Monsters, hunch-backed, broken
Or distorted, let us love them! they still have souls.
Clothed in tattered petticoats and flimsy dresses

They creep, lashed by the iniquitous wind,
Trembling at the clatter of the omnibuses,
Each pressing to her side, as if it were a relic,
A small purse embroidered with rebuses or flowers;

They trot exactly like marionettes;
They drag themselves along like wounded animals,
Or dance, against their will, poor little bells
Pulled constantly by a heartless Demon! Broken

Though they are, they have eyes as piercing as gimlets,
That shine like those holes in which water sleeps at night;
They have the divine eyes of little girls
Who are amazed and laugh at everything that gleams.

—Have you observed how frequently coffins
For old women are almost as small as a child's?
Clever Death brings to these similar biers
A symbol of a strange and captivating taste,

And when I catch a glimpse of a feeble specter
Crossing the swarming scene that is Paris,
It always seems to me that that fragile creature
Is going quietly toward a second cradle;

Unless, pondering on geometry,
I try, at the sight of those discordant members,
To figure how many times the workman changes
The shape of the boxes where those bodies are laid.

—Those eyes are wells filled with a million tears,
Crucibles which a quenched metal spangled...
Those mysterious eyes have invincible charms
For one whom austere Misfortune has suckled!

II

Vestal in love with the late Frascati;
High priestess of Thalia, whose name is known
To her buried prompter; vanished celebrity
Whom Tivoli sheltered at the peak of her fame,

They all enrapture me; among those frail beings
There are some who, making honey out of sorrow,
Have said to Devotion who had lent them his wings:
"Powerful hippogriff, carry me to the sky!"

One, inured to misfortune by her fatherland,
Another, overwhelmed with grief by her husband,
Another, a Madonna transfixed by her child,
Each could have made a river with her tears!

III

Ah! how many of these women I have followed!
One, among others, at the hour when the sunset
Makes the sky bloody with vermilion wounds,
Pensive, used to sit alone on a bench

To hear one of those concerts rich in brass,
With which the soldiers sometimes flood our public parks
On those golden evenings when one feels new life within
And which inspire heroism in the townsman's heart.

Proud, still erect, feeling she must sit thus,
She thirstily drank in that stirring, martial song;
Her eyes opened at times like the eyes of an old eagle;
Her marble brow seemed to be made for the laurel!

IV

Thus you trudge along, stoical, uncomplaining,
Amid the confusion of cities full of life,
Mothers with bleeding hearts, courtesans, saints,
Whose names in years gone by were on everyone's lips.

O you who were charming or who were glorious,
None recognizes you! A drunken ruffian
Passing by insults you with an obscene remark;
A dirty, nasty child frisks about at your heels.

Wizened shadows, ashamed of existing,
With bent backs, you timidly keep close to the walls
And no person greets you, strange destinies!
Human wreckage, ripe for eternity!

But I, I watch you tenderly from a distance;
My anxious eyes are fixed on your uncertain steps,
As if I were your own father; how wonderful!
I taste unknown to you clandestine pleasures:

I see your untried passions come into full bloom;
I live your vanished days, gloomy or filled with light;
My heart multiplied enjoys all of your vices!
My soul is resplendent with all of your virtues!

Ruins! my family! O kindred minds!
I bid you each evening a solemn farewell!
Octogenarian Eves, upon whom rests
God's terrible claw, where will you be tomorrow?

LES AVEUGLES

Contemple-les, mon âme; ils sont vraiment affreux!
Pareils aux mannequins; vaguement ridicules;
Terribles, singuliers comme les somnambules;
Dardant on ne sait où leurs globes ténébreux.

Leurs yeux, d'où la divine étincelle est partie,
Comme s'ils regardaient au loin, restent levés
Au ciel; on ne les voit jamais vers les pavés
Pencher rêveusement leur tête appesantie.

Ils traversent ainsi le noir illimité,
Ce frère du silence éternel. Ô cité!
Pendant qu'autour de nous tu chantes, ris et beugles,

Eprise du plaisir jusqu'à l'atrocité,
Vois! je me traîne aussi! mais, plus qu'eux hébété,
Je dis: Que cherchent-ils au Ciel, tous ces aveugles?

THE BLIND

Contemplate them, my soul; they are truly frightful!
Like mannequins; vaguely ridiculous;
Strange and terrible, like somnambulists;
Darting, one never knows where, their tenebrous orbs.

Their eyes, from which the divine spark has departed,
Remain raised to the sky, as if they were looking
Into space: one never sees them toward the pavement
Dreamily bend their heavy heads.

Thus they go across the boundless darkness,
That brother of eternal silence. O city!
While about us you sing, laugh, and bellow,

In love with pleasure to the point of cruelty,
See! I drag along also! but, more dazed than they,
I say: "What do they seek in Heaven, all those blind?"

À UNE PASSANTE

La rue assourdissante autour de moi hurlait.
Longue, mince, en grand deuil, douleur majestueuse,
Une femme passa, d'une main fastueuse
Soulevant, balançant le feston et l'ourlet;

Agile et noble, avec sa jambe de statue.
Moi, je buvais, crispé comme un extravagant,
Dans son oeil, ciel livide où germe l'ouragan,
La douceur qui fascine et le plaisir qui tue.

Un éclair... puis la nuit!—Fugitive beauté
Dont le regard m'a fait soudainement renaître,
Ne te verrai-je plus que dans l'éternité?

Ailleurs, bien loin d'ici! trop tard! *jamais* peut-être!
Car j'ignore où tu fuis, tu ne sais où je vais,
Ô toi que j'eusse aimée, ô toi qui le savais!

TO A PASSER-BY

The street about me roared with a deafening sound.
Tall, slender, in heavy mourning, majestic grief,
A woman passed, with a glittering hand
Raising, swinging the hem and flounces of her skirt;

Agile and graceful, her leg was like a statue's.
Tense as in a delirium, I drank
From her eyes, pale sky where tempests germinate,
The sweetness that enthralls and the pleasure that kills.

A lightning flash... then night! Fleeting beauty
By whose glance I was suddenly reborn,
Will I see you no more before eternity?

Elsewhere, far, far from here! too late! *never* perhaps!
For I know not where you fled, you know not where I go,
O you whom I would have loved, O you who knew it!

LE SQUELETTE LABOUREUR

I

Dans les planches d'anatomie
Qui traînent sur ces quais poudreux
Où maint livre cadavéreux
Dort comme une antique momie,

Dessins auxquels la gravité
Et le savoir d'un vieil artiste,
Bien que le sujet en soit triste,
Ont communiqué la Beauté,

On voit, ce qui rend plus complètes
Ces mystérieuses horreurs,
Bêchant comme des laboureurs,
Des Ecorchés et des Squelettes.

II

De ce terrain que vous fouillez,
Manants résignés et funèbres
De tout l'effort de vos vertèbres,
Ou de vos muscles dépouillés,

Dites, quelle moisson étrange,
Forçats arrachés au charnier,
Tirez-vous, et de quel fermier
Avez-vous à remplir la grange?

Voulez-vous (d'un destin trop dur
Epouvantable et clair emblème!)
Montrer que dans la fosse même
Le sommeil promis n'est pas sûr;

Qu'envers nous le Néant est traître;
Que tout, même la Mort, nous ment,
Et que sempiternellement
Hélas! il nous faudra peut-être

Dans quelque pays inconnu
Ecorcher la terre revêche
Et pousser une lourde bêche
Sous notre pied sanglant et nu?

SKELETON WITH A SPADE

I

In the anatomical plates
That lie about on dusty quais
Where many cadaverous books
Sleep like an ancient mummy,

Engravings to which the staidness
And knowledge of some old artist
Have communicated beauty,
Although the subject is gloomy,

One sees, and it makes more complete
These mysteries full of horror,
Skinless bodies and skeletons,
Spading as if they were farmhands.

II

From the soil that you excavate,
Resigned, macabre villagers,
From all the effort of your backs,
Or of your muscles stripped of skin,

Tell me, what singular harvest,
Convicts torn from cemeteries,
Do you reap, and of what farmer
Do you have to fill the barn?

Do you wish (clear, frightful symbol
Of too cruel a destiny!)
To show that even in the grave
None is sure of the promised sleep;

That Annihilation betrays us;
That all, even Death, lies to us,
And that forever and ever,
Alas! we shall be forced perhaps

In some unknown country
To scrape the hard and stony ground
And to push a heavy spade in
With our bare and bleeding feet?

LE CREPUSCULE DU SOIR

Voici le soir charmant, ami du criminel;
Il vient comme un complice, à pas de loup; le ciel
Se ferme lentement comme une grande alcôve,
Et l'homme impatient se change en bête fauve.

Ô soir, aimable soir, désiré par celui
Dont les bras, sans mentir, peuvent dire: Aujourd'hui
Nous avons travaillé!—C'est le soir qui soulage
Les esprits que dévore une douleur sauvage,
Le savant obstiné dont le front s'alourdit,

Et l'ouvrier courbé qui regagne son lit.
Cependant des démons malsains dans l'atmosphère
S'éveillent lourdement, comme des gens d'affaire,
Et cognent en volant les volets et l'auvent.
À travers les lueurs que tourmente le vent
La Prostitution s'allume dans les rues;
Comme une fourmilière elle ouvre ses issues;
Partout elle se fraye un occulte chemin,
Ainsi que l'ennemi qui tente un coup de main;
Elle remue au sein de la cité de fange
Comme un ver qui dérobe à l'Homme ce qu'il mange.
On entend çà et là les cuisines siffler,
Les théâtres glapir, les orchestres ronfler;
Les tables d'hôte, dont le jeu fait les délices,
S'emplissent de catins et d'escrocs, leurs complices,
Et les voleurs, qui n'ont ni trêve ni merci,
Vont bientôt commencer leur travail, eux aussi,
Et forcer doucement les portes et les caisses
Pour vivre quelques jours et vêtir leurs maîtresses.

Recueille-toi, mon âme, en ce grave moment,
Et ferme ton oreille à ce rugissement.
C'est l'heure où les douleurs des malades s'aigrissent!
La sombre Nuit les prend à la gorge; ils finissent
Leur destinée et vont vers le gouffre commun;
L'hôpital se remplit de leurs soupirs.—Plus d'un
Ne viendra plus chercher la soupe parfumée,
Au coin du feu, le soir, auprès d'une âme aimée.

Encore la plupart n'ont-ils jamais connu
La douceur du foyer et n'ont jamais vécu!

TWILIGHT

Behold the sweet evening, friend of the criminal;
It comes like an accomplice, stealthily; the sky
Closes slowly like an immense alcove,
And impatient man turns into a beast of prey.
O evening, kind evening, desired by him
Whose arms can say, without lying: "Today
We labored!"—It is the evening that comforts
Those minds that are consumed by a savage sorrow,
The obstinate scholar whose head bends with fatigue
And the bowed laborer who returns to his bed.

Meanwhile in the atmosphere malefic demons
Awaken sluggishly, like businessmen,
And take flight, bumping against porch roofs and shutters.
Among the gas flames worried by the wind
Prostitution catches alight in the streets;
Like an ant-hill she lets her workers out;
Everywhere she blazes a secret path,
Like an enemy who plans a surprise attack;
She moves in the heart of the city of mire
Like a worm that steals from Man what he eats.
Here and there one hears food sizzle in the kitchens,
The theaters yell, the orchestras moan;

The gambling dens, where games of chance delight,
Fill up with whores and cardsharps, their accomplices;
The burglars, who know neither respite nor mercy,
Are soon going to begin their work, they also,
And quietly force open cash-boxes and doors
To enjoy life awhile and dress their mistresses.

Meditate, O my soul, in this solemn moment,
And close your ears to this uproar;
It is now that the pains of the sick grow sharper!
Somber Night grabs them by the throat; they reach the end
Of their destinies and go to the common pit;
The hospitals are filled with their sighs.—More than one
Will come no more to get his fragrant soup
By the fireside, in the evening, with a loved one.

However, most of them have never known
The sweetness of a home, have never lived!

LE JEU

Dans des fauteuils fanés des courtisanes vieilles,
Pâles, le sourcil peint, l'oeil câlin et fatal,
Minaudant, et faisant de leurs maigres oreilles
Tomber un cliquetis de pierre et de métal;

Autour des verts tapis des visages sans lèvre,
Des lèvres sans couleur, des mâchoires sans dent,
Et des doigts convulsés d'une infernale fièvre,
Fouillant la poche vide ou le sein palpitant;

Sous de sales plafonds un rang de pâles lustres
Et d'énormes quinquets projetant leurs lueurs
Sur des fronts ténébreux de poètes illustres
Qui viennent gaspiller leurs sanglantes sueurs;

Voilà le noir tableau qu'en un rêve nocturne
Je vis se dérouler sous mon oeil clairvoyant.
Moi-même, dans un coin de l'antre taciturne,
Je me vis accoudé, froid, muet, enviant,

Enviant de ces gens la passion tenace,
De ces vieilles putains la funèbre gaieté,
Et tous gaillardement trafiquant à ma face,
L'un de son vieil honneur, l'autre de sa beauté!

Et mon coeur s'effraya d'envier maint pauvre homme
Courant avec ferveur à l'abîme béant,
Et qui, soûl de son sang, préférerait en somme
La douleur à la mort et l'enfer au néant!

GAMBLING

In faded armchairs aged courtesans,
Pale, eyebrows penciled, with alluring fatal eyes,
Smirking and sending forth from wizened ears
A jingling sound of metal and of gems;

Around the gaming tables faces without lips,
Lips without color and jaws without teeth,
Fingers convulsed with a hellborn fever
Searching empty pockets and fluttering bosoms;

Under dirty ceilings a row of bright lusters
And enormous oil-lamps casting their rays
On the tenebrous brows of distinguished poets
Who come there to squander the blood they have sweated;

That is the black picture that in a dream one night
I saw unfold before my penetrating eyes.
I saw myself at the back of that quiet den,
Leaning on my elbows, cold, silent, envying,

Envying the stubborn passion of those people,
The dismal merriment of those old prostitutes,
All blithely selling right before my eyes,
One his ancient honor, another her beauty!

My heart took fright at its envy of so many
Wretches running fiercely to the yawning chasm,
Who, drunk with their own blood, would prefer, in a word,
Suffering to death and hell to nothingness!

DANSE MACABRE

À Ernest Christophe

Fière, autant qu'un vivant, de sa noble stature
Avec son gros bouquet, son mouchoir et ses gants
Elle a la nonchalance et la désinvolture
D'une coquette maigre aux airs extravagants.

Vit-on jamais au bal une taille plus mince?
Sa robe exagérée, en sa royale ampleur,
S'écroule abondamment sur un pied sec que pince
Un soulier pomponné, joli comme une fleur.

La ruche qui se joue au bord des clavicules,
Comme un ruisseau lascif qui se frotte au rocher,
Défend pudiquement des lazzi ridicules
Les funèbres appas qu'elle tient à cacher.

Ses yeux profonds sont faits de vide et de ténèbres,
Et son crâne, de fleurs artistement coiffé,
Oscille mollement sur ses frêles vertèbres.
Ô charme d'un néant follement attifé.

Aucuns t'appelleront une caricature,
Qui ne comprennent pas, amants ivres de chair,
L'élégance sans nom de l'humaine armature.
Tu réponds, grand squelette, à mon goût le plus cher!

Viens-tu troubler, avec ta puissante grimace,
La fête de la Vie? ou quelque vieux désir,
Eperonnant encor ta vivante carcasse,
Te pousse-t-il, crédule, au sabbat du Plaisir?

Au chant des violons, aux flammes des bougies,
Espères-tu chasser ton cauchemar moqueur,
Et viens-tu demander au torrent des orgies
De rafraîchir l'enfer allumé dans ton coeur?

Inépuisable puits de sottise et de fautes!
De l'antique douleur éternel alambic!
À travers le treillis recourbé de tes côtes
Je vois, errant encor, l'insatiable aspic.

Pour dire vrai, je crains que ta coquetterie
Ne trouve pas un prix digne de ses efforts
Qui, de ces coeurs mortels, entend la raillerie?
Les charmes de l'horreur n'enivrent que les forts!

Le gouffre de tes yeux, plein d'horribles pensées,
Exhale le vertige, et les danseurs prudents
Ne contempleront pas sans d'amères nausées
Le sourire éternel de tes trente-deux dents.

Pourtant, qui n'a serré dans ses bras un squelette,
Et qui ne s'est nourri des choses du tombeau?
Qu'importe le parfum, l'habit ou la toilette?
Qui fait le dégoûté montre qu'il se croit beau.

Bayadère sans nez, irrésistible gouge,
Dis donc à ces danseurs qui font les offusqués:
«Fiers mignons, malgré l'art des poudres et du rouge
Vous sentez tous la mort! Ô squelettes musqués,

Antinoüs flétris, dandys à face glabre,
Cadavres vernissés, lovelaces chenus,
Le branle universel de la danse macabre
Vous entraîne en des lieux qui ne sont pas connus!

Des quais froids de la Seine aux bords brûlants du Gange,
Le troupeau mortel saute et se pâme, sans voir
Dans un trou du plafond la trompette de l'Ange
Sinistrement béante ainsi qu'un tromblon noir.

En tout climat, sous tout soleil, la Mort t'admire
En tes contorsions, risible Humanité
Et souvent, comme toi, se parfumant de myrrhe,
Mêle son ironie à ton insanité!»

THE DANCE OF DEATH

To Ernest Christophe

Proud as a living person of her noble stature,
With her big bouquet, her handkerchief and gloves,
She has the nonchalance and easy manner
Of a slender coquette with bizarre ways.

Did one ever see a slimmer waist at a ball?
Her ostentatious dress in its queenly fullness
Falls in ample folds over thin feet, tightly pressed
Into slippers with pompons pretty as flowers.

The swarm of bees that plays along her collar-bones
Like a lecherous brook that rubs against the rocks
Modestly protects from cat-calls and jeers
The funereal charms that she's anxious to hide.

Her deep eye-sockets are empty and dark,
And her skull, skillfully adorned with flowers,
Oscillates gently on her fragile vertebrae.
Charm of a non-existent thing, madly arrayed!

Some, lovers drunken with flesh, will call you
A caricature; they don't understand
The marvelous elegance of the human frame.
You satisfy my fondest taste, tall skeleton!

Do you come to trouble with your potent grimace
The festival of Life? Or does some old desire
Still goading your living carcass
Urge you on, credulous one, toward Pleasure's sabbath?

With the flames of candles, with songs of violins,
Do you hope to chase away your mocking nightmare,
And do you come to ask of the flood of orgies
To cool the hell set ablaze in your heart?

Inexhaustible well of folly and of sins!
Eternal alembic of ancient suffering!
Through the curved trellis of your ribs
I see, still wandering, the insatiable asp.

To tell the truth, I fear your coquetry
Will not find a reward worthy of its efforts;
Which of these mortal hearts understands raillery?
The charms of horror enrapture only the strong!

The abyss of your eyes, full of horrible thoughts,
Exhales vertigo, and discreet dancers
Cannot look without bitter nausea
At the eternal smile of your thirty-two teeth.

Yet who has not clasped a skeleton in his arms,
Who has not fed upon what belongs to the grave?
What matters the perfume, the costume or the dress?
He who shows disgust believes that he is handsome.

Noseless dancer, irresistible whore,
Tell those dancing couples who act so offended:
"Proud darlings, despite the art of make-up
You all smell of death! Skeletons perfumed with musk,

Withered Antinoi, dandies with smooth faces,
Varnished corpses, hoary-haired Lovelaces,
The universal swing of the *danse macabre*
Sweeps you along into places unknown!

From the Seine's cold quays to the Ganges' burning shores,
The human troupe skips and swoons with delight, sees not
In a hole in the ceiling the Angel's trumpet
Gaping ominously like a black blunderbuss.

In all climes, under every sun, Death admires you
At your antics, ridiculous Humanity,
And frequently, like you, scenting herself with myrrh,
Mingles her irony with your insanity!"

L'AMOUR DU MENSONGE

Quand je te vois passer, ô ma chère indolente,
Au chant des instruments qui se brise au plafond
Suspendant ton allure harmonieuse et lente,
Et promenant l'ennui de ton regard profond;

Quand je contemple, aux feux du gaz qui le colore,
Ton front pâle, embelli par un morbide attrait,
Où les torches du soir allument une aurore,
Et tes yeux attirants comme ceux d'un portrait,

Je me dis: Qu'elle est belle! et bizarrement fraîche!
Le souvenir massif, royale et lourde tour,
La couronne, et son coeur, meurtri comme une pêche,
Est mûr, comme son corps, pour le savant amour.

Es-tu le fruit d'automne aux saveurs souveraines?
Es-tu vase funèbre attendant quelques pleurs,
Parfum qui fait rêver aux oasis lointaines,
Oreiller caressant, ou corbeille de fleurs?

Je sais qu'il est des yeux, des plus mélancoliques,
Qui ne recèlent point de secrets précieux;
Beaux écrins sans joyaux, médaillons sans reliques,
Plus vides, plus profonds que vous-mêmes, ô Cieux!

Mais ne suffit-il pas que tu sois l'apparence,
Pour réjouir un coeur qui fuit la vérité?
Qu'importe ta bêtise ou ton indifférence?
Masque ou décor, salut! J'adore ta beauté.

THE LOVE OF LIES

When I see you pass by, my indolent darling,
To the sound of music that the ceiling deadens,
Pausing in your slow and harmonious movements,
Turning here and there the boredom of your gaze;

When I study, in the gaslight which colors it,
Your pale forehead, embellished with a morbid charm,
Where the torches of evening kindle a dawn,
And your eyes alluring as a portrait's,

I say within: "How fair she is! How strangely fresh!"
Huge, massive memory, royal, heavy tower,
Crowns her; her heart bruised like a peach
Is ripe like her body for a skillful lover.

Are you the autumn fruit with sovereign taste?
A funereal urn awaiting a few tears?
Perfume that makes one dream of distant oases?
A caressive pillow, a basket of flowers?

I know that there are eyes, most melancholy ones,
In which no precious secrets lie hidden;
Lovely cases without jewels, lockets without relics,
Emptier and deeper than you are, O Heavens!

But is it not enough that you are a semblance
To gladden a heart that flees from the truth?
What matter your obtuseness or your indifference?
Mask or ornament, hail! I adore your beauty.

JE N'AI PAS OUBLIE, VOISINE DE LA VILLE

Je n'ai pas oublié, voisine de la ville,
Notre blanche maison, petite mais tranquille;
Sa Pomone de plâtre et sa vieille Vénus
Dans un bosquet chétif cachant leurs membres nus,
Et le soleil, le soir, ruisselant et superbe,
Qui, derrière la vitre où se brisait sa gerbe
Semblait, grand oeil ouvert dans le ciel curieux,
Contempler nos dîners longs et silencieux,
Répandant largement ses beaux reflets de cierge
Sur la nappe frugale et les rideaux de serge.

I HAVE NOT FORGOTTEN OUR WHITE COTTAGE

I have not forgotten our white cottage,
Small but peaceful, near the city,
Its plaster Pomona, its old Venus,
Hiding their bare limbs in a stunted grove.
In the evening streamed down the radiant sun,
That great eye which stares from the inquisitive sky.
From behind the window that scattered its bright rays
It seemed to gaze upon our long, quiet dinners,
Spreading wide its candle-like reflections
On the frugal table-cloth and the serge curtains.

LA SERVANTE AU GRAND COEUR DONT VOUS ETIEZ JALOUSE

La servante au grand coeur dont vous étiez jalouse,
Et qui dort son sommeil sous une humble pelouse,
Nous devrions pourtant lui porter quelques fleurs.
Les morts, les pauvres morts, ont de grandes douleurs,
Et quand Octobre souffle, émondeur des vieux arbres,
Son vent mélancolique à l'entour de leurs marbres,
Certe, ils doivent trouver les vivants bien ingrats,
À dormir, comme ils font, chaudement dans leurs draps,
Tandis que, dévorés de noires songeries,
Sans compagnon de lit, sans bonnes causeries,
Vieux squelettes gelés travaillés par le ver,
Ils sentent s'égoutter les neiges de l'hiver
Et le siècle couler, sans qu'amis ni famille
Remplacent les lambeaux qui pendent à leur grille.
Lorsque la bûche siffle et chante, si le soir
Calme, dans le fauteuil je la voyais s'asseoir,
Si, par une nuit bleue et froide de décembre,
Je la trouvais tapie en un coin de ma chambre,
Grave, et venant du fond de son lit éternel
Couver l'enfant grandi de son oeil maternel,
Que pourrais-je répondre à cette âme pieuse,
Voyant tomber des pleurs de sa paupière creuse?

THE KIND-HEARTED SERVANT OF WHOM YOU WERE JEALOUS

The kind-hearted servant of whom you were jealous,
Who sleeps her sleep beneath a humble plot of grass,
We must by all means take her some flowers.
The dead, ah! the poor dead suffer great pains,
And when October, the pruner of old trees, blows
His melancholy breath about their marble tombs,
Surely they must think the living most ungrateful,
To sleep, as they do, between warm, white sheets,
While, devoured by gloomy reveries,
Without bedfellows, without pleasant causeries,
Old, frozen skeletons, belabored by the worm,
They feel the drip of winter's snow,
The passing of the years; nor friends, nor family
Replace the dead flowers that hang on their tombs.

If, some evening, when the fire-log whistles and sings
I saw her sit down calmly in the great armchair,
If, on a cold, blue night in December,
I found her ensconced in a corner of my room,
Grave, having come from her eternal bed
Maternally to watch over her grown-up child,
What could I reply to that pious soul,
Seeing tears fall from her hollow eyelids?

BRUMES ET PLUIES

Ô fins d'automne, hivers, printemps trempés de boue,
Endormeuses saisons! je vous aime et vous loue
D'envelopper ainsi mon coeur et mon cerveau
D'un linceul vaporeux et d'un vague tombeau.

Dans cette grande plaine où l'autan froid se joue,
Où par les longues nuits la girouette s'enroue,
Mon âme mieux qu'au temps du tiède renouveau
Ouvrira largement ses ailes de corbeau.

Rien n'est plus doux au coeur plein de choses funèbres,
Et sur qui dès longtemps descendent les frimas,
Ô blafardes saisons, reines de nos climats,

Que l'aspect permanent de vos pâles ténèbres,
—Si ce n'est, par un soir sans lune, deux à deux,
D'endormir la douleur sur un lit hasardeux.

MIST AND RAIN

O ends of autumn, winters, springtimes drenched with mud,
Seasons that lull to sleep! I love you, I praise you
For enfolding my heart and mind thus
In a misty shroud and a filmy tomb.

On that vast plain where the cold south wind plays,
Where in the long, dark nights the weather-cock grows hoarse,
My soul spreads wide its raven wings
More easily than in the warm springtide.

Nothing is sweeter to a gloomy heart
On which the hoar-frost has long been falling,
Than the permanent aspect of your pale shadows,

O wan seasons, queens of our clime
—Unless it be to deaden suffering, side by side
In a casual bed, on a moonless night.

REVE PARISIEN

À Constantin Guys

I

De ce terrible paysage,
Tel que jamais mortel n'en vit,
Ce matin encore l'image,
Vague et lointaine, me ravit.

Le sommeil est plein de miracles!
Par un caprice singulier
J'avais banni de ces spectacles
Le végétal irrégulier,

Et, peintre fier de mon génie,
Je savourais dans mon tableau
L'enivrante monotonie
Du métal, du marbre et de l'eau.

Babel d'escaliers et d'arcades,
C'était un palais infini
Plein de bassins et de cascades
Tombant dans l'or mat ou bruni;

Et des cataractes pesantes,
Comme des rideaux de cristal
Se suspendaient, éblouissantes,
À des murailles de métal.

Non d'arbres, mais de colonnades
Les étangs dormants s'entouraient
Où de gigantesques naïades,
Comme des femmes, se miraient.

Des nappes d'eau s'épanchaient, bleues,
Entre des quais roses et verts,
Pendant des millions de lieues,
Vers les confins de l'univers:

C'étaient des pierres inouïes
Et des flots magiques, c'étaient
D'immenses glaces éblouies
Par tout ce qu'elles reflétaient!

Insouciants et taciturnes,
Des Ganges, dans le firmament,
Versaient le trésor de leurs urnes
Dans des gouffres de diamant.

Architecte de mes féeries,
Je faisais, à ma volonté,
Sous un tunnel de pierreries
Passer un océan dompté;

Et tout, même la couleur noire,
Semblait fourbi, clair, irisé;
Le liquide enchâssait sa gloire
Dans le rayon cristallisé.

Nul astre d'ailleurs, nuls vestiges
De soleil, même au bas du ciel,
Pour illuminer ces prodiges,
Qui brillaient d'un feu personnel!

Et sur ces mouvantes merveilles
Planait (terrible nouveauté!
Tout pour l'oeil, rien pour les oreilles!)
Un silence d'éternité.

II

En rouvrant mes yeux pleins de flamme
J'ai vu l'horreur de mon taudis,
Et senti, rentrant dans mon âme,
La pointe des soucis maudits;

La pendule aux accents funèbres
Sonnait brutalement midi,
Et le ciel versait des ténèbres
Sur le triste monde engourdi.

PARISIAN DREAM

To Constantin Guys

I

This morning I am still entranced
By the image, distant and dim,
Of that awe-inspiring landscape
Such as no mortal ever saw.

Sleep is full of miracles!
Obeying a curious whim,
I had banned from that spectacle
Irregular vegetation,

And, painter proud of his genius,
I savored in my picture
The delightful monotony
Of water, marble, and metal.

Babel of arcades and stairways,
It was a palace infinite,
Full of basins and of cascades
Falling on dull or burnished gold,

And heavy waterfalls,
Like curtains of crystal,
Were hanging, bright and resplendent,
From ramparts of metal.

Not with trees but with colonnades
The sleeping ponds were encircled;
In these mirrors huge naiads
Admired themselves like women.

Streams of blue water flowed along
Between rose and green embankments,
Stretching away millions of leagues
Toward the end of the universe;

There were indescribable stones
And magic waves; there were
Enormous glaciers bedazzled
By everything they reflected!

Insouciant and taciturn,
Ganges, in the firmament,
Poured out the treasure of their urns
Into chasms made of diamonds.

Architect of my fairyland,
Whenever it pleased me I made
A vanquished ocean flow
Into a tunnel of jewels;

And all, even the color black,
Seemed polished, bright, iridescent,
Liquid enchased its own glory
In the crystallized rays of light.

Moreover, no star, no glimmer
Of sun, even at the sky's rim,
Illuminated these marvels
That burned with a personal fire!

And over these shifting wonders
Hovered (terrible novelty!
All for the eye, naught for the ear!)
The silence of eternity.

II

Opening my eyes full of flames
I saw my miserable room
And felt the cursed blade of care
Sink deep into my heart again;

The clock with its death-like accent
Was brutally striking noon;
The sky was pouring down its gloom
Upon the dismal, torpid world.

LE CREPUSCULE DU MATIN

La diane chantait dans les cours des casernes,
Et le vent du matin soufflait sur les lanternes.

C'était l'heure où l'essaim des rêves malfaisants
Tord sur leurs oreillers les bruns adolescents;
Où, comme un oeil sanglant qui palpite et qui bouge,
La lampe sur le jour fait une tache rouge;
Où l'âme, sous le poids du corps revêche et lourd,
Imite les combats de la lampe et du jour.
Comme un visage en pleurs que les brises essuient,
L'air est plein du frisson des choses qui s'enfuient,
Et l'homme est las d'écrire et la femme d'aimer.

Les maisons çà et là commençaient à fumer.
Les femmes de plaisir, la paupière livide,
Bouche ouverte, dormaient de leur sommeil stupide;
Les pauvresses, traînant leurs seins maigres et froids,
Soufflaient sur leurs tisons et soufflaient sur leurs doigts.
C'était l'heure où parmi le froid et la lésine
S'aggravent les douleurs des femmes en gésine;
Comme un sanglot coupé par un sang écumeux
Le chant du coq au loin déchirait l'air brumeux
Une mer de brouillards baignait les édifices,
Et les agonisants dans le fond des hospices
Poussaient leur dernier râle en hoquets inégaux.
Les débauchés rentraient, brisés par leurs travaux.

L'aurore grelottante en robe rose et verte
S'avançait lentement sur la Seine déserte,
Et le sombre Paris, en se frottant les yeux
Empoignait ses outils, vieillard laborieux.

DAWN

They were sounding reveille in the barracks' yards,
And the morning wind was blowing on the lanterns.

It was the hour when swarms of harmful dreams
Make the sun-tanned adolescents toss in their beds;
When, like a bloody eye that twitches and rolls,
The lamp makes a red splash against the light of day;
When the soul within the heavy, fretful body

Imitates the struggle of the lamp and the sun.
Like a tear-stained face being dried by the breeze,
The air is full of the shudders of things that flee,
And man is tired of writing and woman of making love.

Here and there the houses were beginning to smoke.
The ladies of pleasure, with eyelids yellow-green
And mouths open, were sleeping their stupefied sleep;
The beggar-women, their breasts hanging thin and cold,
Were blowing on their fires, blowing on their fingers.
It was the hour when amid poverty and cold
The pains of women in labor grow more cruel;
The cock's crow in the distance tore the foggy air
Like a sob stifled by a bloody froth;

The buildings were enveloped in a sea of mist,
And in the charity-wards, the dying
Hiccupped their death-sobs at uneven intervals.
The rakes were going home, exhausted by their work.

The dawn, shivering in her green and rose garment,
Was moving slowly along the deserted Seine,
And somber Paris, the industrious old man,
Was rubbing his eyes and gathering up his tools.

LE VIN — WINE

L'AME DU VIN

Un soir, l'âme du vin chantait dans les bouteilles:
«Homme, vers toi je pousse, ô cher déshérité,
Sous ma prison de verre et mes cires vermeilles,
Un chant plein de lumière et de fraternité!

Je sais combien il faut, sur la colline en flamme,
De peine, de sueur et de soleil cuisant
Pour engendrer ma vie et pour me donner l'âme;
Mais je ne serai point ingrat ni malfaisant,

Car j'éprouve une joie immense quand je tombe
Dans le gosier d'un homme usé par ses travaux,
Et sa chaude poitrine est une douce tombe
Où je me plais bien mieux que dans mes froids caveaux.

Entends-tu retentir les refrains des dimanches
Et l'espoir qui gazouille en mon sein palpitant?
Les coudes sur la table et retroussant tes manches,
Tu me glorifieras et tu seras content;

J'allumerai les yeux de ta femme ravie;
À ton fils je rendrai sa force et ses couleurs
Et serai pour ce frêle athlète de la vie
L'huile qui raffermit les muscles des lutteurs.

En toi je tomberai, végétale ambroisie,
Grain précieux jeté par l'éternel Semeur,
Pour que de notre amour naisse la poésie
Qui jaillira vers Dieu comme une rare fleur!»

THE SOUL OF WINE

One night, the soul of wine was singing in the flask:
"O man, dear disinherited! to you I sing
This song full of light and of brotherhood
From my prison of glass with its scarlet wax seals.

I know the cost in pain, in sweat,
And in burning sunlight on the blazing hillside,
Of creating my life, of giving me a soul:
I shall not be ungrateful or malevolent,

For I feel a boundless joy when I flow
Down the throat of a man worn out by his labor;
His warm breast is a pleasant tomb
Where I'm much happier than in my cold cellar.

Do you hear the choruses resounding on Sunday
And the hopes that warble in my fluttering breast?
With sleeves rolled up, elbows on the table,
You will glorify me and be content;

I shall light up the eyes of your enraptured wife,
And give back to your son his strength and his color;
I shall be for that frail athlete of life
The oil that hardens a wrestler's muscles.

Vegetal ambrosia, precious grain scattered
By the eternal Sower, I shall descend in you
So that from our love there will be born poetry,
Which will spring up toward God like a rare flower!"

LE VIN DE CHIFFONNIERS

Souvent à la clarté rouge d'un réverbère
Dont le vent bat la flamme et tourmente le verre,
Au coeur d'un vieux faubourg, labyrinthe fangeux
Où l'humanité grouille en ferments orageux,

On voit un chiffonnier qui vient, hochant la tête,
Butant, et se cognant aux murs comme un poète,
Et, sans prendre souci des mouchards, ses sujets,
Epanche tout son coeur en glorieux projets.

Il prête des serments, dicte des lois sublimes,
Terrasse les méchants, relève les victimes,
Et sous le firmament comme un dais suspendu
S'enivre des splendeurs de sa propre vertu.

Oui, ces gens harcelés de chagrins de ménage
Moulus par le travail et tourmentés par l'âge
Ereintés et pliant sous un tas de débris,
Vomissement confus de l'énorme Paris,

Reviennent, parfumés d'une odeur de futailles,
Suivis de compagnons, blanchis dans les batailles,
Dont la moustache pend comme les vieux drapeaux.
Les bannières, les fleurs et les arcs triomphaux

Se dressent devant eux, solennelle magie!
Et dans l'étourdissante et lumineuse orgie
Des clairons, du soleil, des cris et du tambour,
Ils apportent la gloire au peuple ivre d'amour!

C'est ainsi qu'à travers l'Humanité frivole
Le vin roule de l'or, éblouissant Pactole;
Par le gosier de l'homme il chante ses exploits
Et règne par ses dons ainsi que les vrais rois.

Pour noyer la rancoeur et bercer l'indolence
De tous ces vieux maudits qui meurent en silence,
Dieu, touché de remords, avait fait le sommeil;
L'Homme ajouta le Vin, fils sacré du Soleil!

THE RAG-PICKER'S WINE

Often, in the red light of a street-lamp
Of which the wind whips the flame and worries the glass,
In the heart of some old suburb, muddy labyrinth,
Where humanity crawls in a seething ferment,

One sees a rag-picker go by, shaking his head,
Stumbling, bumping against the walls like a poet,
And, with no thought of the stool-pigeons, his subjects,
He pours out his whole heart in grandiose projects.

He takes oaths, dictates sublime laws,
Lays low the wicked and succors victims;
Beneath the firmament spread like a canopy
He gets drunk with the splendor of his own virtues.

Yes, these people harassed by domestic worries,
Ground down by their work, distorted by age,
Worn-out, and bending beneath a load of debris,
The commingled vomit of enormous Paris,

Come back, smelling of the wine-cask,
Followed by companions whitened by their battles,
And whose moustaches bang down like old flags;
Banners, flowers, and triumphal arches

Rise up before them, a solemn magic!
And in the deafening, brilliant orgy
Of clarions and drums, of sunlight and of shouts,
They bring glory to the crowd drunk with love!

It is thus that throughout frivolous Humanity
Wine, the dazzling Pactolus, carries flakes of gold;
By the throats of men he sings his exploits
And reigns by his gifts like a veritable king.

To drown the bitterness and lull the indolence
Of all these accurst old men who die in silence,
God, touched with remorse, had created sleep;
Man added Wine, divine child of the Sun!

LE VIN DE L'ASSASSIN

Ma femme est morte, je suis libre!
Je puis donc boire tout mon soûl.
Lorsque je rentrais sans un sou,
Ses cris me déchiraient la fibre.

Autant qu'un roi je suis heureux;
L'air est pur, le ciel admirable...
Nous avions un été semblable
Lorsque j'en devins amoureux!

L'horrible soif qui me déchire
Aurait besoin pour s'assouvir
D'autant de vin qu'en peut tenir
Son tombeau;—ce n'est pas peu dire:

Je l'ai jetée au fond d'un puits,
Et j'ai même poussé sur elle
Tous les pavés de la margelle.
—Je l'oublierai si je le puis!

Au nom des serments de tendresse,
Dont rien ne peut nous délier,
Et pour nous réconcilier
Comme au beau temps de notre ivresse,

J'implorai d'elle un rendez-vous,
Le soir, sur une route obscure.
Elle y vint—folle créature!
Nous sommes tous plus ou moins fous!

Elle était encore jolie,
Quoique bien fatiguée! et moi,
Je l'aimais trop! voilà pourquoi
Je lui dis: Sors de cette vie!

Nul ne peut me comprendre. Un seul
Parmi ces ivrognes stupides
Songea-t-il dans ses nuits morbides
À faire du vin un linceul?

Cette crapule invulnérable
Comme les machines de fer
Jamais, ni l'été ni l'hiver,
N'a connu l'amour véritable,

Avec ses noirs enchantements,
Son cortège infernal d'alarmes,
Ses fioles de poison, ses larmes,
Ses bruits de chaîne et d'ossements!

—Me voilà libre et solitaire!
Je serai ce soir ivre mort;
Alors, sans peur et sans remords,
Je me coucherai sur la terre,

Et je dormirai comme un chien!
Le chariot aux lourdes roues
Chargé de pierres et de boues,
Le wagon enragé peut bien

Ecraser ma tête coupable
Ou me couper par le milieu,
Je m'en moque comme de Dieu,
Du Diable ou de la Sainte Table!

THE MURDERER'S WINE

My wife is dead and I am free!
Now I can drink my fill;
When I'd come home without a sou,
Her screaming would drive me crazy.

I am as happy as a king;
The air is pure, the sky superb...
We had a summer like this
When I fell in love with her!

To satisfy the awful thirst
That tortures me, I'd have to drink
All the wine it would take to fill
Her grave—that is not a little:

I threw her down a well,
And what is more, I dropped on her
All the stones of the well's rim.
I will forget her if I can!

In the name of love's vows,
From which nothing can release us,
And to become the friends we were
When we first knew passion's rapture,

I begged of her a rendezvous
At night, on a deserted road.
She came there!—mad creature!
We're all more or less mad!

She was still attractive,
Although very tired! and I,
I loved her too much! that is why
I said to her: Depart this life!

None can understand me. Did one
Among all those stupid drunkards
Ever dream in his morbid nights
Of making a shroud of wine?

That dissolute crowd, unfeeling
As an iron machine,
Never, nor summer, nor winter,
Has known what true love is,

With its black enchantments,
Its hellish cortege of alarms,
Its phials of poison, and its tears,
Its noise of chains and dead men's bones!

—Here I am free and all alone!
I'll get blind drunk tonight;
Then without fear, without remorse,
I'll lie down on the ground

And I'll sleep like a dog!
The dump-cart with its heavy wheels
Loaded with mud and rocks,
The careening wagon may well

Crush in my guilty head
Or cut my body in two;
I laugh at God, at the Devil,
And at the Holy Table as well!

LE VIN DU SOLITAIRE

Le regard singulier d'une femme galante
Qui se glisse vers nous comme le rayon blanc
Que la lune onduleuse envoie au lac tremblant,
Quand elle y veut baigner sa beauté nonchalante;

Le dernier sac d'écus dans les doigts d'un joueur;
Un baiser libertin de la maigre Adeline;
Les sons d'une musique énervante et câline,
Semblable au cri lointain de l'humaine douleur,

Tout cela ne vaut pas, ô bouteille profonde,
Les baumes pénétrants que ta panse féconde
Garde au coeur altéré du poète pieux;

Tu lui verses l'espoir, la jeunesse et la vie,
—Et l'orgueil, ce trésor de toute gueuserie,
Qui nous rend triomphants et semblables aux Dieux!

THE WINE OF THE SOLITARY

The strange look of a lady of pleasure
Turned slyly toward us like the white beam
Which the undulous moon casts on the trembling lake
When she wishes to bathe her nonchalant beauty;

The last bag of crowns between a gambler's fingers;
A lustful kiss from slender Adeline;
The sound of music, tormenting and caressing,
Resembling the distant cry of a man in pain,

All that is not worth, O deep, deep bottle,
The penetrating balm that your fruitful belly
Holds for the thirsty heart of the pious poet;

You pour out for him hope, and youth, and life
—And pride, the treasure of all beggary,
Which makes us triumphant and equal to the gods!

LE VIN DES AMANTS

Aujourd'hui l'espace est splendide!
Sans mors, sans éperons, sans bride,
Partons à cheval sur le vin
Pour un ciel féerique et divin!

Comme deux anges que torture
Une implacable calenture
Dans le bleu cristal du matin
Suivons le mirage lointain!

Mollement balancés sur l'aile
Du tourbillon intelligent,
Dans un délire parallèle,

Ma soeur, côte à côte nageant,
Nous fuirons sans repos ni trêves
Vers le paradis de mes rêves!

THE WINE OF LOVERS

Today space is magnificent!
Without bridle or bit or spurs
Let us ride away on wine
To a divine, fairy-like heaven!

Like two angels who are tortured
By a relentless delirium,
Let us follow the far mirage
Through the crystal blue of the morning!

Gently balanced upon the wings
Of the intelligent whirlwind,
In a similar ecstasy,

My sister, floating side by side,
We'll flee without ever stopping
To the paradise of my dreams!

FLEURS DU MAL — FLOWERS OF EVIL

LA DESTRUCTION

Sans cesse à mes côtés s'agite le Démon;
Il nage autour de moi comme un air impalpable;
Je l'avale et le sens qui brûle mon poumon
Et l'emplit d'un désir éternel et coupable.

Parfois il prend, sachant mon grand amour de l'Art,
La forme de la plus séduisante des femmes,
Et, sous de spécieux prétextes de cafard,
Accoutume ma lèvre à des philtres infâmes.

Il me conduit ainsi, loin du regard de Dieu,
Haletant et brisé de fatigue, au milieu
Des plaines de l'Ennui, profondes et désertes,

Et jette dans mes yeux pleins de confusion
Des vêtements souillés, des blessures ouvertes,
Et l'appareil sanglant de la Destruction!

DESTRUCTION

The Demon is always moving about at my side;
He floats about me like an impalpable air;
I swallow him, I feel him burn my lungs
And fill them with an eternal, sinful desire.

Sometimes, knowing my deep love for Art, he assumes
The form of a most seductive woman,
And, with pretexts specious and hypocritical,
Accustoms my lips to infamous philtres.

He leads me thus, far from the sight of God,
Panting and broken with fatigue, into the midst
Of the plains of Ennui, endless and deserted,

And thrusts before my eyes full of bewilderment,
Dirty filthy garments and open, gaping wounds,
And all the bloody instruments of Destruction!

UNE MARTYRE

Dessin d'un Maître inconnu

Au milieu des flacons, des étoffes lamées
Et des meubles voluptueux,
Des marbres, des tableaux, des robes parfumées
Qui traînent à plis somptueux,

Dans une chambre tiède où, comme en une serre,
L'air est dangereux et fatal,
Où des bouquets mourants dans leurs cercueils de verre
Exhalent leur soupir final,

Un cadavre sans tête épanche, comme un fleuve,
Sur l'oreiller désaltéré
Un sang rouge et vivant, dont la toile s'abreuve
Avec l'avidité d'un pré.

Semblable aux visions pâles qu'enfante l'ombre
Et qui nous enchaînent les yeux,
La tête, avec l'amas de sa crinière sombre
Et de ses bijoux précieux,

Sur la table de nuit, comme une renoncule,
Repose; et, vide de pensers,
Un regard vague et blanc comme le crépuscule
S'échappe des yeux révulsés.

Sur le lit, le tronc nu sans scrupules étale
Dans le plus complet abandon
La secrète splendeur et la beauté fatale
Dont la nature lui fit don;

Un bas rosâtre, orné de coins d'or, à la jambe,
Comme un souvenir est resté;
La jarretière, ainsi qu'un oeil secret qui flambe,
Darde un regard diamanté.

Le singulier aspect de cette solitude
Et d'un grand portrait langoureux,
Aux yeux provocateurs comme son attitude,
Révèle un amour ténébreux,

Une coupable joie et des fêtes étranges
Pleines de baisers infernaux,
Dont se réjouissait l'essaim des mauvais anges
Nageant dans les plis des rideaux;

Et cependant, à voir la maigreur élégante
De l'épaule au contour heurté,
La hanche un peu pointue et la taille fringante
Ainsi qu'un reptile irrité,

Elle est bien jeune encor!—Son âme exaspérée
Et ses sens par l'ennui mordus
S'étaient-ils entr'ouverts à la meute altérée
Des désirs errants et perdus?

L'homme vindicatif que tu n'as pu, vivante,
Malgré tant d'amour, assouvir,
Combla-t-il sur ta chair inerte et complaisante
L'immensité de son désir?

Réponds, cadavre impur! et par tes tresses roides
Te soulevant d'un bras fiévreux,
Dis-moi, tête effrayante, a-t-il sur tes dents froides
Collé les suprêmes adieux?

—Loin du monde railleur, loin de la foule impure,
Loin des magistrats curieux,
Dors en paix, dors en paix, étrange créature,
Dans ton tombeau mystérieux;

Ton époux court le monde, et ta forme immortelle
Veille près de lui quand il dort;
Autant que toi sans doute il te sera fidèle,
Et constant jusques à la mort.

A MARTYR

Drawing by an unknown master

In the midst of perfume flasks, of sequined fabrics
And voluptuous furniture,
Of marble statues, pictures, and perfumed dresses
That trail in sumptuous folds,

In a warm room where, as in a hothouse,
The air is dangerous, fatal,
Where bouquets dying in their glass coffins
Exhale their final breath,

A headless cadaver pours out, like a river,
On the saturated pillow
Red, living blood, that the linen drinks up
As greedily as a meadow.

Like the pale visions engendered by shadows
And which hold our eyes riveted,
The head, its mane of hair piled up in a dark mass
And wearing precious jewels,

On the bedside table, like a ranunculus,
Reposes; and, empty of thoughts,
A stare, blank and pallid as the dawn,
Escapes from the upturned eyeballs.

On the bed, the nude torso shamelessly displays
With the most complete abandon
The secret splendor and fatal beauty
That nature had bestowed on her;

A rose stocking embroidered with gold clocks remains
On her leg like a souvenir;
The garter, like a hidden flashing eye,
Darts its glance of diamond brilliance.

The bizarre aspect of that solitude
And of a large, languid portrait
With eyes as provocative as the pose,
Reveals an unwholesome love,

Guilty joys and exotic revelries,
With infernal kisses
That delighted the swarm of bad angels
Hovering in the curtains' folds;

And yet one sees from the graceful slimness
Of the angular shoulders.
The haunches slightly sharp, and the waist sinuous
As a snake poised to strike,

That she's still quite young!—Had her exasperated soul
And her senses gnawed by ennui
Thrown open their gates to the thirsty pack
Of lost and wandering desires?

The vengeful man whom you could not with all your love
Satisfy when you were alive,
Did he use your inert, complacent flesh to fill
The immensity of his lust?

Reply, impure cadaver! and by your stiffened tresses
Raising you with a fevered arm,
Tell me, ghastly head, did he glue on your cold teeth
The kisses of the last farewell?

—Far from the sneering world, far from the impure crowd,
Far from curious magistrates,
Sleep in peace, sleep in peace, bizarre creature,
In your mysterious tomb;

Your mate roams o'er the world, and your immortal form
Watches over him when he sleeps;
Even as you, he will doubtless be faithful
And constant until death.

FEMMES DAMNEES

Comme un bétail pensif sur le sable couchées,
Elles tournent leurs yeux vers l'horizon des mers,
Et leurs pieds se cherchant et leurs mains rapprochées
Ont de douces langueurs et des frissons amers.

Les unes, coeurs épris des longues confidences,
Dans le fond des bosquets où jasent les ruisseaux,
Vont épelant l'amour des craintives enfances
Et creusent le bois vert des jeunes arbrisseaux;

D'autres, comme des soeurs, marchent lentes et graves
À travers les rochers pleins d'apparitions,
Où saint Antoine a vu surgir comme des laves
Les seins nus et pourprés de ses tentations;

Il en est, aux lueurs des résines croulantes,
Qui dans le creux muet des vieux antres païens
T'appellent au secours de leurs fièvres hurlantes,
Ô Bacchus, endormeur des remords anciens!

Et d'autres, dont la gorge aime les scapulaires,
Qui, recélant un fouet sous leurs longs vêtements,
Mêlent, dans le bois sombre et les nuits solitaires,
L'écume du plaisir aux larmes des tourments.

Ô vierges, ô démons, ô monstres, ô martyres,
De la réalité grands esprits contempteurs,
Chercheuses d'infini, dévotes et satyres,
Tantôt pleines de cris, tantôt pleines de pleurs,

Vous que dans votre enfer mon âme a poursuivies,
Pauvres soeurs, je vous aime autant que je vous plains,
Pour vos mornes douleurs, vos soifs inassouvies,
Et les urnes d'amour dont vos grands coeurs sont pleins

DAMNED WOMEN

Lying on the sand like ruminating cattle,
They turn their eyes toward the horizon of the sea,
And their clasped hands and their feet which seek the other's
Know both sweet languor and shudders of pain.

Some, whose hearts grew amorous from long confessions,
In the depth of the woods, among the babbling brooks,
Spell out the love of their timid adolescence
By carving the green wood of young saplings;

Others, like sisters, walk gravely and with slow steps
Among the high rocks peopled with apparitions,
Where Saint Anthony saw the naked, purple breasts
Of his temptations rise up like lava;

There are some who by the light of crumbling resin
In the silent void of the old pagan caverns
Call out for help from their screaming fevers to you
O Bacchus, who lull to sleep the ancient remorse!

And others, whose breasts love the feel of scapulars,
Who, concealing a whip under their long habits,
Mingle, in the dark woods and solitary nights,
The froth of pleasure with tears of torment.

O virgins, O demons, O monsters, O martyrs,
Great spirits, contemptuous of reality,
Seekers of the infinite, pious and satyric,
Sometimes full of cries, sometimes full of tears,

You whom my spirit has followed into your hell,
Poor sisters, I love you as much as I pity you,
For your gloomy sorrows, your unsatisfied thirsts,
And the urns of love with which your great hearts are filled!

LES DEUX BONNES SOEURS

La Débauche et la Mort sont deux aimables filles,
Prodigues de baisers et riches de santé,
Dont le flanc toujours vierge et drapé de guenilles
Sous l'éternel labeur n'a jamais enfanté.

Au poète sinistre, ennemi des familles,
Favori de l'enfer, courtisan mal renté,
Tombeaux et lupanars montrent sous leurs charmilles
Un lit que le remords n'a jamais fréquenté.

Et la bière et l'alcôve en blasphèmes fécondes
Nous offrent tour à tour, comme deux bonnes soeurs,
De terribles plaisirs et d'affreuses douceurs.

Quand veux-tu m'enterrer, Débauche aux bras immondes?
Ô Mort, quand viendras-tu, sa rivale en attraits,
Sur ses myrtes infects enter tes noirs cyprès?

THE TWO GOOD SISTERS

Debauchery and Death are two lovable girls,
Lavish with their kisses and rich with health,
Whose ever-virgin loins, draped with tattered clothes and
Burdened with constant work, have never given birth.

To the sinister poet, foe of families,
Poorly paid courtier, favorite of hell,
Graves and brothels show beneath their bowers
A bed in which remorse has never slept.

The bier and the alcove, fertile in blasphemies
Like two good sisters, offer to us in turn
Terrible pleasures and frightful sweetness.

When will you bury me, Debauch with the filthy arms?
Death, her rival in charms, when will you come
To graft black cypress on her infected myrtle?

LA FONTAINE DE SANG

Il me semble parfois que mon sang coule à flots,
Ainsi qu'une fontaine aux rythmiques sanglots.
Je l'entends bien qui coule avec un long murmure,
Mais je me tâte en vain pour trouver la blessure.

À travers la cité, comme dans un champ clos,
Il s'en va, transformant les pavés en îlots,
Désaltérant la soif de chaque créature,
Et partout colorant en rouge la nature.

J'ai demandé souvent à des vins captieux
D'endormir pour un jour la terreur qui me mine;
Le vin rend l'oeil plus clair et l'oreille plus fine!

J'ai cherché dans l'amour un sommeil oublieux;
Mais l'amour n'est pour moi qu'un matelas d'aiguilles
Fait pour donner à boire à ces cruelles filles!

THE FOUNTAIN OF BLOOD

It seems to me at times my blood flows out in waves
Like a fountain that gushes in rhythmical sobs.
I hear it clearly, escaping with long murmurs,
But I feel my body in vain to find the wound.

Across the city, as in a tournament field,
It courses, making islands of the paving stones,
Satisfying the thirst of every creature
And turning the color of all nature to red.

I have often asked insidious wines
To lull to sleep for a day my wasting terror;
Wine makes the eye sharper, the ear more sensitive!

I have sought in love a forgetful sleep;
But love is to me only a bed of needles
Made to slake the thirst of those cruel prostitutes!

ALLEGORIE

C'est une femme belle et de riche encolure,
Qui laisse dans son vin traîner sa chevelure.
Les griffes de l'amour, les poisons du tripot,
Tout glisse et tout s'émousse au granit de sa peau.
Elle rit à la Mort et nargue la Débauche,
Ces monstres dont la main, qui toujours gratte et fauche,
Dans ses jeux destructeurs a pourtant respecté
De ce corps ferme et droit la rude majesté.
Elle marche en déesse et repose en sultane;
Elle a dans le plaisir la foi mahométane,
Et dans ses bras ouverts, que remplissent ses seins,
Elle appelle des yeux la race des humains.
Elle croit, elle sait, cette vierge inféconde
Et pourtant nécessaire à la marche du monde,
Que la beauté du corps est un sublime don
Qui de toute infamie arrache le pardon.
Elle ignore l'Enfer comme le Purgatoire,
Et quand l'heure viendra d'entrer dans la Nuit noire
Elle regardera la face de la Mort,
Ainsi qu'un nouveau-né,—sans haine et sans remords.

ALLEGORY

She's a beautiful woman with opulent shoulders
Who lets her long hair trail in her goblet of wine.
The claws of love, the poisons of brothels,
All slips and all is blunted on her granite skin.
She laughs at Death and snaps her fingers at Debauch.
The hands of those monsters, ever cutting and scraping,
Have respected nonetheless the pristine majesty
Of her firm, straight body at its destructive games.
She walks like a goddess, rests like a sultana;
She has a Mohammedan's faith in pleasure
And to her open arms which are filled by her breasts,

She lures all mortals with her eyes.
She believes, she knows, this virgin, sterile
And yet essential to the march of the world,
That a beautiful body is a sublime gift
That wrings a pardon for any foul crime.
She is unaware of Hell and Purgatory
And when the time comes for her to enter
The black Night, she will look into the face of Death
As a new-born child,—without hatred or remorse.

LA BEATRICE

Dans des terrains cendreux, calcinés, sans verdure,
Comme je me plaignais un jour à la nature,
Et que de ma pensée, en vaguant au hasard,
J'aiguisais lentement sur mon coeur le poignard,
Je vis en plein midi descendre sur ma tête
Un nuage funèbre et gros d'une tempête,
Qui portait un troupeau de démons vicieux,
Semblables à des nains cruels et curieux.
À me considérer froidement ils se mirent,
Et, comme des passants sur un fou qu'ils admirent,
Je les entendis rire et chuchoter entre eux,
En échangeant maint signe et maint clignement d'yeux:

—«Contemplons à loisir cette caricature
Et cette ombre d'Hamlet imitant sa posture,
Le regard indécis et les cheveux au vent.
N'est-ce pas grand'pitié de voir ce bon vivant,
Ce gueux, cet histrion en vacances, ce drôle,
Parce qu'il sait jouer artistement son rôle,
Vouloir intéresser au chant de ses douleurs
Les aigles, les grillons, les ruisseaux et les fleurs,
Et même à nous, auteurs de ces vieilles rubriques,
Réciter en hurlant ses tirades publiques?»

J'aurais pu (mon orgueil aussi haut que les monts
Domine la nuée et le cri des démons)
Détourner simplement ma tête souveraine,
Si je n'eusse pas vu parmi leur troupe obscène,
Crime qui n'a pas fait chanceler le soleil!
La reine de mon coeur au regard nonpareil
Qui riait avec eux de ma sombre détresse
Et leur versait parfois quelque sale caresse.

BEATRICE

One day as I was making complaint to nature
In a burnt, ash-gray land without vegetation,
And as I wandered aimlessly, slowly whetting
Upon my heart the dagger of my thought,
I saw in broad daylight descending on my head
A leaden cloud, pregnant with a tempest,
That carried a herd of vicious demons
Who resembled curious, cruel dwarfs.
They began to look at me coldly,
And I heard them laugh and whisper to each other,
Exchanging many a sign and many a wink
Like passers-by who discuss a fool they admire:

—"Let us look leisurely at this caricature,
This shade of Hamlet who imitates his posture
With indecisive look, hair streaming in the wind.
Is it not a pity to see this bon vivant,
This tramp, this queer fish, this actor without a job,
Because he knows how to play skillfully his role,
Wish to interest in the song of his woes
The eagles, the crickets, the brooks, and the flowers,
And even to us, authors of that hackneyed drivel,
Bellow the recital of his public tirades?"

I could have (my pride as high as mountains
Dominates the clouds and the cries of the demons)
Simply turned away my sovereign head
If I had not seen in that obscene troop
A crime which did not make the sun reel in its course!
The queen of my heart with the peerless gaze
Laughing with them at my somber distress
And giving them at times a lewd caress.

UN VOYAGE A CYTHERE

Mon coeur, comme un oiseau, voltigeait tout joyeux
Et planait librement à l'entour des cordages;
Le navire roulait sous un ciel sans nuages;
Comme un ange enivré d'un soleil radieux.

Quelle est cette île triste et noire?—C'est Cythère,
Nous dit-on, un pays fameux dans les chansons
Eldorado banal de tous les vieux garçons.
Regardez, après tout, c'est une pauvre terre.

—Île des doux secrets et des fêtes du coeur!
De l'antique Vénus le superbe fantôme
Au-dessus de tes mers plane comme un arôme
Et charge les esprits d'amour et de langueur.

Belle île aux myrtes verts, pleine de fleurs écloses,
Vénérée à jamais par toute nation,
Où les soupirs des coeurs en adoration
Roulent comme l'encens sur un jardin de roses

Ou le roucoulement éternel d'un ramier!
—Cythère n'était plus qu'un terrain des plus maigres,
Un désert rocailleux troublé par des cris aigres.
J'entrevoyais pourtant un objet singulier!

Ce n'était pas un temple aux ombres bocagères,
Où la jeune prêtresse, amoureuse des fleurs,
Allait, le corps brûlé de secrètes chaleurs,
Entrebâillant sa robe aux brises passagères;

Mais voilà qu'en rasant la côte d'assez près
Pour troubler les oiseaux avec nos voiles blanches,
Nous vîmes que c'était un gibet à trois branches,
Du ciel se détachant en noir, comme un cyprès.

De féroces oiseaux perchés sur leur pâture
Détruisaient avec rage un pendu déjà mûr,
Chacun plantant, comme un outil, son bec impur
Dans tous les coins saignants de cette pourriture;

Les yeux étaient deux trous, et du ventre effondré
Les intestins pesants lui coulaient sur les cuisses,
Et ses bourreaux, gorgés de hideuses délices,
L'avaient à coups de bec absolument châtré.

Sous les pieds, un troupeau de jaloux quadrupèdes,
Le museau relevé, tournoyait et rôdait;
Une plus grande bête au milieu s'agitait
Comme un exécuteur entouré de ses aides.

Habitant de Cythère, enfant d'un ciel si beau,
Silencieusement tu souffrais ces insultes
En expiation de tes infâmes cultes
Et des péchés qui t'ont interdit le tombeau.

Ridicule pendu, tes douleurs sont les miennes!
Je sentis, à l'aspect de tes membres flottants,
Comme un vomissement, remonter vers mes dents
Le long fleuve de fiel des douleurs anciennes;

Devant toi, pauvre diable au souvenir si cher,
J'ai senti tous les becs et toutes les mâchoires
Des corbeaux lancinants et des panthères noires
Qui jadis aimaient tant à triturer ma chair.

—Le ciel était charmant, la mer était unie;
Pour moi tout était noir et sanglant désormais,
Hélas! et j'avais, comme en un suaire épais,
Le coeur enseveli dans cette allégorie.

Dans ton île, ô Vénus! je n'ai trouvé debout
Qu'un gibet symbolique où pendait mon image...
—Ah! Seigneur! donnez-moi la force et le courage
De contempler mon coeur et mon corps sans dégoût!

A VOYAGE TO CYTHERA

My heart like a bird was fluttering joyously
And soaring freely around the rigging;
Beneath a cloudless sky the ship was rolling
Like an angel drunken with the radiant sun.

What is this black, gloomy island?—It's Cythera,
They tell us, a country celebrated in song,
The banal Eldorado of old bachelors.
Look at it; after all, it is a wretched land.

—Island of sweet secrets, of the heart's festivals!
The beautiful shade of ancient Venus
Hovers above your seas like a perfume
And fills all minds with love and languidness.

Fair isle of green myrtle filled with full-blown flowers
Ever venerated by all nations,
Where the sighs of hearts in adoration
Roll like incense over a garden of roses

Or like the eternal cooing of wood-pigeons!
—Cythera was now no more than the barrenest land,
A rocky desert disturbed by shrill cries.
But I caught a glimpse of a singular object!

It was not a temple in the shade of a grove
Where the youthful priestess, amorous of flowers,
Was walking, her body hot with hidden passion,
Half-opening her robe to the passing breezes;

But behold! as we passed, hugging the shore
So that we disturbed the sea-birds with our white sails,
We saw it was a gallows with three arms
Outlined in black like a cypress against the sky.

Ferocious birds perched on their feast were savagely
Destroying the ripe corpse of a hanged man;
Each plunged his filthy beak as though it were a tool
Into every corner of that bloody putrescence;

The eyes were two holes and from the gutted belly
The heavy intestines hung down along his thighs
And his torturers, gorged with hideous delights,
Had completely castrated him with their sharp beaks.

Below his feet a pack of jealous quadrupeds
Prowled with upraised muzzles and circled round and round;
One beast, larger than the others, moved in their midst
Like a hangman surrounded by his aides.

Cytherean, child of a sky so beautiful,
You endured those insults in silence
To expiate your infamous adorations
And the sins which denied to you a grave.

Ridiculous hanged man, your sufferings are mine!
I felt at the sight of your dangling limbs
The long, bitter river of my ancient sorrows
Rise up once more like vomit to my teeth;

Before you, poor devil of such dear memory
I felt all the stabbing beaks of the crows
And the jaws of the black panthers who loved so much
In other days to tear my flesh to shreds.

—The sky was charming and the sea was smooth;
For me thenceforth all was black and bloody,
Alas! and I had in that allegory
Wrapped up my heart as in a heavy shroud.

On your isle, O Venus! I found upright only
A symbolic gallows from which hung my image...
O! Lord! give me the strength and the courage
To contemplate my body and soul without loathing!

L'AMOUR ET LE CRANE

Vieux cul-de-lampe

L'Amour est assis sur le crâne
De l'Humanité,
Et sur ce trône le profane,
Au rire effronté,

Souffle gaiement des bulles rondes
Qui montent dans l'air,
Comme pour rejoindre les mondes
Au fond de l'éther.

Le globe lumineux et frêle
Prend un grand essor,
Crève et crache son âme grêle
Comme un songe d'or.

J'entends le crâne à chaque bulle
Prier et gémir:
—«Ce jeu féroce et ridicule,
Quand doit-il finir?

Car ce que ta bouche cruelle
Eparpille en l'air,
Monstre assassin, c'est ma cervelle,
Mon sang et ma chair!»

CUPID AND THE SKULL

An Old Lamp Base

Cupid is seated on the skull
Of Humanity;
On this throne the impious one
With the shameless laugh

Is gaily blowing round bubbles
That rise in the air
As if they would rejoin the globes
At the ether's end.

The sphere, fragile and luminous,
Takes flight rapidly,
Bursts and spits out its flimsy soul
Like a golden dream.

I hear the skull groan and entreat
At every bubble:
"When is this fierce, ludicrous game
To come to an end?

Because what your pitiless mouth
Scatters in the air,
Monstrous murderer—is my brain,
My flesh and my blood!"

RÉVOLTE—REVOLT

LE RENIEMENT DE SAINT PIERRE

Qu'est-ce que Dieu fait donc de ce flot d'anathèmes
Qui monte tous les jours vers ses chers Séraphins?
Comme un tyran gorgé de viande et de vins,
Il s'endort au doux bruit de nos affreux blasphèmes.

Les sanglots des martyrs et des suppliciés
Sont une symphonie enivrante sans doute,
Puisque, malgré le sang que leur volupté coûte,
Les cieux ne s'en sont point encore rassasiés!

—Ah! Jésus, souviens-toi du Jardin des Olives!
Dans ta simplicité tu priais à genoux
Celui qui dans son ciel riait au bruit des clous
Que d'ignobles bourreaux plantaient dans tes chairs vives,

Lorsque tu vis cracher sur ta divinité
La crapule du corps de garde et des cuisines,
Et lorsque tu sentis s'enfoncer les épines
Dans ton crâne où vivait l'immense Humanité;

Quand de ton corps brisé la pesanteur horrible
Allongeait tes deux bras distendus, que ton sang
Et ta sueur coulaient de ton front pâlissant,
Quand tu fus devant tous posé comme une cible,

Rêvais-tu de ces jours si brillants et si beaux
Où tu vins pour remplir l'éternelle promesse,
Où tu foulais, monté sur une douce ânesse,
Des chemins tout jonchés de fleurs et de rameaux,

Où, le coeur tout gonflé d'espoir et de vaillance,
Tu fouettais tous ces vils marchands à tour de bras,
Où tu fus maître enfin? Le remords n'a-t-il pas
Pénétré dans ton flanc plus avant que la lance?

—Certes, je sortirai, quant à moi, satisfait
D'un monde où l'action n'est pas la soeur du rêve;
Puissé-je user du glaive et périr par le glaive!
Saint Pierre a renié Jésus... il a bien fait!

THE DENIAL OF SAINT PETER

What does God do with the wave of curses
That rises every day toward his dear Seraphim?
Like a tyrant gorged with food and wine, he falls asleep
To the sweet sound of our horrible blasphemies.

The sobs of martyrs and of tortured criminals
Are doubtless an enchanting symphony,
Since, despite the blood that this pleasure costs,
The heavens have not yet been surfeited with it!

—Ah Jesus, remember the Garden of Olives!
In your naïveté you prayed on your knees to
Him Who in His heaven laughed at the sound of the nails
Being driven into your living flesh;

When you saw them spitting on your divinity,
That vile mob of body-guards and scullions,
And when you felt the thorns go deep
Into your skull where lived immense Humanity,

When the horrible weight of your broken body
Lengthened your two outstretched arms, when your blood
And sweat flowed from your paling brow,
When you were placed before them all like a target,

Did you dream of those days so brilliant and so fair
When you came to fulfill the eternal promise,
When the gentle donkey you were riding trampled
The branches and flowers strewn in your path,

When, your heart swollen with courage and hope,
You lashed those vile money-changers with all your might,
In a word, when you were master? Did not remorse
Penetrate your side deeper than the spear?

—For my part, I shall indeed be content to leave
A world where action is not the sister of dreams;
Would that I could take up the sword and perish by the sword!
Saint Peter denied Jesus—he did well!

ABEL ET CAÏN

I

Race d'Abel, dors, bois et mange;
Dieu te sourit complaisamment.

Race de Caïn, dans la fange
Rampe et meurs misérablement.

Race d'Abel, ton sacrifice
Flatte le nez du Séraphin!

Race de Caïn, ton supplice
Aura-t-il jamais une fin?

Race d'Abel, vois tes semailles
Et ton bétail venir à bien;

Race de Caïn, tes entrailles
Hurlent la faim comme un vieux chien.

Race d'Abel, chauffe ton ventre
À ton foyer patriarcal;

Race de Caïn, dans ton antre
Tremble de froid, pauvre chacal!

Race d'Abel, aime et pullule!
Ton or fait aussi des petits.

Race de Caïn, coeur qui brûle,
Prends garde à ces grands appétits.

Race d'Abel, tu croîs et broutes
Comme les punaises des bois!

Race de Caïn, sur les routes
Traîne ta famille aux abois.

II

Ah! race d'Abel, ta charogne
Engraissera le sol fumant!

Race de Caïn, ta besogne
N'est pas faite suffisamment;

Race d'Abel, voici ta honte:
Le fer est vaincu par l'épieu!

Race de Caïn, au ciel monte,
Et sur la terre jette Dieu!

CAIN AND ABEL

I

Race of Abel, sleep, eat and drink;
God smiles on you complacently.

Race of Cain, crawl on your belly,
Die in the mire wretchedly.

Race of Abel, your sacrifice
Delights the nose of the Seraphim!

Race of Cain, will there ever be
An ending to your punishment?

Race of Abel, see your sowing
And your cattle thrive and flourish;

Race of Cain, your bowels
Howl with hunger like an old dog.

Race of Abel, warm your belly
At your patriarchal hearth;

Race of Cain, shiver with the cold
In your cavern, wretched jackal!

Race of Abel, love, pullulate!
Even your gold has progeny.

Race of Cain, with the burning heart,
Beware of those intense desires.

Race of Abel, you browse and grow
Like the insects of the forest!

Race of Cain, along the highways
Drag your destitute family.

II

Ah! race of Abel, your carcass
Will fertilize the steaming soil!

Race of Cain, your appointed task
Has not been adequately done;

Race of Abel, your disgrace is:
The sword is conquered by the pike!

Race of Cain, ascend to heaven,
And cast God down upon the earth!

LES LITANIES DE SATAN

Ô toi, le plus savant et le plus beau des Anges,
Dieu trahi par le sort et privé de louanges,

Ô Satan, prends pitié de ma longue misère!

Ô Prince de l'exil, à qui l'on a fait tort
Et qui, vaincu, toujours te redresses plus fort,

Ô Satan, prends pitié de ma longue misère!

Toi qui sais tout, grand roi des choses souterraines,
Guérisseur familier des angoisses humaines,

Ô Satan, prends pitié de ma longue misère!

Toi qui, même aux lépreux, aux parias maudits,
Enseignes par l'amour le goût du Paradis,

Ô Satan, prends pitié de ma longue misère!

Ô toi qui de la Mort, ta vieille et forte amante,
Engendras l'Espérance,—une folle charmante!

Ô Satan, prends pitié de ma longue misère!

Toi qui fais au proscrit ce regard calme et haut
Qui damne tout un peuple autour d'un échafaud.

Ô Satan, prends pitié de ma longue misère!

Toi qui sais en quels coins des terres envieuses
Le Dieu jaloux cacha les pierres précieuses,

Ô Satan, prends pitié de ma longue misère!

Toi dont l'oeil clair connaît les profonds arsenaux
Où dort enseveli le peuple des métaux,

Ô Satan, prends pitié de ma longue misère!

Toi dont la large main cache les précipices
Au somnambule errant au bord des édifices,

Ô Satan, prends pitié de ma longue misère!

Toi qui, magiquement, assouplis les vieux os
De l'ivrogne attardé foulé par les chevaux,

Ô Satan, prends pitié de ma longue misère!

Toi qui, pour consoler l'homme frêle qui souffre,
Nous appris à mêler le salpêtre et le soufre,

Ô Satan, prends pitié de ma longue misère!

Toi qui poses ta marque, ô complice subtil,
Sur le front du Crésus impitoyable et vil,

Ô Satan, prends pitié de ma longue misère!

Toi qui mets dans les yeux et dans le coeur des filles
Le culte de la plaie et l'amour des guenilles,

Ô Satan, prends pitié de ma longue misère!

Bâton des exilés, lampe des inventeurs,
Confesseur des pendus et des conspirateurs,

Ô Satan, prends pitié de ma longue misère!

Père adoptif de ceux qu'en sa noire colère
Du paradis terrestre a chassés Dieu le Père,

Ô Satan, prends pitié de ma longue misère!

Prière

Gloire et louange à toi, Satan, dans les hauteurs
Du Ciel, où tu régnas, et dans les profondeurs
De l'Enfer, où, vaincu, tu rêves en silence!
Fais que mon âme un jour, sous l'Arbre de Science,
Près de toi se repose, à l'heure où sur ton front
Comme un Temple nouveau ses rameaux s'épandront!

THE LITANY OF SATAN

O you, the wisest and fairest of the Angels,
God betrayed by destiny and deprived of praise,

O Satan, take pity on my long misery!

O Prince of Exile, you who have been wronged
And who vanquished always rise up again more strong,

O Satan, take pity on my long misery!

You who know all, great king of hidden things,
The familiar healer of human sufferings,

O Satan, take pity on my long misery!

You who teach through love the taste for Heaven
To the cursed pariah, even to the leper,

O Satan, take pity on my long misery!

You who of Death, your mistress old and strong,
Have begotten Hope,—a charming madcap!

O Satan, take pity on my long misery!

You who give the outlaw that calm and haughty look
That damns the whole multitude around his scaffold.

O Satan, take pity on my long misery!

You who know in what nooks of the miserly earth
A jealous God has hidden precious stones,

O Satan, take pity on my long misery!

You whose clear eye sees the deep arsenals
Where the tribe of metals sleeps in its tomb,

O Satan, take pity on my long misery!

You whose broad hand conceals the precipice
From the sleep-walker wandering on the building's ledge,

O Satan, take pity on my long misery!

You who soften magically the old bones
Of belated drunkards trampled by the horses,

O Satan, take pity on my long misery!

You who to console frail mankind in its sufferings
Taught us to mix sulphur and saltpeter,

O Satan, take pity on my long misery!

You who put your mark, O subtle accomplice,
Upon the brow of Croesus, base and pitiless,

O Satan, take pity on my long misery!

You who put in the eyes and hearts of prostitutes
The cult of sores and the love of rags and tatters,

O Satan, take pity on my long misery!

Staff of those in exile, lamp of the inventor,
Confessor of the hanged and of conspirators,

O Satan, take pity on my long misery!

Adopted father of those whom in black rage
—God the Father drove from the earthly paradise,

O Satan, take pity on my long misery!

Prayer

Glory and praise to you, O Satan, in the heights
Of Heaven where you reigned and in the depths
Of Hell where vanquished you dream in silence!
Grant that my soul may someday repose near to you
Under the Tree of Knowledge, when, over your brow,
Its branches will spread like a new Temple!

LA MORT — DEATH

LA MORT DES AMANTS

Nous aurons des lits pleins d'odeurs légères,
Des divans profonds comme des tombeaux,
Et d'étranges fleurs sur des étagères,
Ecloses pour nous sous des cieux plus beaux.

Usant à l'envi leurs chaleurs dernières,
Nos deux coeurs seront deux vastes flambeaux,
Qui réfléchiront leurs doubles lumières
Dans nos deux esprits, ces miroirs jumeaux.

Un soir fait de rose et de bleu mystique,
Nous échangerons un éclair unique,
Comme un long sanglot, tout chargé d'adieux;

Et plus tard un Ange, entr'ouvrant les portes,
Viendra ranimer, fidèle et joyeux,
Les miroirs ternis et les flammes mortes.

THE DEATH OF LOVERS

We shall have beds full of subtle perfumes,
Divans as deep as graves, and on the shelves
Will be strange flowers that blossomed for us
Under more beautiful heavens.

Using their dying flames emulously,
Our two hearts will be two immense torches
Which will reflect their double light
In our two souls, those twin mirrors.

Some evening made of rose and of mystical blue
A single flash will pass between us
Like a long sob, charged with farewells;

And later an Angel, setting the doors ajar,
Faithful and joyous, will come to revive
The tarnished mirrors, the extinguished flames.

LA MORT DES PAUVRES

C'est la Mort qui console, hélas! et qui fait vivre;
C'est le but de la vie, et c'est le seul espoir
Qui, comme un élixir, nous monte et nous enivre,
Et nous donne le coeur de marcher jusqu'au soir;

À travers la tempête, et la neige, et le givre,
C'est la clarté vibrante à notre horizon noir
C'est l'auberge fameuse inscrite sur le livre,
Où l'on pourra manger, et dormir, et s'asseoir;

C'est un Ange qui tient dans ses doigts magnétiques
Le sommeil et le don des rêves extatiques,
Et qui refait le lit des gens pauvres et nus;

C'est la gloire des Dieux, c'est le grenier mystique,
C'est la bourse du pauvre et sa patrie antique,
C'est le portique ouvert sur les Cieux inconnus!

THE DEATH OF THE POOR

It's Death that comforts us, alas! and makes us live;
It is the goal of life; it is the only hope
Which, like an elixir, makes us inebriate
And gives us the courage to march until evening;

Through the storm and the snow and the hoar-frost
It is the vibrant light on our black horizon;
It is the famous inn inscribed upon the book,
Where one can eat, and sleep, and take his rest;

It's an Angel who holds in his magnetic hands
Sleep and the gift of ecstatic dreams
And who makes the beds for the poor, naked people;

It's the glory of the gods, the mystic granary,
It is the poor man's purse, his ancient fatherland,
It is the portal opening on unknown Skies!

LA MORT DES ARTISTES

Combien faut-il de fois secouer mes grelots
Et baiser ton front bas, morne caricature?
Pour piquer dans le but, de mystique nature,
Combien, ô mon carquois, perdre de javelots?

Nous userons notre âme en de subtils complots,
Et nous démolirons mainte lourde armature,
Avant de contempler la grande Créature
Dont l'infernal désir nous remplit de sanglots!

Il en est qui jamais n'ont connu leur Idole,
Et ces sculpteurs damnés et marqués d'un affront,
Qui vont se martelant la poitrine et le front,

N'ont qu'un espoir, étrange et sombre Capitole!
C'est que la Mort, planant comme un soleil nouveau,
Fera s'épanouir les fleurs de leur cerveau!

THE DEATH OF ARTISTS

How many times must I shake my bauble and bells
And kiss your low forehead, dismal caricature?
To strike the target of mystic nature,
How many javelins must I waste, O my quiver?

We shall wear out our souls in subtle schemes
And we shall demolish many an armature
Before contemplating the glorious Creature
For whom a tormenting desire makes our hearts grieve!

There are some who have never known their Idol
And those sculptors, damned and branded with shame,
Who are always hammering their brows and their breasts,

Have but one hope, bizarre and somber Capitol!
It is that Death, soaring like a new sun,
Will bring to bloom the flowers of their brains!

LA FIN DE LA JOURNEE

Sous une lumière blafarde
Court, danse et se tord sans raison
La Vie, impudente et criarde.
Aussi, sitôt qu'à l'horizon

La nuit voluptueuse monte,
Apaisant tout, même la faim,
Effaçant tout, même la honte,
Le Poète se dit: «Enfin!

Mon esprit, comme mes vertèbres,
Invoque ardemment le repos;
Le coeur plein de songes funèbres,

Je vais me coucher sur le dos
Et me rouler dans vos rideaux,
Ô rafraîchissantes ténèbres!»

THE END OF THE DAY

Under a pallid light, noisy,
Impudent Life runs and dances,
Twists and turns, for no good reason
So, as soon as voluptuous

Night rises from the horizon,
Assuaging all, even hunger,
Effacing all, even shame,
The Poet says to himself: "At last!

My spirit, like my vertebrae,
Passionately invokes repose;
With a heart full of gloomy dreams,

I shall lie down flat on my back
And wrap myself in your curtains,
O refreshing shadows!"

LE REVE D'UN CURIEUX

À Félix Nadar

Connais-tu, comme moi, la douleur savoureuse
Et de toi fais-tu dire: «Oh! l'homme singulier!»
—J'allais mourir. C'était dans mon âme amoureuse
Désir mêlé d'horreur, un mal particulier;

Angoisse et vif espoir, sans humeur factieuse.
Plus allait se vidant le fatal sablier,
Plus ma torture était âpre et délicieuse;
Tout mon coeur s'arrachait au monde familier.

J'étais comme l'enfant avide du spectacle,
Haïssant le rideau comme on hait un obstacle...
Enfin la vérité froide se révéla:

J'étais mort sans surprise, et la terrible aurore
M'enveloppait.—Eh quoi! n'est-ce donc que cela?
La toile était levée et j'attendais encore.

THE DREAM OF A CURIOUS MAN

To Félix Nadar

Do you know as I do, delectable suffering?
And do you have them say of you: "O! the strange man!"
—I was going to die. In my soul, full of love,
A peculiar illness; desire mixed with horror,

Anguish and bright hopes; without internal strife.
The more the fatal hour-glass continued to flow,
The fiercer and more delightful grew my torture;
My heart was being torn from this familiar world.

I was like a child eager for the play,
Hating the curtain as one hates an obstacle...
Finally the cold truth revealed itself:

I had died and was not surprised; the awful dawn
Enveloped me.—What! is that all there is to it?
The curtain had risen and I was still waiting.

LE VOYAGE

À Maxime du Camp

I

Pour l'enfant, amoureux de cartes et d'estampes,
L'univers est égal à son vaste appétit.
Ah! que le monde est grand à la clarté des lampes!
Aux yeux du souvenir que le monde est petit!

Un matin nous partons, le cerveau plein de flamme,
Le coeur gros de rancune et de désirs amers,
Et nous allons, suivant le rythme de la lame,
Berçant notre infini sur le fini des mers:

Les uns, joyeux de fuir une patrie infâme;
D'autres, l'horreur de leurs berceaux, et quelques-uns,
Astrologues noyés dans les yeux d'une femme,
La Circé tyrannique aux dangereux parfums.

Pour n'être pas changés en bêtes, ils s'enivrent
D'espace et de lumière et de cieux embrasés;
La glace qui les mord, les soleils qui les cuivrent,
Effacent lentement la marque des baisers.

Mais les vrais voyageurs sont ceux-là seuls qui partent
Pour partir; coeurs légers, semblables aux ballons,
De leur fatalité jamais ils ne s'écartent,
Et, sans savoir pourquoi, disent toujours: Allons!

Ceux-là dont les désirs ont la forme des nues,
Et qui rêvent, ainsi qu'un conscrit le canon,
De vastes voluptés, changeantes, inconnues,
Et dont l'esprit humain n'a jamais su le nom!

II

Nous imitons, horreur! la toupie et la boule
Dans leur valse et leurs bonds; même dans nos sommeils
La Curiosité nous tourmente et nous roule
Comme un Ange cruel qui fouette des soleils.

Singulière fortune où le but se déplace,
Et, n'étant nulle part, peut être n'importe où!
Où l'Homme, dont jamais l'espérance n'est lasse,
Pour trouver le repos court toujours comme un fou!

Notre âme est un trois-mâts cherchant son Icarie;
Une voix retentit sur le pont: «Ouvre l'oeil!»
Une voix de la hune, ardente et folle, crie:
«Amour... gloire... bonheur!» Enfer! c'est un écueil!

Chaque îlot signalé par l'homme de vigie
Est un Eldorado promis par le Destin;
L'Imagination qui dresse son orgie
Ne trouve qu'un récif aux clartés du matin.

Ô le pauvre amoureux des pays chimériques!
Faut-il le mettre aux fers, le jeter à la mer,
Ce matelot ivrogne, inventeur d'Amériques
Dont le mirage rend le gouffre plus amer?

Tel le vieux vagabond, piétinant dans la boue,
Rêve, le nez en l'air, de brillants paradis;
Son oeil ensorcelé découvre une Capoue
Partout où la chandelle illumine un taudis.

III

Etonnants voyageurs! quelles nobles histoires
Nous lisons dans vos yeux profonds comme les mers!
Montrez-nous les écrins de vos riches mémoires,
Ces bijoux merveilleux, faits d'astres et d'éthers.

Nous voulons voyager sans vapeur et sans voile!
Faites, pour égayer l'ennui de nos prisons,
Passer sur nos esprits, tendus comme une toile,
Vos souvenirs avec leurs cadres d'horizons.

Dites, qu'avez-vous vu?

IV

«Nous avons vu des astres
Et des flots, nous avons vu des sables aussi;
Et, malgré bien des chocs et d'imprévus désastres,
Nous nous sommes souvent ennuyés, comme ici.

La gloire du soleil sur la mer violette,
La gloire des cités dans le soleil couchant,
Allumaient dans nos coeurs une ardeur inquiète
De plonger dans un ciel au reflet alléchant.

Les plus riches cités, les plus grands paysages,
Jamais ne contenaient l'attrait mystérieux
De ceux que le hasard fait avec les nuages.
Et toujours le désir nous rendait soucieux!

—La jouissance ajoute au désir de la force.
Désir, vieil arbre à qui le plaisir sert d'engrais,
Cependant que grossit et durcit ton écorce,
Tes branches veulent voir le soleil de plus près!

Grandiras-tu toujours, grand arbre plus vivace
Que le cyprès?—Pourtant nous avons, avec soin,
Cueilli quelques croquis pour votre album vorace
Frères qui trouvez beau tout ce qui vient de loin!

Nous avons salué des idoles à trompe;
Des trônes constellés de joyaux lumineux;
Des palais ouvragés dont la féerique pompe
Serait pour vos banquiers un rêve ruineux;

Des costumes qui sont pour les yeux une ivresse;
Des femmes dont les dents et les ongles sont teints,
Et des jongleurs savants que le serpent caresse.»

V

Et puis, et puis encore?

VI

«Ô cerveaux enfantins!

Pour ne pas oublier la chose capitale,
Nous avons vu partout, et sans l'avoir cherché,
Du haut jusques en bas de l'échelle fatale,
Le spectacle ennuyeux de l'immortel péché:

La femme, esclave vile, orgueilleuse et stupide,
Sans rire s'adorant et s'aimant sans dégoût;
L'homme, tyran goulu, paillard, dur et cupide,
Esclave de l'esclave et ruisseau dans l'égout;

Le bourreau qui jouit, le martyr qui sanglote;
La fête qu'assaisonne et parfume le sang;
Le poison du pouvoir énervant le despote,
Et le peuple amoureux du fouet abrutissant;

Plusieurs religions semblables à la nôtre,
Toutes escaladant le ciel; la Sainteté,
Comme en un lit de plume un délicat se vautre,
Dans les clous et le crin cherchant la volupté;

L'Humanité bavarde, ivre de son génie,
Et, folle maintenant comme elle était jadis,
Criant à Dieu, dans sa furibonde agonie:
»Ô mon semblable, mon maître, je te maudis!«

Et les moins sots, hardis amants de la Démence,
Fuyant le grand troupeau parqué par le Destin,
Et se réfugiant dans l'opium immense!
—Tel est du globe entier l'éternel bulletin.»

VII

Amer savoir, celui qu'on tire du voyage!
Le monde, monotone et petit, aujourd'hui,
Hier, demain, toujours, nous fait voir notre image:
Une oasis d'horreur dans un désert d'ennui!

Faut-il partir? rester? Si tu peux rester, reste;
Pars, s'il le faut. L'un court, et l'autre se tapit
Pour tromper l'ennemi vigilant et funeste,
Le Temps! Il est, hélas! des coureurs sans répit,

Comme le Juif errant et comme les apôtres,
À qui rien ne suffit, ni wagon ni vaisseau,
Pour fuir ce rétiaire infâme; il en est d'autres
Qui savent le tuer sans quitter leur berceau.

Lorsque enfin il mettra le pied sur notre échine,
Nous pourrons espérer et crier: En avant!
De même qu'autrefois nous partions pour la Chine,
Les yeux fixés au large et les cheveux au vent,

Nous nous embarquerons sur la mer des Ténèbres
Avec le coeur joyeux d'un jeune passager.
Entendez-vous ces voix charmantes et funèbres,
Qui chantent: «Par ici vous qui voulez manger

Le Lotus parfumé! c'est ici qu'on vendange
Les fruits miraculeux dont votre coeur a faim;
Venez vous enivrer de la douceur étrange
De cette après-midi qui n'a jamais de fin!»

À l'accent familier nous devinons le spectre;
Nos Pylades là-bas tendent leurs bras vers nous.
«Pour rafraîchir ton coeur nage vers ton Electre!»
Dit celle dont jadis nous baisions les genoux.

VIII

Ô Mort, vieux capitaine, il est temps! levons l'ancre!
Ce pays nous ennuie, ô Mort! Appareillons!
Si le ciel et la mer sont noirs comme de l'encre,
Nos coeurs que tu connais sont remplis de rayons!

Verse-nous ton poison pour qu'il nous réconforte!
Nous voulons, tant ce feu nous brûle le cerveau,
Plonger au fond du gouffre, Enfer ou Ciel, qu'importe?
Au fond de l'Inconnu pour trouver du *nouveau*!

THE VOYAGE

To Maxime du Camp

To a child who is fond of maps and engravings
The universe is the size of his immense hunger.
Ah! how vast is the world in the light of a lamp!
In memory's eyes how small the world is!

One morning we set out, our brains aflame,
Our hearts full of resentment and bitter desires,
And we go, following the rhythm of the wave,
Lulling our infinite on the finite of the seas:

Some, joyful at fleeing a wretched fatherland;
Others, the horror of their birthplace; a few,
Astrologers drowned in the eyes of some woman,
Some tyrannic Circe with dangerous perfumes.

Not to be changed into beasts, they get drunk
With space, with light, and with fiery skies;
The ice that bites them, the suns that bronze them,
Slowly efface the bruise of the kisses.

But the true voyagers are only those who leave
Just to be leaving; hearts light, like balloons,
They never turn aside from their fatality
And without knowing why they always say: "Let's go!"

Those whose desires have the form of the clouds,
And who, as a raw recruit dreams of the cannon,
Dream of vast voluptuousness, changing and strange,
Whose name the human mind has never known!

II

Horror! We imitate the top and bowling ball,
Their bounding and their waltz; even in our slumber
Curiosity torments us, rolls us about,
Like a cruel Angel who lashes suns.

Singular destiny where the goal moves about,
And being nowhere can be anywhere!
Toward which Man, whose hope never grows weary,
Is ever running like a madman to find rest!

Our soul's a three-master seeking Icaria;
A voice resounds upon the bridge: "Keep a sharp eye!"
From aloft a voice, ardent and wild, cries:
"Love... glory... happiness!" –Damnation! It's a shoal!

Every small island sighted by the man on watch
Is the Eldorado promised by Destiny;
Imagination preparing for her orgy
Finds but a reef in the light of the dawn.

O the poor lover of imaginary lands!
Must he be put in irons, thrown into the sea,
That drunken tar, inventor of Americas,
Whose mirage makes the abyss more bitter?

Thus the old vagabond tramping through the mire
Dreams with his nose in the air of brilliant Edens;
His enchanted eye discovers a Capua
Wherever a candle lights up a hut.

III

Astonishing voyagers! What splendid stories
We read in your eyes as deep as the seas!
Show us the chest of your rich memories,
Those marvelous jewels, made of ether and stars.

We wish to voyage without steam and without sails!
To brighten the ennui of our prisons,
Make your memories, framed in their horizons,
Pass across our minds stretched like canvasses.

Tell us what you have seen.

IV

"We have seen stars
And waves; we have also seen sandy wastes;
And in spite of many a shock and unforeseen
Disaster, we were often bored, as we are here.

The glory of sunlight upon the purple sea,
The glory of cities against the setting sun,
Kindled in our hearts a troubling desire
To plunge into a sky of alluring colors.

The richest cities, the finest landscapes,
Never contained the mysterious attraction
Of the ones that chance fashions from the clouds
And desire was always making us more avid!

—Enjoyment fortifies desire.
Desire, old tree fertilized by pleasure,
While your bark grows thick and hardens,
Your branches strive to get closer to the sun!

Will you always grow, tall tree more hardy
Than the cypress?—However, we have carefully
Gathered a few sketches for your greedy album,
Brothers who think lovely all that comes from afar!

We have bowed to idols with elephantine trunks;
Thrones studded with luminous jewels;
Palaces so wrought that their fairly-like splendor
Would make your bankers have dreams of ruination;

And costumes that intoxicate the eyes;
Women whose teeth and fingernails are dyed
And clever mountebanks whom the snake caresses."

V

And then, and then what else?

VI

"O childish minds!

Not to forget the most important thing,
We saw everywhere, without seeking it,
From the foot to the top of the fatal ladder,
The wearisome spectacle of immortal sin:

Woman, a base slave, haughty and stupid,
Adoring herself without laughter or disgust;
Man, a greedy tyrant, ribald, hard and grasping,
A slave of the slave, a gutter in the sewer;

The hangman who feels joy and the martyr who sobs,
The festival that blood flavors and perfumes;
The poison of power making the despot weak,
And the people loving the brutalizing whip;

Several religions similar to our own,
All climbing up to heaven; Saintliness
Like a dilettante who sprawls in a feather bed,
Seeking voluptuousness on horsehair and nails;

Prating humanity, drunken with its genius,
And mad now as it was in former times,
Crying to God in its furious death-struggle:
'O my fellow, O my master, may you be damned!'

The less foolish, bold lovers of Madness,
Fleeing the great flock that Destiny has folded,
Taking refuge in opium's immensity!
—That's the unchanging report of the entire globe."

VII

Bitter is the knowledge one gains from voyaging!
The world, monotonous and small, today,
Yesterday, tomorrow, always, shows us our image:
An oasis of horror in a desert of ennui!

Must one depart? Remain? If you can stay, remain;
Leave, if you must. One runs, another hides
To elude the vigilant, fatal enemy,
Time! There are, alas! those who rove without respite,

Like the Wandering Jew and like the Apostles,
Whom nothing suffices, neither coach nor vessel,
To flee this infamous retiary; and others
Who know how to kill him without leaving their cribs.

And when at last he sets his foot upon our spine,
We can hope and cry out: Forward!
Just as in other times we set out for China,
Our eyes fixed on the open sea, hair in the wind,

We shall embark on the sea of Darkness
With the glad heart of a young traveler.
Do you hear those charming, melancholy voices
Singing: "Come this way! You who wish to eat

The perfumed Lotus! It's here you gather
The miraculous fruits for which your heart hungers;
Come and get drunken with the strange sweetness
Of this eternal afternoon?"

By the familiar accent we know the specter;
Our Pylades yonder stretch out their arms towards us.
"To refresh your heart swim to your Electra!"
Cries she whose knees we kissed in other days.

VIII

O Death, old captain, it is time! let's weigh anchor!
This country wearies us, O Death! Let us set sail!
Though the sea and the sky are black as ink,
Our hearts which you know well are filled with rays of light

Pour out your poison that it may refresh us!
This fire burns our brains so fiercely, we wish to plunge
To the abyss' depths, Heaven or Hell, does it matter?
To the depths of the Unknown to find something new!"

PIÈCES CONDAMNÉES — CONDEMNED POEMS

LESBOS

Mère des jeux latins et des voluptés grecques,
Lesbos, où les baisers, languissants ou joyeux,
Chauds comme les soleils, frais comme les pastèques,
Font l'ornement des nuits et des jours glorieux,
Mère des jeux latins et des voluptés grecques,

Lesbos, où les baisers sont comme les cascades
Qui se jettent sans peur dans les gouffres sans fonds,
Et courent, sanglotant et gloussant par saccades,
Orageux et secrets, fourmillants et profonds;
Lesbos, où les baisers sont comme les cascades!

Lesbos, où les Phrynés l'une l'autre s'attirent,
Où jamais un soupir ne resta sans écho,
À l'égal de Paphos les étoiles t'admirent,
Et Vénus à bon droit peut jalouser Sapho!
Lesbos où les Phrynés l'une l'autre s'attirent,

Lesbos, terre des nuits chaudes et langoureuses,
Qui font qu'à leurs miroirs, stérile volupté!
Les filles aux yeux creux, de leur corps amoureuses,
Caressent les fruits mûrs de leur nubilité;
Lesbos, terre des nuits chaudes et langoureuses,

Laisse du vieux Platon se froncer l'oeil austère;
Tu tires ton pardon de l'excès des baisers,
Reine du doux empire, aimable et noble terre,
Et des raffinements toujours inépuisés.
Laisse du vieux Platon se froncer l'oeil austère.

Tu tires ton pardon de l'éternel martyre,
Infligé sans relâche aux coeurs ambitieux,
Qu'attire loin de nous le radieux sourire
Entrevu vaguement au bord des autres cieux!
Tu tires ton pardon de l'éternel martyre!

Qui des Dieux osera, Lesbos, être ton juge
Et condamner ton front pâli dans les travaux,
Si ses balances d'or n'ont pesé le déluge
De larmes qu'à la mer ont versé tes ruisseaux?
Qui des Dieux osera, Lesbos, être ton juge?

Que nous veulent les lois du juste et de l'injuste ?
Vierges au coeur sublime, honneur de l'archipel,
Votre religion comme une autre est auguste,
Et l'amour se rira de l'Enfer et du Ciel!
Que nous veulent les lois du juste et de l'injuste?

Car Lesbos entre tous m'a choisi sur la terre
Pour chanter le secret de ses vierges en fleurs,
Et je fus dès l'enfance admis au noir mystère
Des rires effrénés mêlés aux sombres pleurs;
Car Lesbos entre tous m'a choisi sur la terre.

Et depuis lors je veille au sommet de Leucate,
Comme une sentinelle à l'oeil perçant et sûr,
Qui guette nuit et jour brick, tartane ou frégate,
Dont les formes au loin frissonnent dans l'azur;
Et depuis lors je veille au sommet de Leucate,

Pour savoir si la mer est indulgente et bonne,
Et parmi les sanglots dont le roc retentit
Un soir ramènera vers Lesbos, qui pardonne,
Le cadavre adoré de Sapho, qui partit
Pour savoir si la mer est indulgente et bonne!

De la mâle Sapho, l'amante et le poète,
Plus belle que Vénus par ses mornes pâleurs!
—L'oeil d'azur est vaincu par l'oeil noir que tachète
Le cercle ténébreux tracé par les douleurs
De la mâle Sapho, l'amante et le poète!

—Plus belle que Vénus se dressant sur le monde
Et versant les trésors de sa sérénité
Et le rayonnement de sa jeunesse blonde
Sur le vieil Océan de sa fille enchanté;
Plus belle que Vénus se dressant sur le monde!

—De Sapho qui mourut le jour de son blasphème,
Quand, insultant le rite et le culte inventé,
Elle fit son beau corps la pâture suprême
D'un brutal dont l'orgueil punit l'impiété
De celle qui mourut le jour de son blasphème.

Et c'est depuis ce temps que Lesbos se lamente,
Et, malgré les honneurs que lui rend l'univers,
S'enivre chaque nuit du cri de la tourmente
Que poussent vers les cieux ses rivages déserts.
Et c'est depuis ce temps que Lesbos se lamente!

LESBOS

Mother of Latin games and Greek delights,
Lesbos, where kisses, languishing or joyous,
Burning as the sun's light, cool as melons,
Adorn the nights and the glorious days;
Mother of Latin games and Greek delights,

Lesbos, where the kisses are like cascades
That throw themselves boldly into bottomless chasms
And flow, sobbing and gurgling intermittently,
Stormy and secret, teeming and profound;
Lesbos, where the kisses are like cascades!

Lesbos, where courtesans feel drawn toward each other,
Where for every sigh there is an answering sigh,
The stars admire you as much as Paphos,
And Venus may rightly be jealous of Sappho!
Lesbos, where courtesans feel drawn toward each other,

Lesbos, land of hot and languorous nights,
That make the hollow-eyed girls, amorous
Of their own bodies, caress before their mirrors
The ripe fruits of their nubility, O sterile pleasure!
Lesbos, land of hot and languorous nights,

Let old Plato look on you with an austere eye;
You earn pardon by the excess of your kisses
And the inexhaustible refinements of your love,
Queen of the sweet empire, pleasant and noble land.
Let old Plato look on you with an austere eye.

You earn pardon by the eternal martyrdom
Inflicted ceaselessly upon aspiring hearts
Who are lured far from us by radiant smiles
Vaguely glimpsed at the edge of other skies!
You earn pardon by that eternal martyrdom!

Which of the gods will dare to be your judge, Lesbos,
And condemn your brow, grown pallid from your labors,
If his golden scales have not weighed the flood
Of tears your streams have poured into the sea?
Which of the gods will dare to be your judge, Lesbos?

What are to us the laws of the just and unjust
Virgins with sublime hearts, honor of these islands;
Your religion, like any other, is august,
And love will laugh at Heaven and at Hell!
What are to us the laws of the just and unjust?

For Lesbos chose me among all other poets
To sing the secret of her virgins in their bloom,
And from childhood I witnessed the dark mystery
Of unbridled laughter mingled with tears of gloom;
For Lesbos chose me among all other poets.

And since then I watch from Leucadia's summit,
Like a sentry with sure and piercing eyes
Who looks night and day for tartane, brig or frigate,
Whose forms in the distance flutter against the blue;
And since then I watch from Leucadia's summit,

To find out if the sea is indulgent and kind,
If to the sobs with which the rocks resound
It will bring back some night to Lesbos, who forgives,
The worshipped body of Sappho, who departed
To find out if the sea is indulgent and kind!

Of the virile Sappho, paramour and poet,
With her wan pallor, more beautiful than Venus!
—The blue eyes were conquered by the black eyes, ringed
With dark circles, traced by the sufferings
Of the virile Sappho, paramour and poet!

—Lovelier than Venus dominating the world,
Pouring out the treasures of her serenity
And the radiance of her golden-haired youth
Upon old Ocean, delighted with his daughter;
Lovelier than Venus dominating the world!

—Of Sappho who died the day of her blasphemy,
When, insulting the rite and the established cult,
She made of her body the supreme pabulum
Of a cruel brute whose pride punished the sacrilege
Of her who died on the day of her blasphemy.

And it is since that time that Lesbos mourns,
And in spite of the homage the world renders her,
Gets drunk every night with the tempest's howls
Which are hurled at the skies by her deserted shores.
And it is since that time that Lesbos mourns.

FEMMES DAMNÉES (DELPHINE ET HIPPOLYTE)

À la pâle clarté des lampes languissantes,
Sur de profonds coussins tout imprégnés d'odeur
Hippolyte rêvait aux caresses puissantes
Qui levaient le rideau de sa jeune candeur.

Elle cherchait, d'un oeil troublé par la tempête,
De sa naïveté le ciel déjà lointain,
Ainsi qu'un voyageur qui retourne la tête
Vers les horizons bleus dépassés le matin.

De ses yeux amortis les paresseuses larmes,
L'air brisé, la stupeur, la morne volupté,
Ses bras vaincus, jetés comme de vaines armes,
Tout servait, tout parait sa fragile beauté.

Étendue à ses pieds, calme et pleine de joie,
Delphine la couvait avec des yeux ardents,
Comme un animal fort qui surveille une proie,
Après l'avoir d'abord marquée avec les dents.

Beauté forte à genoux devant la beauté frêle,
Superbe, elle humait voluptueusement
Le vin de son triomphe, et s'allongeait vers elle,
Comme pour recueillir un doux remerciement.

Elle cherchait dans l'oeil de sa pâle victime
Le cantique muet que chante le plaisir,
Et cette gratitude infinie et sublime
Qui sort de la paupière ainsi qu'un long soupir.

—«Hippolyte, cher coeur, que dis-tu de ces choses?
Comprends-tu maintenant qu'il ne faut pas offrir
L'holocauste sacré de tes premières roses
Aux souffles violents qui pourraient les flétrir ?

Mes baisers sont légers comme ces éphémères
Qui caressent le soir les grands lacs transparents,
Et ceux de ton amant creuseront leurs ornières
Comme des chariots ou des socs déchirants;

Ils passeront sur toi comme un lourd attelage
De chevaux et de boeufs aux sabots sans pitié...
Hippolyte, ô ma soeur! tourne donc ton visage,
Toi, mon âme et mon coeur, mon tout et ma moitié,

Tourne vers moi tes yeux pleins d'azur et d'étoiles!
Pour un de ces regards charmants, baume divin,
Des plaisirs plus obscurs je lèverai les voiles,
Et je t'endormirai dans un rêve sans fin!»

Mais Hippolyte alors, levant sa jeune tête:
—«Je ne suis point ingrate et ne me repens pas,
Ma Delphine, je souffre et je suis inquiète,
Comme après un nocturne et terrible repas.

Je sens fondre sur moi de lourdes épouvantes
Et de noirs bataillons de fantômes épars,
Qui veulent me conduire en des routes mouvantes
Qu'un horizon sanglant ferme de toutes parts.

Avons-nous donc commis une action étrange ?
Explique, si tu peux, mon trouble et mon effroi:
Je frissonne de peur quand tu me dis: 'Mon ange!'
Et cependant je sens ma bouche aller vers toi.

Ne me regarde pas ainsi, toi, ma pensée!
Toi que j'aime à jamais, ma soeur d'élection,
Quand même tu serais une embûche dressée
Et le commencement de ma perdition!»

Delphine secouant sa crinière tragique,
Et comme trépignant sur le trépied de fer,
L'oeil fatal, répondit d'une voix despotique:
—«Qui donc devant l'amour ose parler d'enfer ?

Maudit soit à jamais le rêveur inutile
Qui voulut le premier, dans sa stupidité,
S'éprenant d'un problème insoluble et stérile,
Aux choses de l'amour mêler l'honnêteté!

Celui qui veut unir dans un accord mystique
L'ombre avec la chaleur, la nuit avec le jour,
Ne chauffera jamais son corps paralytique
À ce rouge soleil que l'on nomme l'amour!

Va, si tu veux, chercher un fiancé stupide;
Cours offrir un coeur vierge à ses cruels baisers;
Et, pleine de remords et d'horreur, et livide,
Tu me rapporteras tes seins stigmatisés...

On ne peut ici-bas contenter qu'un seul maître!»
Mais l'enfant, épanchant une immense douleur,
Cria soudain:—«Je sens s'élargir dans mon être
Un abîme béant; cet abîme est mon coeur!

Brûlant comme un volcan, profond comme le vide!
Rien ne rassasiera ce monstre gémissant
Et ne rafraîchira la soif de l'Euménide
Qui, la torche à la main, le brûle jusqu'au sang.

Que nos rideaux fermés nous séparent du monde,
Et que la lassitude amène le repos!
Je veux m'anéantir dans ta gorge profonde,
Et trouver sur ton sein la fraîcheur des tombeaux!»

—Descendez, descendez, lamentables victimes,
Descendez le chemin de l'enfer éternel!
Plongez au plus profond du gouffre, où tous les crimes
Flagellés par un vent qui ne vient pas du ciel,

Bouillonnent pêle-mêle avec un bruit d'orage.
Ombres folles, courez au but de vos désirs;
Jamais vous ne pourrez assouvir votre rage,
Et votre châtiment naîtra de vos plaisirs.

Jamais un rayon frais n'éclaira vos cavernes;
Par les fentes des murs des miasmes fiévreux
Filtrent en s'enflammant ainsi que des lanternes
Et pénètrent vos corps de leurs parfums affreux.

L'âpre stérilité de votre jouissance
Altère votre soif et roidit votre peau,
Et le vent furibond de la concupiscence
Fait claquer votre chair ainsi qu'un vieux drapeau.

Loin des peuples vivants, errantes, condamnées,
À travers les déserts courez comme les loups;
Faites votre destin, âmes désordonnées,
Et fuyez l'infini que vous portez en vous!

DAMNED WOMEN (DELPHINE AND HIPPOLYTA)

In the pallid light of languishing lamps,
In deep cushions redolent of perfume,
Hippolyta dreamed of the potent caresses
That drew aside the veil of her young innocence.

She was seeking, with an eye disturbed by the storm,
The already distant skies of her naiveté,
Like a voyager who turns to look back
Toward the blue horizons passed early in the day.

The listless tears from her lacklustrous eyes,
The beaten, bewildered look, the dulled delight,
Her defeated arms thrown wide like futile weapons,
All served, all adorned her fragile beauty.

Lying at her feet, calm and filled with joy,
Delphine gazed at her hungrily, with burning eyes,
Like a strong animal watching a prey
Which it has already marked with its teeth.

The strong beauty kneeling before the frail beauty,
Superb, she savored voluptuously
The wine of her triumph and stretched out toward the girl
As if to reap her reward of sweet thankfulness.

She was seeking in the eyes of her pale victim
The silent canticle that pleasure sings
And that gratitude, sublime and infinite,
Which the eyes give forth like a long drawn sigh.

"Hippolyta, sweet, what do you think of our love?
Do you understand now that you need not offer
The sacred burnt-offering of your first roses
To a violent breath which could make them wither?

My kisses are as light as the touch of May flies
That caress in the evening the great limpid lakes,
But those of your lover will dig furrows
As a wagon does, or a tearing ploughshare;

They will pass over you like heavy teams
Of horses or oxen, with cruel iron-shod hooves...
Hippolyta, sister! please turn your face to me,
You, my heart and soul, my all, half of my own self,

Turn toward me your eyes brimming with azure and stars!
For one of those bewitching looks, O divine balm,
I will lift the veil of the more subtle pleasures
And lull you to sleep in an endless dream!"

Hippolyta then raised her youthful head:
"I am not ungrateful and I do not repent,
Delphine darling; I feel restless and ill,
As I do after a rich midnight feast.

I feel heavy terrors pouncing on me
And black battalions of scattered phantoms
Who wish to lead me onto shifting roads
That a bloody horizon shuts in on all sides.

Is there something strange in what we have done?
Explain if you can my confusion and my fright:
I shudder with fear when you say: 'My angel!'
And yet I feel my mouth moving toward you.

Do not look at me that way, you, my dearest thought:
The sister of my choice whom I'd love forever
Even if you were an ambush prepared for me
And the beginning of my perdition."

Delphine, shaking her tragic mane and stamping her foot
As if she were stamping on the iron Tripod,
Her eyes fatal, replied in a despotic voice:
"Who dares to speak of hell in the presence of love?

May he be cursed forever, that idle dreamer,
The first one who in his stupidity
Entranced by a sterile, insoluble problem,
Wished to mix honesty with what belongs to love!

He who would unite in a mystic harmony
Coolness with warmth and the night with the day
Will never warm his palsied flesh
With that red sun whose name is love!

Go if you wish and find a stupid sweetheart, run
To offer your virgin heart to his cruel kisses;
Full of remorse and horror, and livid,
You will bring back to me your stigmatized breasts...

Woman here below can serve only one master!"
But the girl pouring out the vast grief in her heart,
Suddenly cried: "I feel opening within me
A yawning abyss; that abyss is my heart!

Burning like a volcano and deep as the void!
Nothing will satiate that wailing monster
Nor cool the thirst of the Eumenides
Who with torch in hand burn his very blood.

Let our drawn curtains separate us from the world
And let lassitude bring to us repose!
I want to bury my head in your deep bosom
And find in your breast the cool of the tomb!"

—Go down, go down, lamentable victims,
Go down the pathway to eternal hell!
Plunge to the bottom of the abyss where all crime
Whipped by a wind that comes not from heaven,

Boil pell-mell with the sound of a tempest.
Mad shades, run to the goal of your desires;
You will never be able to sate your passion
And your punishment will be born of your pleasures.

Never will a cool ray light your caverns;
Through the chinks in the walls feverish miasmas
Filter through, burst into flame like lanterns
And permeate your bodies with frightful odors.

The bleak sterility of your pleasures
Increases your thirst and makes your skin taut
And the raging wind of carnal desire
Makes your flesh snap like an old flag.

Damned, wandering, far from living people,
Roam like the wolves across the desert waste;
Fulfill your destinies, dissolute souls,
And flee the infinite you carry in your hearts!

LE LETHE

Viens sur mon coeur, âme cruelle et sourde,
Tigre adoré, monstre aux airs indolents;
Je veux longtemps plonger mes doigts tremblants
Dans l'épaisseur de ta crinière lourde;

Dans tes jupons remplis de ton parfum
Ensevelir ma tête endolorie,
Et respirer, comme une fleur flétrie,
Le doux relent de mon amour défunt.

Je veux dormir! dormir plutôt que vivre!
Dans un sommeil aussi doux que la mort,
J'étalerai mes baisers sans remords
Sur ton beau corps poli comme le cuivre.

Pour engloutir mes sanglots apaisés
Rien ne me vaut l'abîme de ta couche;
L'oubli puissant habite sur ta bouche,
Et le Léthé coule dans tes baisers.

À mon destin, désormais mon délice,
J'obéirai comme un prédestiné;
Martyr docile, innocent condamné,
Dont la ferveur attise le supplice,

Je sucerai, pour noyer ma rancoeur,
Le népenthès et la bonne ciguë
Aux bouts charmants de cette gorge aiguë
Qui n'a jamais emprisonné de coeur.

LETHE

Come, lie upon my breast, cruel, insensitive soul,
Adored tigress, monster with the indolent air;
I want to plunge trembling fingers for a long time
In the thickness of your heavy mane,

To bury my head, full of pain
In your skirts redolent of your perfume,
To inhale, as from a withered flower,
The moldy sweetness of my defunct love.

I wish to sleep! to sleep rather than live!
In a slumber doubtful as death,
I shall remorselessly cover with my kisses
Your lovely body polished like copper.

To bury my subdued sobbing
Nothing equals the abyss of your bed,
Potent oblivion dwells upon your lips
And Lethe flows in your kisses.

My fate, hereafter my delight,
I'll obey like one predestined;
Docile martyr, innocent man condemned,
Whose fervor aggravates the punishment.

I shall suck, to drown my rancor,
Nepenthe and the good hemlock
From the charming tips of those pointed breasts
That have never guarded a heart.

À CELLE QUI EST TROP GAIE

Ta tête, ton geste, ton air
Sont beaux comme un beau paysage;
Le rire joue en ton visage
Comme un vent frais dans un ciel clair.

Le passant chagrin que tu frôles
Est ébloui par la santé
Qui jaillit comme une clarté
De tes bras et de tes épaules.

Les retentissantes couleurs
Dont tu parsèmes tes toilettes
Jettent dans l'esprit des poètes
L'image d'un ballet de fleurs.

Ces robes folles sont l'emblème
De ton esprit bariolé;
Folle dont je suis affolé,
Je te hais autant que je t'aime!

Quelquefois dans un beau jardin
Où je traînais mon atonie,
J'ai senti, comme une ironie,
Le soleil déchirer mon sein,

Et le printemps et la verdure
Ont tant humilié mon coeur,
Que j'ai puni sur une fleur
L'insolence de la Nature.

Ainsi je voudrais, une nuit,
Quand l'heure des voluptés sonne,
Vers les trésors de ta personne,
Comme un lâche, ramper sans bruit,

Pour châtier ta chair joyeuse,
Pour meurtrir ton sein pardonné,
Et faire à ton flanc étonné
Une blessure large et creuse,

Et, vertigineuse douceur!
À travers ces lèvres nouvelles,
Plus éclatantes et plus belles,
T'infuser mon venin, ma soeur!

TO ONE WHO IS TOO GAY

Your head, your bearing, your gestures
Are fair as a fair countryside;
Laughter plays on your face
Like a cool wind in a clear sky.

The gloomy passer-by you meet
Is dazzled by the glow of health
Which radiates resplendently
From your arms and shoulders.

The touches of sonorous color
That you scatter on your dresses
Cast into the minds of poets
The image of a flower dance.

Those crazy frocks are the emblem
Of your multi-colored nature;
Mad woman whom I'm mad about,
I hate and love you equally!

At times in a lovely garden
Where I dragged my atony,
I have felt the sun tear my breast,
As though it were in mockery;

Both the springtime and its verdure
So mortified my heart
That I punished a flower
For the insolence of Nature.

Thus I should like, some night,
When the hour for pleasure sounds,
To creep softly, like a coward,
Toward the treasures of your body,

To whip your joyous flesh
And bruise your pardoned breast,
To make in your astonished flank
A wide and gaping wound,

And, intoxicating sweetness!
Through those new lips,
More bright, more beautiful,
To infuse my venom, my sister!

LES BIJOUX

La très chère était nue, et, connaissant mon coeur,
Elle n'avait gardé que ses bijoux sonores,
Dont le riche attirail lui donnait l'air vainqueur
Qu'ont dans leurs jours heureux les esclaves des Mores.

Quand il jette en dansant son bruit vif et moqueur,
Ce monde rayonnant de métal et de pierre
Me ravit en extase, et j'aime à la fureur
Les choses où le son se mêle à la lumière.

Elle était donc couchée et se laissait aimer,
Et du haut du divan elle souriait d'aise
À mon amour profond et doux comme la mer,
Qui vers elle montait comme vers sa falaise.

Les yeux fixés sur moi, comme un tigre dompté,
D'un air vague et rêveur elle essayait des poses,
Et la candeur unie à la lubricité
Donnait un charme neuf à ses métamorphoses;

Et son bras et sa jambe, et sa cuisse et ses reins,
Polis comme de l'huile, onduleux comme un cygne,
Passaient devant mes yeux clairvoyants et sereins;
Et son ventre et ses seins, ces grappes de ma vigne,

S'avançaient, plus câlins que les Anges du mal,
Pour troubler le repos où mon âme était mise,
Et pour la déranger du rocher de cristal
Où, calme et solitaire, elle s'était assise.

Je croyais voir unis par un nouveau dessin
Les hanches de l'Antiope au buste d'un imberbe,
Tant sa taille faisait ressortir son bassin.
Sur ce teint fauve et brun, le fard était superbe!

—Et la lampe s'étant résignée à mourir,
Comme le foyer seul illuminait la chambre
Chaque fois qu'il poussait un flamboyant soupir,
Il inondait de sang cette peau couleur d'ambre!

THE JEWELS

My darling was naked, and knowing my heart well,
She was wearing only her sonorous jewels,
Whose opulent display made her look triumphant
Like Moorish concubines on their fortunate days.

When it dances and flings its lively, mocking sound,
This radiant world of metal and of gems
Transports me with delight; I passionately love
All things in which sound is mingled with light.

She had lain down; and let herself be loved
From the top of the couch she smiled contentedly
Upon my love, deep and gentle as the sea,
Which rose toward her as toward a cliff.

Her eyes fixed upon me, like a tamed tigress,
With a vague, dreamy air she was trying poses,
And by blending candor with lechery,
Her metamorphoses took on a novel charm;

And her arm and her leg, and her thigh and her loins,
Shiny as oil, sinuous as a swan,
Passed in front of my eyes, clear-sighted and serene;
And her belly, her breasts, grapes of my vine,

Advanced, more cajoling than angels of evil,
To trouble the quiet that had possessed my soul,
To dislodge her from the crag of crystal,
Where calm and alone she had taken her seat.

I thought I saw blended in a novel design
Antiope's haunches and the breast of a boy,
Her waist set off so well the fullness of her hips.
On that tawny brown skin the rouge stood out superb!

—And when at last the lamp allowed itself to die,
Since the fire alone lighted the room,
Each time that it uttered a flaming sigh,
It drenched with blood that amber colored skin!

LES METAMORPHOSES DU VAMPIRE

La femme cependant, de sa bouche de fraise,
En se tordant ainsi qu'un serpent sur la braise,
Et pétrissant ses seins sur le fer de son busc,
Laissait couler ces mots tout imprégnés de musc:
—«Moi, j'ai la lèvre humide, et je sais la science
De perdre au fond d'un lit l'antique conscience.
Je sèche tous les pleurs sur mes seins triomphants,
Et fais rire les vieux du rire des enfants.
Je remplace, pour qui me voit nue et sans voiles,
La lune, le soleil, le ciel et les étoiles!
Je suis, mon cher savant, si docte aux voluptés,
Lorsque j'étouffe un homme en mes bras redoutés,
Ou lorsque j'abandonne aux morsures mon buste,
Timide et libertine, et fragile et robuste,
Que sur ces matelas qui se pâment d'émoi,
Les anges impuissants se damneraient pour moi!»

Quand elle eut de mes os sucé toute la moelle,
Et que languissamment je me tournai vers elle
Pour lui rendre un baiser d'amour, je ne vis plus
Qu'une outre aux flancs gluants, toute pleine de pus!
Je fermai les deux yeux, dans ma froide épouvante,
Et quand je les rouvris à la clarté vivante,
À mes côtés, au lieu du mannequin puissant
Qui semblait avoir fait provision de sang,
Tremblaient confusément des débris de squelette,
Qui d'eux-mêmes rendaient le cri d'une girouette
Ou d'une enseigne, au bout d'une tringle de fer,
Que balance le vent pendant les nuits d'hiver.

THE VAMPIRE'S METAMORPHOSES

The woman meanwhile, twisting like a snake
On hot coals and kneading her breasts against the steel
Of her corset, from her mouth red as strawberries
Let flow these words impregnated with musk:
—"I, I have moist lips, and I know the art
Of losing old Conscience in the depths of a bed.
I dry all tears on my triumphant breasts
And make old men laugh with the laughter of children.
I replace, for him who sees me nude, without veils,
The moon, the sun, the stars and the heavens!
I am, my dear scholar, so learned in pleasure
That when I smother a man in my fearful arms,
Or when, timid and licentious, frail and robust,
I yield my bosom to biting kisses
On those two soft cushions which swoon with emotion,
The powerless angels would damn themselves for me!"

When she had sucked out all the marrow from my bones
And I languidly turned toward her
To give back an amorous kiss, I saw no more
Than a wine-skin with gluey sides, all full of pus!
Frozen with terror, I closed both my eyes,
And when I opened them to the bright light,
At my side, instead of the robust manikin
Who seemed to have laid in a store of blood,
There quivered confusedly a heap of old bones,
Which of themselves gave forth the cry of a weather-cock
Or of a sign on the end of an iron rod
That the wind swings to and fro on a winter night.

THE END